FROM THE LIBRARY OF
David Wiczynski

THE ARRIVAL OF GODOT

THE ARRIVAL OF GODOT

Ritual Patterns in Modern Drama

KATHERINE H. BURKMAN

Rutherford • Madison • Teaneck
Fairleigh Dickinson University Press
London and Toronto: Associated University Presses

© 1986 by Associated University Presses, Inc.

Associated University Presses
440 Forsgate Drive
Cranbury, NJ 08512

Associated University Presses
25 Sicilian Avenue
London WC1A 2QH, England

Associated University Presses
2133 Royal Windsor Drive
Unit 1
Mississauga, Ontario
Canada L5J 1K5

The paper used in this publication meets the requirements of the American National Standard for Permanence of Paper for Printed Materials Z39.48-1984.

Library of Congress Cataloging-in-Publication Data

Burkman, Katherine H.
   The arrival of Godot.

   Bibliography: p.
   Includes index.
   1. Drama—20th century—History and criticism.
2. Ritual in literature. I. Title.
PN1861.B87   1986   809.2′04   85-45786
ISBN 0-8386-3264-5 (alk. paper)

Printed in the United States of America

For my sister, Linda Blumberg

"If Godot comes, tell him to wait."
(graffito)

Contents

Acknowledgments		9
1	Farewell to Firs: An Introduction	13
2	The Nonarrival of Godot: Initiation into the Sacred Void	33
3	Farcical False Arrivals: The Dying-Reviving God	54
4	Another False Arrival and Several Unhappy Birthdays	66
5	Exorcising Godot: Possession and Self-Possession in Genet's *The Maids* and Pinter's *Old Times*	81
6	In Search of Godot	96
7	And Who's Godot When He's at Home?	117
8	Godot Arrives: *The Homecoming*	125
9	Awakenings	149
Works Cited		161
Index		168

Acknowledgments

I am especially grateful to Jane Cottrell for her research assistance and her helpful criticism. For their many suggestions and their encouragement I also thank Jim Battersby, Rolf H. Soellner, Stanley J. Kahrl, Morris Beja, and Julian H. Markels. Martina Ebert was kind enough to read and criticize my analysis of Günter Grass's play *The Wicked Cooks* and offered some excellent suggestions, and Roger Pierce has generously allowed me to draw substantially from a long piece that I collaborated on with him on Harold Pinter's *The Homecoming*. I am also grateful to The Ohio State University College of Humanities for a faculty leave and grant-in-aid that facilitated my work, to Barbara Austin for her expert editing, and to Linda Fairchild for her expert word processing. Finally, I must thank June Schlueter for her perceptive reading of the manuscript and her helpful suggestions.

I also wish to thank the following publishers and journals for their permission to reprint from published works:

Faber and Faber Ltd. and Grove Press, Inc., for permission to quote from *Waiting for Godot*, by Samuel Beckett.

Eyre Methuen Ltd. and Grove Press, Inc., for permission to quote from *The Homecoming*, by Harold Pinter.

Albert Frank Gegenheimer, Editor, *Arizona Quarterly*, for permission to use portions of my article "Hirst as Godot: Pinter in Beckett's Land," *Arizona Quarterly* 39, no. 1 (Spring 1983).

Armand E. Singer, Editor in Chief, *West Virginia University Philological Papers*, for permission to use portions of my article "Earth and Water: The Question of Renewal in Harold Pinter's *Old Times* and *No Man's Land*," *West Virginia University Philological Papers* 25, series 79, no. 8-3 (February 1979).

Marilyn R. Waldman, Editor, *Papers in Comparative Studies*, for permission to use portions of my article "Initiation Rites in Samuel Beckett's *Waiting for Godot*," *Papers in Comparative Studies* 3 (1984).

THE ARRIVAL OF GODOT

1

Farewell to Firs: An Introduction

In Anton Chekhov's tragicomic farce, *The Cherry Orchard,* the homecoming comes first, departure and exile from a disintegrating home, last. Chekhov's portrayal of the passing of an age sets the stage for those modern dramatists, sometimes called absurdists, who have taken up their mentor's tragicomic tone and have followed his exiles down a variety of roads. Following the descendants of the guilt-ridden, love-seeking Madame Ranevskaya, or those of the ambitious Lopakhin, who cannot possess what he has bought, modern playwrights have left Firs, even as Chekhov's characters did, to die with the house that has been his spiritual home and without which he cannot exist.

The tendency of the absurdists, however, has been to reverse the rhythms of Chekhov's final masterpiece. Rather than fixing on the homecoming/departure structure of that play,[1] the playwrights with whom I will be especially concerned in this study—Samuel Beckett, Harold Pinter, Eugène Ionesco, Edward Albee, Günter Grass, and Jean Genet—have begun with the exiled. Beckett places his tramps at first and last on a country road where they pass the time while waiting for Godot. Günter Grass has his cooks in *The Wicked Cooks* in hot pursuit, from first to last, of a recipe for soup. The seaside resort in Harold Pinter's *The Birthday Party,* like the other rooms in which his dramas are often set, is not so much a haven as a hideout; Stanley senses that he is lost from the outset. Genet's maids invade their mistress's domain, his blacks invade the white man's world, but possession is as uncertain as it was for Lopakhin. Starting, then, in exile, like Bérenger in Ionesco's play *The Killer,* what the characters in these plays seek is an ideal city—a home.

Friedrich Nietzsche, who characterized modern man as homeless, associated man's consequent loss of a sense of self with his loss of belief in God. For Nietzsche, Hamlet becomes an absurd hero; as he returns to a lost home, throne, family, lover, and friends, he looks into the essence of things and, contemplating the horror or absurdity of existence, becomes inactive with nausea.² Hamlet, however, hovering as he does on the brink of the modern world and contemplating the basic existential questions, does have a second and authentic homecoming. Returning from his voyage to England, he descends into Ophelia's grave and emerges with a new sense of self. Announcing that self as "Hamlet, the Dane," Shakespeare's hero eventually comes to accept himself both as a scapegoat and as part of a providential order in which the fall of a sparrow is not accidental and "the readiness is all."

While the protagonist of modern drama inherits Hamlet's nausea and his propensity for inaction (witness Madame Ranevskaya), or is, in Prufrock fashion, as busy with meaningless action as Polonius, he does not succeed, as Hamlet does, in overcoming his inertia, nor does he seem to find his place in life, remaining, in effect, homeless.³ "Nothing to be done," moans Estragon in *Waiting for Godot,* and even after Pozzo and Lucky arrive, Estragon agonizes that "Nothing happens, nobody comes, nobody goes, it's awful."⁴ Without the repeatedly promised arrival of Godot, action is so ephemeral that the characters often recognize neither each other nor themselves. While Hamlet's final coming to grips with action makes his death significant and his story worth telling by Horatio, Hamlet's foils, Rosencrantz and Guildenstern, who take center stage in Tom Stoppard's *Rosencrantz and Guildenstern Are Dead* (1967), are such passive victims of chance that they are not even capable of death—they merely disappear.

Still, their story, which as much as Hamlet's may be ours, is also worth telling. And the quest for meaning remains, its romantic strain persisting and informing the life of the modern play.⁵ Indeed, Robert Brustein has brilliantly demonstrated how many of the great giants of modern drama—Ibsen, Strindberg, Chekhov, Shaw, Brecht, Pirandello, O'Neill, and Genet—ride "on the second wave of Romanticism—not the cheerful optimism of Rousseau, with his emphasis on institutional reform, but rather the dark fury of Nietzsche with his radical demands for a total transformation of man's spiritual life." With Nietzsche, Brustein writes in *The Theatre of Revolt,* the modern dramatist envisions a termination of exile. "In a world without God, he must shape a congregation, invent a liturgy, create a faith." The goal of the modern dramatist is "to make a new union out of his secession—to make his initial act of revolt the occasion for a new kind of grace."⁶

Even before Samuel Beckett wrote his absurdist classic *Waiting for Godot* in 1949 (first published in French in 1952, in English in 1954), and certainly after he wrote it, the issue of Godot's arrival has been of paramount concern in modern drama. This is so, of course, only if one takes Beckett's Godot as a symbol for a savior figure whose arrival may bring salvation or damnation to those who wait for him. Such a savior

Farewell to Firs

figure need not be equated with God; Beckett himself refuses to equate Godot with God and what little information can be gathered about Godot in his play suggests a rather secular savior figure. Nor does the savior figure in modern drama always arrive. In Beckett's own dramatic world the arrival of Godot is something of a contradiction in terms: the Godot tramps may desire that arrival or wait for it, but it is his nonarrival that they confront and his absence that is most at issue. In Beckett's play, however, it is the possibility of Godot's arrival that keeps Vladimir and Estragon going, and in other important dramas written before and after *Waiting for Godot,* the pressing question of salvation often revolves around what I will call in this study a Godot figure, one in whom the characters, to some degree, place their faith.

The playwrights of the absurd, so labeled by Martin Esslin, certainly follow in the footsteps of their predecessors, seeking a new kind of grace even more fervently the more lost, godless, and homeless they feel. Eugene O'Neill insisted that all the serious art of his day dealt with man's failure in a materialistic world to find a new god to replace the old.[7] No less than O'Neill and no less than other modern playwrights, the absurdists, despite their despairing depiction of a choatic world, still undertake the religious quest. Surely one of the reasons Godot has become such a potent symbol for our time is that the subject of art today, as in O'Neill's day, remains the quest for meaning in a world in which the old gods no longer serve.

One may overlook the modern hero's quest for salvation—I use the term *salvation* not in any narrowly religious sense, but in the broader sense in which man pursues a life of meaning—because so much of his energy seems today to go into mere questions of survival. How Etienne in Fernando Arrabal's *Labyrinth* will extricate himself from a park of blankets into which he has wandered or even whether he will be able to extricate himself at all are such pressing questions that he and the reader may have little time to ponder the metaphorical meaning of his predicament. Does he deserve to be so trapped? What power has arranged life in such Kafkaesque fashion? In the *Endgame* of life, can one move at all, much less move with meaning?

The questions of survival and salvation, however, remain as irremediably mixed in modern drama as they have been in dramatic literature through the ages. "We're not beginning ... to ... to mean something?"[8], Hamm asks Clov with decided ambivalence in *Endgame,* but the question persists. Speaking of the absurdists' mentor, Joyce Carol Oates says of Chekhov what is true for his followers: "as in Beckett, the less tangible the means of salvation, the greater the urge for salvation becomes."[9]

While the rhythms of the double quest for survival and salvation that have informed dramatic literature since its inception in Greek ritual have persisted in modern drama and specifically in absurdist drama, in some instances the rhythms have changed or have been modified. In his seminal work, *The Idea of a Theater,* Francis Fergusson has suggested that the full rhythm of dramatic action, that of purpose, passion, and perception, is the full rhythm of those rituals central to all religions in which a sacrificial scapegoat redeems the land.[10] Taking Aristotle's favorite play, Fergusson demonstrates how Sophocles' Oedipus took up the terrible search for the killer of Laius (immediate purpose) in order to insure the survival of his plague-ridden people and redeem the land (a central purpose of all ritual and drama), a search that led to terrible premonitions and suffering (passion) and finally, ironically, to that tragic finding of the self (perception) that completes and defines tragedy. Taking Hamlet as another archetype of the tragic hero, Fergusson again finds the hero moving through the complete rhythm that provides both self-realization and redemption of his people.[11] But whereas the tragic hero's death involves a victory since he achieves salvation for himself in terms of self-discovery and renewal for his people, the absurdist protagonist rarely achieves that redeeming sense of self and is even more rarely able to bring renewal to others.

This emphasis on the role of the absurd hero as victim rather than the victim/victor of tragedy along with the antirealistic techniques of the absurdists has led several critics to deal with absurdist drama as if it were toally un-Aristotelian. Esslin notes that the absurdists have redefined all of the six Aristotelian elements of theater—plot, character, thought, diction, music, and spectacle—and that their plays are structured less as imitations of an action than as poetic patterns that unfold or situations that intensify.[12] Others have sought in vain for the Aristotelian beginning, middle, and end or the unity of action that, with its threefold rhythm. Fergusson insists embodies the very "idea" of theater.

Fergusson himself offers an important clue, however, to how these plays are structured as he points out that the rhythms in the drama of all ages persist but receive different emphasis. Chekhov, for example, is a playwright whose major emphasis is on the "passion" part of the full dramatic rhythm; his characters suffer their fates and make what seem like minimal gestures regarding their purposes. All of the characters in *The Cherry Orchard* may wish, on some level, to save the orchard, but mostly they suffer its loss and have only flashes of perception about the meaning of that loss.[13] "Hence, what they [Chekhov's characters] experience is the result not of action carried out but of action begun and left unfinished."[14] What happens in a Checkhov play, according to Tom Driver, is not only an emphasis on the suffering part of the rhythm of action, but a shift of perception from the protagonist to the audience, who are able to endure insights that are too overwhelming for the characters involved.[15]

Despite Estragon's claim that nothing happens in *Waiting for Godot* or the claim of one of Beckett's critics that "nothing happens—*twice*"[16] in that play, something does happen in it and in all of Beckett's dramas. "Something," as Clov often remarks in *Endgame*, "is taking its course" (p. 13). One may miss the climax of a Beckett or Genet or Pinter play because of shifts in rhythm, texture, or technique, but if the absurdists are giving new definition to the Aristotelian elements of drama, they are in no way deserting them. Nor are they deserting the rituals out of which drama emerges and which the rhythms of the Aristotelian action reflect. Despite the cultural diversity of their audiences and what Fergusson has called "the centerless diversity of our theater,"[17] the most significant modern playwrights still deal with the sacrificial rites that have traditionally promised renewal both outside and inside the theater.

Given the diversity of present-day culture, in which there are so few rituals in common, Antonin Artaud (1896–1948) sought to make the theatrical experience itself a ritual. Artaud wished to break the barriers between actor and audience and envisioned the artist as one who signals to us "through the flames."[18] In his fascinating book, *Holy Theatre: Ritual and the Avant Garde,* Christopher Innes has traced the influence of Artaud on much avant-garde drama. Touching briefly on some of the playwrights I will consider, Innes concerns himself more with performance groups, such as The Living Theatre or Richard Schechner's The Performance Group, and with directors, such as Jean-Louis Barrault or Jerzi Grotowski, who, in Artaudian fashion, have borrowed "ritual forms to manipulate the audience."[19]

Several of the playwrights upon whom I will focus have been influenced by Artaud, but they have chosen, on the whole, to retain the aesthetic distance he was willing to forsake and to work more traditionally with some of the basic ritual structures that are still common to all cultures. Although they have experimented as Artaud did with spectacle and silence, they have continued to use language as an essential part of the poetry of their plays and have retained some of the tragic elements that Artaud lost through his particular use of spectacle. Although Artaud desired a ritual drama that would provide the kind of catharsis that would renew an effete society, his emphasis on shocking kinds of spectacle was quite foreign to Aristotle's idea of tragedy.[20]

Artaud's dramas suffered not only from an overabundance of violence, but from an underabundance of the kind of humor that permeates the absurdist play. Not only does the audience laugh at the absurd hero, looking down at him from within what Northrop Frye has called the ironic mode,[21] from the safety of which one can feel somewhat superior, but the hero also often laughs at himself, distancing himself from his agony. "There is nothing funnier than unhappiness" (p. 18), Nell informs Nag in *Endgame,* and Estragon wisely calls the tramps' inability to laugh "any more" a "dreadful privation" (p. 8). Camus's Sisyphus achieves joy as an absurd hero, not by laughing at himself, but by mocking the very gods he holds responsible for his unproductive labor in the underworld. The discharge of nausea, Nietzsche tells us, is accomplished through laughter.[22] Artaud saw the value of the comic—"the contemporary theater is decadent because it has lost the feeling on the one hand for seriousness and on the other for laughter . . . because it has lost a sense of real humor, a sense of laughter's power of physical and anarchic dissociation"[23]—but he was not able to employ such humor, leaving only his theory as a bequest to those who were to put it to better use.

It is not surprising that the ironic mode of modern writers shades back, as Frye suggests, into the mythic mode. Whether or not the modern dramatist attempts, as Brustein suggests, to become God,[24] the concern of many of today's playwrights is with the need for new gods. Frye has proposed the current return to myth as part of a kind of cycle in literature in which he sees a movement from myth to romance to the high mimetic mode of tragedy to the low mimetic to irony and back to myth. "Irony descends," he writes, "from the low mimetic; it begins in realism and dispassionate observation. But as it does so it moves steadily towards myth, and dim outlines of sacrificial rituals and dying gods begin to reappear in it. Our five modes evidently go around in a circle."[25]

Some of the ritual patterns that I will explore in several plays by Beckett, Pinter, Ionesco, Grass, Albee, and Genet may be seen very clearly in two earlier dramas, Henrik Ibsen's *The Wild Duck* (1894) and Eugene O'Neill's *The Iceman Cometh* (1939). Ibsen's and O'Neill's ironical use of myth in their ostensibly realistic and naturalistic plays also provides a key to the use of myth in the later dramas I will explore.

In both plays, the playwrights offer arriving Godots. In both cases, however, the savior figure is revealed as a false messiah, and the rituals of renewal turn out to be as false as the Godots who initiate them. Ibsen and O'Neill also both employ the ritual of a birthday party to crystallize the seasonal nature of the drama of the dying-and-reviving god.

In that year drama, which Sir James George Frazer explored in his many-volumed work, *The Golden Bough* (1907-15, 3rd ed.), the battle between winter and spring unfolds as a battle between old kings and new kings. In this work, which John B. Vickery has described as "the discursive archetype and hence matrix"[26] of twentieth-century literature, Frazer explores primitive customs of killing kings, sometimes when they show signs of decay through illness, sexual impotence, or mere old age, sometimes on a periodic basis, whatever the state of their health or well-being, the period being variable, sometimes several years, one year, or even a week. Often regarding their rulers, not just as kings, but as priests and gods as well, primitive people, according to Frazer, feel that their own health and well-being is tied up with their leader's and hence find his death unacceptable. The strange remedy for this danger to life lies in killing the king-god while he is still in his prime and transferring his soul to a new king-god. Frazer suggests that this sacrifice of the king-priest-god or of a substitute for him became associated in time with the sacrifice of a scapegoat, one who could take upon him the sins of his tribe. The method of sacrifice of the scapegoat, be he king, a human or animal substitute for the king, or a mere image, sometimes involved a battle between a new and old king (the battle between winter and spring), and sometimes involved the death and resurrection of a single god-king. Examples of the former may be seen in the Nemi ritual in which the battle for succession to the priesthood of Nemi took place between the current ruler and whoever could wrest that rule from him. Examples of the latter may be seen in the dying-reviving Dionysus or in Jesus Christ, whom Frazer regards as but one fertility god among others. Frazer explains the sacrifice of the scapegoat-king as a fertility rite, the means to renewal of the crops and the overcoming of death (survival) and the means to spiritual renewal (salvation) as well.[27]

Such renewal is of central concern to Ibsen and O'Neill in their plays. Gregers Werle, a self-proclaimed savior of the Ekdal family in Ibsen's *The Wild Duck,* is summoned home from the outpost of his father's business in Hoydal by his father, who wishes to procure his blessing for his upcoming marriage with his mistress, Mrs. Soerby. Rejecting his father, Gregers leaves home and moves in with the Ekdal family in order to bring them the truth: Gregers perceives his father as having foisted Gina Ekdal, pregnant by him, on her husband Gregers. His intention is to offer the Ekdals the renewal that must come from building their marriage on the firm ground of "truth" or "reality," a truth that calls Hjalmar Ekdal's paternity of Hedvig into question. Similarly, O'Neill's salesman, Theodore Hickman, makes his yearly visit to Harry Hope's saloon for deadbeat drunks, seeing himself as a savior who will relieve Hope's inhabitants of their illusions about tomorrow; each one convinces himself that he will return to the working world and reestablish either what he has lost or achieve what he thinks he once had. Hickey feels that he can help them leave their illusions behind and find the peace of living new lives based on the truth of their irreparable situations.

The arrival of these particular self-styled Godots is disastrous. Treating these figures with biting irony, Ibsen and O'Neill, respectively, expose their protagonists as neurotic, self-deluded peddlers of "truth," false messiahs who suffer from the very illusions from which they would free the others. Gregers, it soon appears, is in the grip of an Oedipal struggle with his father, and he so misinterprets the nature of his friend Hjalmar that he causes irreparable harm to him and brings about the suicide of his daughter, Hedvig. Hickey, who believes that he has killed his wife Evelyn out of a compassionate desire to free her of his unreformable, drunken ways, has actually killed her out of malice and revenge. "I remember I heard myself speaking to her, as if it was something I'd always wanted to say: 'Well, you know what you can do with your pipe dreams now, you damned bitch!' "[28] Unable to live with the truth he so strongly advocates for his friends, Hickey quickly withdraws from his inadvertent acknowledgment of his real feelings. "No! That's a lie! I never said—! Good God, I couldn't have said that! If I did, I'd gone insane! Why, I loved Evelyn better than anything in life!" (p. 242).

To interpret Ibsen's and O'Neill's masterpieces as thesis plays in which the playwrights advocate Dr. Relling's position in *The Wild Duck* that doses of illusion or vital lies are the way to survival, if not to salvation, is, however, a gross oversimplification. Behind the action of these plays is the ritual battle of spring and winter that involves not only the battle for survival, renewal of the year, but the battle for salvation, renewal of the year in a meaningful way. The treatment of ritual in these plays complicates the action, and one must look beyond their seeming advocacy of illusion as all that modern man can tolerate to the treatment of their rituals for their more complex meanings.

The ritual birthday party in *The Wild Duck* does not take place. Mrs. Soerby delivers a letter to Hedvig from Old Werle, on the eve of her thirteenth birthday, which Hjalmar, his suspicions aroused by Gregers about Hedvig's paternity, insists upon opening. The letter leaves a monthly sum of money to the child's grandfather for as long as he lives, then to be paid to Hedvig as long as she lives. With Gregers at his side to fuel his suspicions ("Gregers: Hjalmar, this is a trap which has been laid for you."[29]), Hjalmar is now convinced that Hedvig is Old Werle's daughter, and tearing up the letter, he rejects her cruelly. Gregers, who has envisioned Hjalmar and Gina rebuilding their marriage without illusion, has himself suffered false illusions about Hjalmar, who flees his home in a melodramatic huff, returning later to paste the latter back together and to be talked into returning.

Hedvig, however, shares the admiration of Gregers for her father and is tempted by his suggestion that she sacrifice her wounded wild duck to prove her love for her father and reclaim his love. But when the returning Hjalmar continues to reject her, she does not sacrifice the wild duck;

she sacrifices herself, killing herself on her birthday. Her act seems clearly to be a response to her father's question to Gregers, "If I were to ask her: 'Hedvig, will you sacrifice your life for me?'—*(He laughs scornfully)* Oh, yes! You'd hear what answer she'd give me!" (p. 212). The fatal shot she inflicts upon herself is that answer.

While Gregers is shocked at the deed, about which he now feels some guilt, he still expects renewal from the sacrifice. "Hedvig has not died in vain," he insists. "Did you see how grief set free all that is most noble in him?" (p. 216). The audience, however, knowing Hjalmar as they do by the end of act 5, cannot help sharing Relling's view that Hedvig has died in vain. "In nine months," Relling insists, "little Hedvig will be nothing more to him than a theme for a recitation" (p. 216).

Why in nine months time—the time of gestation? According to Relling the death on this birthday will only bring about the birth of new illusions, new self-deluding poses, from one whom, like all the characters in the play, Relling diagnoses as sick. The absent birthday party, then, soon to be replaced by a funeral and, in Relling's terms, a false renewal of the Ekdal marriage, suggests the victory of winter over spring and falsehood over truth. The ritual rhythms of sacrifice and renewal are there, but the mode is ironic and the renewal is both questioned and mocked. "Let's talk about it again," Relling suggests to Gregers, "when the first grasses have withered on her grave. Then you'll hear him gulping about 'the child untimely ripped from her father's bosom.' You'll see him stewing in emotion and self-admiration and self-pity. Just you wait" (p. 216).

Ibsen's use of the birthday party, in which the celebration of birth turns into a bitter confrontation with death, casts its shadow over the many other modern dramas that have employed this ironical kind of birthday celebration similarly in their plays. But Relling is neither Isben's nor any subsequent dramatist's hero, and the ironical implications of the birthday parties in all of the plays need further examination than the one given by that astute doctor.

Ibsen's drama, however, not only anticipates numerous dramas and absurdist plays to come, but also goes back to the tragic, ritual rhythms of Sophocles' *Oedipus the King*. This play may not contain a birthday party, but it is one that focuses, as Ibsen's does subsequently, on the ambiguities of birth and salvation.

Like *Oedipus*, *The Wild Duck's* structure involves emerging revelations from the past, and, as in *Oedipus*, many of the ironies of the action revolve around images of vision and blindness, lightness and darkness—ways of seeing. Indeed, the game of blindman's buff played by Mrs. Soerby and the hangers-on who enjoy Old Werle's hospitality in the opening scene becomes a significant poetic image for the entire drama. Here, however, the high tragic search of Oedipus for his city and himself has become a game of hide-and-seek played out in the narrow, middle-class landscape of the modern parlor.

But if neither Hjalmar nor Gregers attains that tragic, redeeming insight that the blinded Oedipus achieves, the minor characters, Hedvig and her grandfather, do achieve something of a new vision. Hedvig has trouble digesting Gregers's idea of sacrifice

> HEDVIG: I don't know. Yesterday evening, when you first mentioned it, I thought there was something so beautiful in the idea; but when I'd slept on it and thought about it again, it didn't seem so good.
>
> (P. 203)

What she arrives at instead, the sacrifice of herself, is something quite beyond Gregers's understanding. To sacrifice means to make sacred, and Hedvig, in her adolescent despair, has the acute insight to see through Gregers's melodramatic suggestion and find her way to a more authentic sacred act. Confused by her father's rejection, and guessing that she may not be his child, Hedvig reasons that she does not love the wounded duck Old Werle's servant has given them any the less because it was given to them. "Yes, I think he should love me just the same," Hedvig explains to Gregers. "Or even more. After all, we got the wild duck sent to us as a present, but I love it very much" (p. 196).

Both Hedvig and her grandfather have done all in their power to save and preserve the wild duck, and her grandfather, when sounded out, even though he hunts rabbit in the attic, would not dream of destroying the creature. In wishing to preserve the duck, most of the characters identify with it; Hedvig does so in her loneliness, and the grandfather, who has suffered a jail sentence for the illegal chopping down of trees on government property, senses that his wounded dignity is like the duck's wound. Gregers sees Hjalmar as a wounded wild duck that he must save from the poisonous marshes of illusion he inhabits, but he also identifies with the wounded duck himself and knows that his efforts to save Hjalmar are actually efforts to save himself. Suffering from a guilty conscience over not speaking out earlier against his father, whom he is sure made Old Ekdal pay for his own crime, and possibly from the Oedipal feelings he harbors, Gregers admits his illness to his father: "And besides—if I am to go on living, I must try to find some cure for my sick conscience" (p. 175).

James Hurt, who clearly grasps the mythic overtones of the forest loft of the wild duck, sees the action of the play as a "maimed rite" executed by Gregers.[30] Gregers has badly misread both Hjalmar's and Hedvig's characters. His romantic vision of Hedvig sacrificing her wild duck to prove her love for a father, who will now appreciate that love and rebuild his family life, falls to pieces with Hedvig's death and Relling's cynical predictions of the new illusions about reality that will follow. Hedvig's suicide, however, is a gesture that suggests more than a maimed rite. Hedvig may associate herself with the wild duck, but she also loves the duck as another being. By killing herself instead of the animal, she is preserving the duck—saving it and, on another level, herself.

As John Northam points out in his valuable study of the play, Hedvig presents an alternative to Gregers's warped idealism and Relling's cynical diagnosis of men. Speaking of Hedvig, Northam writes:

> Her act of love, for however unworthy an object and performed in whatever confusion of spirit, is one that Relling's philosophy cannot account for. Nor Gregers'! She provides the human dignity that Relling cannot understand, and the deep untheoretical integrity of emotion that is lacking in Gregers.[31]

The wounded wild duck has been retrieved from the depths of the sea, where it has tried to bury itself in the seaweed, by a trained dog to which Gregers has likened himself. Northam suggests that Hedvig is the only character "for whom the wild duck is an apt symbol. Not the damaged, contented creature in the attic, but the wild duck in nature, wounded and choosing death rather than accept the outrage. The wild duck in the play is a travesty of nature; the wild duck Hedvig becomes is nature itself."[32]

The sacrifice of Hedvig becomes more than a maimed rite, not just through Hedvig's childlike heroism, but also through the understanding of the grandfather, Old Ekdal. When Old Ekdal sees his granddaughter lying dead on the sofa, he says, "The Forest has taken its revenge" (p. 214). When he realizes she is dead, he retreats into the loft, closing the door behind him. "The Forest has taken its revenge," he repeats, adding significantly, "But I'm not afraid of it" (p. 215). Many critics have seen this as a mere retreat from the tragedy by a weakened old man, though Northam perceives minor heroism in Ekdal's relating of the death to his own sins—"The experience he is reminded of lies too deep for words to explain."[33]

The words, however, brief though they are, explain a great deal, especially in the mythical dimension of the play's meaning. The attic loft that holds the wild duck and the other animals, such as rabbits and pigeons, situated as it is on stage behind the studio, is suggestive of something more than the home of the characters' illusions and dreams. True, tending the wounded wild duck is one of Hjalmar's escapes and one of Old Ekdal's ways of caring for his own wounds while his hunting of rabbits is a way of recapturing the days of his hunting past. Nature, however reduced in scope, is alive in the background of the pedestrian life of the three Ekdals, grandfather, father, and daughter. And because the wild duck comes from Old Werle through his secretary, Peterson (Old Werle has shot the duck, his dog has retrieved it, and Peterson has given it to the Edkals rather than destroying it), the nature represented by the loft provides a symbolic background for both the prosperous business world of Werle and the struggling middle-class world of the Ekdals.

Orley I. Holtan points out in his book, *Mythic Patterns in Ibsen's Last Plays,* that this "shrunken world of nature" also exists as a microcosm. "Life and death, time and eternity, nature and art all contained behind its sliding doors." The forest, reduced here to withered Christmas trees, Holtan points out, is specifically full of dangerous powers in Norse myth and folklore, but works traditionally in most mythologies as a place of the unknown and the dangerous—hence its archetypal significance.[34] Old Ekdal's particular crime, that of cutting down trees on government property, is one for which he feels nature as well as mankind must take revenge. When he hears from Gregers that the forest has been thinned out a good deal since his time, he becomes fearful. "That's dangerous," he says. "Bad things'll come of that. The forest'll have its revenge" (p. 148).

When Old Ekdal, then, sees Hedvig's death as the forest's revenge, he is responding, not as Relling does to the maimed sacrifice that Gregers has perpetrated, but to the more profound sacrifice for which Hedvig has sensed the need and that nature has demanded. Ekdal does not retreat at the end to his fantasy world that has sustained him. He identifies Hedvig with himself; "Now she's started hunting too," he notes just before the tragedy is discovered, and his words about the forest's revenge indicate that he sees her fate as the result of his crimes. His new fearless stance suggests that he now sees that his haven in the loft has not been a safe one, and that there is no escape from the past. There is something of tragic recognition in his final exit to what must now be something of a void.[35]

Hedvig's conception of the loft as she reveals it to Gregers is not so much one of a forest as one of the sea depths, "the vasty deep," as she and Gregers call it (p. 163). The sea, which like the forest is a major archetypal image, has all the potentiality of both a life force and a death force. It is in these sea depths that Hedvig dreams of becoming an engraver, not a photographer like her parents, but an artist who can create the kind of pictures that she finds in the English books in the loft;[36] and it is here that she cares for the wild duck who is "separated from her family" and is a figure of mystery. "No one knows her," Hedvig explains to Gregers. "And no one knows where she came from" (p. 163). Here, too, Hedvig experiences both the timelessness of myth through a broken clock—"Gregers: So time has stopped in there with the wild

Farewell to Firs

duck" (p. 162)—and the threat of death in time. On the front of a history of London "There's a picture of death with an hourglass, and a girl. That's horrid, I think" (p. 162).

On one level, then, *The Wild Duck* provides the pattern for those many subsequent modern plays which involve useless sacrifices, false messiahs, and mock renewals, in which birthdays become occasions for funerals, and celebrations of life give way to dismal confrontations with death. On a deeper level, however, and one that is equally suggestive for the plays to follow, *The Wild Duck* provides an authentic sacrifice and the conversion, albeit of a minor character, of Old Ekdal to the possibly renewing message of the false messiah. That Greger's truth offers Old Ekdal only a tragic insight into the void is partly what makes the play so modern and so important for succeeding dramas. But because nature still operates with vindictive force in the play, demanding, in Old Ekdal's vision, the restitution of innocent blood, the void that he encounters reverberates with echoes of primitive justice and order that take one back to Sophocles as well as forward to O'Neill, Beckett, and Pinter.

Eugene O'Neill's *The Iceman Cometh* has little resemblance to Ibsen's play in plot or characterization, but its themes, ritual patterns, and the treatment of those patterns is hauntingly similar.[37] Hickey, the jovial, kidding salesman, who has been wont to take his periodical drunks with his friends who live or work at Harry Hope's saloon, "The Bottom of the Sea Rathskeller," bears little surface resemblance to the idealistic, prudish Gregers, but the message he brings to his old Friends on the eve of Harry Hope's birthday is Gregers's message; the men are to give up their illusions, their pipe dreams, as O'Neill calls them, in order to build life anew on the firm foundation of truth; only in such a fashion will they find peace. Like the self-styled Gregers/Godot before him, however, Hickey brings death rather than new life to his old friends. No Relling is needed to explain that the men of Hope's saloon are incapable of living their half-lives without the illusions Hickey expects them to discard, although Larry Slade, the ex-anarchist "Foolosopher," says this early in the play. "The lie of a pipe dream is what gives life to the whole misbegotten mad lot of us, drunk or sober" (p. 10), he announces. Ironically, Larry, too, is exposed from the beginning as one who also lives on illusion, in his case the illusion that he awaits death with real anticipation and that he is no longer involved in life.

As they await Hickey/Godot's arrival in act 1,[38] the men look for further reinforcement of their way of life, a flow of free booze that will keep them in their dreamlike stupors throughout their celebration of Harry's birthday. "Would that Hickey or Death would come!" (p. 39), Willie Oban wails, a brilliant Harvard Law School alumnus who has escaped the tyranny of his crooked father through whiskey. Later, we will hear the echo of Willie's cry in Vladimir's "We are waiting for Godot to come—. . .Or for night to fall . . ." (p. 51b). In Beckett's *Waiting for Godot,* the tramps, in true O'Neill fashion, await salvation or oblivion.

Vladimir and Estragon sometimes fear that an equation exists between Godot and death, a Godot who is supposed to save them from death or hell but who seems as impotent as they are before the dark promise of the void. In *The Iceman Cometh* that equation is made explicit. Preaching truth or salvation in a series of salesman/preacher clichés, Hickey is perceived by the men and women of Hope's saloon as the iceman of death—both Hickey and death arrive, and the saving grace of the liquor is lost to the men and women as they lose their taste for drink and for life. After an unsuccessful effort to take his long promised walk around the block, Harry himself, the dispenser of their cure, says of the booze, "There's no kick in it" (p. 202).

Just as Gregers brought dissension and suicide to a family who had lived quite comfortably with mutual respect and love, Hickey brings out hatred and intolerance in the men and women who have previously tolerated each others' illusions and formed a miserably happy community. Unable to live without their illusions, the men turn on each other as well as themselves; and without self-protective illusions, the usually peaceful saloon becomes a warlike hell. Margie and Pearl, stripped of their illusions of being tarts, realize that if they are whores, Rocky must be more than the bartender he pretends to be who simply takes care of the money—he must be a pimp. The men turn on Joe, whom they have tolerated as "white," and relegate him to the position of "nigger"; he now is denied the bar after hours. Finally, they all turn on Hickey, sure that his joke about finding his wife in bed with the iceman has come home to roost,[39] which in a sense it has. Hickey, however, is the iceman of death, the Godot who cometh, since it is he who has killed his own wife and who now brings a living death to his old friends.

Hickey sees his mission with the men fail, but he is unable to see the falseness of his own illusion that he has killed his wife out of generosity, not out of revenge for her constant and cloying forgiveness. Unable to bear the thought that he acted out of hate and not out of love, he retreats into a pose of temporary insanity, and the others pick up his notion as a release from the destructive truth he has brought them. They return to their old pipe dreams with the idea that their activities have all been the humoring of a mad man, and they return as well to the initial tolerance, security, and affection that is the basis of life in their haven. As Hickey clings to an explanation of insanity for calling his wife a bitch when he killed her, insisting on such madness as he is carried off to jail, he frees the men, enabling them to return to the drunken, dreaming stupor of their half-lives.

Like Gregers, Hickey remains deluded about his mission of salvation, and like Gregers he fails to see the Oedipal conflict that has spurred him to action. Gregers pits himself against a father whom he sees as destroying his mother; although he speaks of his sick conscience in connection with the evil he thinks his father has perpetrated on Old Werle, one gets the impression that his sick conscience has more to do with the ills he feels he has allowed his mother to suffer at the hands of his straying father. He is possibly less outraged that his father may have let Old Ekdal take the punishment for the two of them than he is at his father's affair with Gina, whom he has married off to Hjalmar. Hickey, who insists on degrading his ultraforgiving wife with his iceman joke, has brought the joke to life in the final debasement of death. The Oedipal nature of his hostility is made clear through the character of Parritt, a young boy who may be Larry's son and who has betrayed his anarchist mother out of jealousy of her relationship with other men—a confession he makes to the reluctant Larry in counterpoint to Hickey's confession of murder to the rest of the characters. Though Hickey hates his wife for the guilt she makes him feel, and Parritt hates his mother out of jealousy, both men, like Gregers, have failed to resolve deeply ambivalent feelings about women.

Despite their different life-styles and characters, then, Hickey and Gregers share similar psychological troubles as well as similar messianic goals. O'Neill, however, by bringing Ibsen's absent birthday party on stage, makes the ritual nature of his drama more explicit than Ibsen has. Rocky refers to Hope's birthday celebration, climaxed by Hickey's news of Evelyn's death, as a funeral, and Larry agrees. "Yes, it turned out it wasn't a birthday feast but a wake!" (p. 156). The ritual nature of the birthday is accentuated as preparations are made in act 2 for a midnight celebration. The six candles on the cake indicate Hope's sixty years. Yet even as Margie, Rocky, and Chuck get ready for the celebration, there is joking reference to Hope's death. Hickey, it seems, wanted sixty candles on the cake, but Rocky suggests that he would "croak" blowing them out. Eating a piece of cake, Rocky suggests, would also "croak him" (p. 95).

Apparently, both the flowers and cake are a new touch at this annual birthday rite, added, Rocky complains, by Hickey who has "taken on de party like it was his boithday" (p. 96). As Hickey appears with champagne, he further undermines the illusions of those gathered, and Parritt feels, "There's something not human behind his damned grinning and kidding" (p. 126). And indeed, as he continues to harass and probe, identifying with Parritt and Jimmy Tomorrow with their masked but hostile feelings toward women, insisting on calling Margie and Pearl whores, the name Parritt insists, over Larry's objection, that Larry called Parritt's mother, one begins to see how much the ritual involves the unmasking of women as whores, who betray their men. Harry and Jimmy, it seems, must be brought to see how they hated their wives before Hickey can glimpse his own hatred, a glimpse from which, we have seen, he retreats.

Needless to say, Harry is a reluctant celebrant. "Harry don't even want to remember it's his birthday now!" (p. 135), Hickey reveals; and when Harry makes his birthday speech, it is a bitter condemnation of his friends. When everyone makes a stab at regaining old times by turning on Hickey, whose joke they are sure has come true, he announces Evelyn's death—the revelation that turns the birthday once and for all into a wake.

Anything but subtle with his symbols, O'Neill is, of course, suggesting that when Hickey kills hope in his friend Harry and the others, he is indeed turning Hope itself into a corpse. The birthday ritual, which is to signal a rebirth similar to the one Hickey feels he has experienced, fails. Hickey, who does indeed take over the party, making it his, means to offer himself as the new scapegoat god, but he only succeeds in making Hope a scapegoat for his own illusions.

As in Ibsen's play, however, O'Neill does more in *The Iceman Cometh* than mock his arriving Godot and the rituals of renewal he offers. Just as Hedvig and Old Ekdal add a tragic dimension to *The Wild Duck,* so something of a tragic vision emerges through the action and awareness of Larry Slade. At play's end, Larry stands aside from the chorus of revelers, terming himself the only true convert to Hickey's doctrine. He is forced to give up the sustaining illusion that he is fearless and eagerly awaiting death without care for his old anarchist ideals, partly because Hickey helps him see his stance as an illusion, but largely through his contact with Parritt. Parritt insists on confessing that he has betrayed his mother and the cause for which she stands. But unlike Hickey, Parritt comes to accept his motivation as one of hate and revenge, and he manages to elicit from Larry a longed-for death sentence. "Go! Get the hell out of life, god damn you, before I choke it out of you!", Larry expostulates. "Go up—! . . . Go, for the love of Christ, you mad tortured bastard, for your own sake!" (p. 248).

Unlike the others, Larry is truly reborn. Between them, Parritt and Hickey have stirred the ashes of his commitment until, partly out of pity, partly out of outrage, he passes judgment on another human being; and by so doing he participates fully in life. If that participation leads him to an honest rather than a posed longing for death, it is a longing that comes from the tragic insight he has gained that the others, in their half-living, lack.

Larry's blank stare of despair, a visual counterpoint to the dissonance of the various songs the others sing in the final tableau, is paradoxically a song of life. The play's celebration does not so much exist, as Leonard Chabrowe suggests, in an aesthetic justification of life as an eternally ongoing dance of death,[40] as it does in Larry's compassionate understanding of the revelers and of life. The hold of the forces of life is what Larry experiences, and it is that which makes him finally friends with death.

Gregers and Hickey fail as new king-gods, and in both plays the wintry half-life of the others is ironically reaffirmed. As Gregers's challenge of his father's reign fails, the characters return to the life of illusion that Old Werle has helped them to sustain. Hickey's challenge to Harry Hope and the living dead he protects also fails as Hickey remains trapped in the life of illusion from which he would save the others. Nevertheless, as we explore the ritual patterns in several important dramas of more recent times, we will often find not only the maimed rites of these earlier plays but the remnants, as well, of ritual renewal that Ibsen and O'Neill have also offered. Just as the sacrifice of Hedvig and Parritt bring a new sense of life and new understanding to Old Ekdal and Larry, releasing them from illusions and giving them a tragic sense of the mystery of life's cycle, so the ritual patterns in the works of Beckett, Pinter, Ionesco, Albee, Grass, and Genet often contain authentic elements of renewal. That which is celebrated may seem bleak, but there is a sustaining strength that Old Ekdal and Larry offer in their release from illusion and their acceptance of life with all its darkness and pain.

In selecting particular plays to discuss by those whom I consider to be potentially the most important and enduring of the modern playwrights who have dealt with the quest for renewal, I will focus, in the following pages, on dramas that I consider to be important landmarks in the spiritual journey that the book will chart. By noting important connections with previous playwrights and their dramas as well as discussing connections among the plays I explore, I hope to demonstrate the shared nature of the journey as well as the different perspectives of the journeyers.

The plays I will discuss may not be peopled with mythic gods of old, but they do deal in significant ways with the nonarrival of, the search for, and the arrival of new gods to replace the old. Their focus is on a quest for renewal, and they are structured around that quest. Although they are all related to the question of renewal, the rituals that accompany Godot's arrival or nonarrival take a variety of forms in these plays. We have seen how the ritual of the absent birthday clouds the action of *The Wild Duck* while Harry Hope's birthday party is at the center of *The Iceman Cometh*. I will next turn to the initiation rite that gives form to Beckett's *Waiting for Godot*, continuing, then, to explore other sacrificial rites and ritual patterns that give life to the other dramas under consideration. My purpose is to explore the way in which several modern playwrights employ such rituals as initiations, birthday parties, exorcisms, and homecomings, all of which involve sacrifices, and use the rituals in both traditional and untraditional ways to afford insight into the nature of the quest. Some of the playwrights who have written since Fergusson worried about the "centerless diversity of our theater," remote though they are from the ritual structures out of which drama grew, are finding their way back to a center and thus finding a way forward to new insights that may sustain modern man in his ongoing quest for survival and salvation.

Godot may never arrive in the dramatic world of Beckett, and the implications of that nonarrival will be my first concern. But if we take Godot as a symbol of that force which sometimes does take shape and change our lives, bringing what Estragon and Vladimir hope may be salvation or what they sometimes fear may be damnation, then he does arrive in the dramas of several of the playwrights I will explore. Sometimes he arrives as a false messiah, sometimes as an evil or negative force to be exorcised, but sometimes, too, as an authentic means to salvation. The nonarrival of Godot, his arrival as a false messiash, his exorcism as an evil force, the search for him, his arrival as an authentic savior, and the rituals that attend his nonarrival or arrival in a variety of modern plays are all part of the forthcoming discussion of modern man's fate as an exile and his own possibilities for arrival—for coming home.

NOTES

1. Arthur Ganz finds homecoming and departure to be the structure of all of Chekhov's major plays. See his *Realms of the Self*, pp. 37–56.
2. Friedrich Nietzsche, *The Birth of Tragedy and The Case of Wagner*, p. 60.
3. See Albert Camus, *The Myth of Sisyphus and Other Essays*, p. 3, for what has become a classical statement on homelessness and the absurd condition of modern man. "A world that can be explained even with bad reasons is a familiar world. But on the other hand, in a universe that is suddenly divested of illusions and lights, man feels an alien, a stranger. His exile is without remedy since he is deprived of the memory of a lost home or the hope of a promised land. This divorce between man and his life, the actor and his setting, is properly the feeling of absurdity."
4. Samuel Beckett, *Waiting for Godot* (New York: Grove Press, 1954), pp. 7, 27. All subsequent quotations from *Waiting for Godot* are from this edition.
5. See Tom Driver's *Romantic Quest and Modern Query: A History of the Modern Theatre*, (New York: Delacorte Press).
6. Robert Brustein, *The Theatre of Revolt*, pp. 8, 11.
7. Ibid., p. 329.
8. Samuel Beckett, *Endgame* (New York, Grove Press, 1958), p. 32. All subsequent quotations from *Endgame* are from this edition.
9. Joyce Carol Oates, "Chekhov and the Theatre of the Absurd," in *Drama and Discussion*, 2nd ed., ed. Stanley A. Clayes, p. 664.

Farewell to Firs 31

10. Francis Fergussion, *The Idea of a Theater*, pp. 26, 27, 118.
11. Ibid., pp. 98–142.
12. Martin Esslin, "Godot and His children: The Theatre of Samuel Beckett and Harold Pinter," in *Modern British Dramatists: A Collection of Critical Essays*, ed. John Russell Brown, pp. 60–63, and Esslin, *The Theatre of the Absurd*, p. 404.
13. Fergusson, *The Idea of a Theater*, p. 165.
14. Driver, *Romantic Quest and Modern Query*, p. 224.
15. Ibid., p. 231.
16. Vivian Mercier, *Beckett/Beckett*, p. 74. Mercier actually suggests that Beckett, like Racine, makes much out of nothing.
17. Fergusson, *The Idea of a Theater*, p. 2.
18. Antonin Artaud, *The Theatre and Its Double*, p. 13. "And if there is still one hellish, truly accursed thing in our time," Artaud writes, "it is our artistic dallying with forms, instead of being like victims burnt at the stake, signaling through the flames."
19. Christopher Innes, *Holy Theatre*, p. 11.
20. "Those who employ spectacular means to create a sense not of the terrible but only the monstrous, are strangers to the purpose of tragedy . . . (Aristotle, *Aristotle's Poetics*, trans. S. H. Butcher, p. 78).
21. Northrop Frye, *Anatomy of Criticism*, pp. 40–42.
22. Nietzsche, *The Birth of Tragedy*, p. 60.
23. Artaud, *The Theatre and Its Double*, p. 42.
24. "Messianic revolt occurs when the dramatist rebels against God and tries to take His place . . . (Brustein *The Theatre of Revolt*, p. 16).
25. Frye, *Anatomy of Criticisn*, p. 42.
26. John B. Vickery, "The Golden Bough: Impact and Archetype," in *Myth and Symbol: Critical Approaches and Applications*, ed. Bernice Slote, p. 196.
27. Sir James Frazer, *The Golden Bough*, pp. 310, 313, 668.
28. Eugene O'Neill, *The Iceman Cometh* (New York: Vintage Books, 1946), p. 241. All subsequent quotations from *The Iceman Cometh* are from this edition.
29. Henrik Ibsen, *The Wild Duck*, in *Henrik Ibsen Plays: One*, trans. Michael Meyer (London: Eyre Methuen, 1980), p. 194. All subsequent quotations from *The Wild Duck* are from this edition.
30. James Hurt, *Cataline's Dream: An Essay on Ibsen's Plays*, p. 125.
31. John Northam, *Ibsen: A Critical Study*, p. 141.
32. Ibid., p. 140.
33. Ibid., p. 145.
34. Orley I. Holtan, *Mythic Patterns in Ibsen's Last Plays*, pp. 41, 45.
35. "At this point he goes into the loft and closes the door, an action which Haàkonsen interprets as indicating that he has at least partly cast away his illusion and is determined to embrace his fate" (ibid., p. 46).
36. Hurt, *Cataline's Dream*, p. 129.
37. O'Neill discovered Ibsen on his own while attending Princeton. "I needed no professor to tell me that Ibsen as dramatist, knew whereof he spoke. I found him for myself outside of college grounds and house. If I had met him inside, I might still be a stranger to Ibsen." Quoted in Arthur Gelb and Barbara Gelb, *O'Neill*, p. 112.
38. ". . . Hickey's entrance is delayed so long that—like another long-awaited figure, Beckett's Godot—he begins to accumulate supernatural qualities" (Brustein, *The Theatre of Revolt*, p. 343).
39. Two different versions of the joke about the iceman that Hickey apparently has told the men and to which they often refer are given by O'Neill. In one version it is "the salesman's old story that when he is stewed he would go sobbing around from table to table in bars, hauling out a picture of his wife and blubbering about 'my poor wife.' 'But she's

safe,' the salesman would say. 'I left her in bed with the iceman'" ("Interview with O'Neill by J. S. Wilson," in *Twentieth Century Interpretations of The Iceman Cometh*, ed. John Henry Raleigh, p. 23). The other version is "of the man who calls upstairs, 'Has the iceman come yet?' and his wife calls back, 'No, but he's breathin' hard'" ("Dudley Nichols on *The Iceman Cometh*," in ibid., p. 34).

40. Leonard Chabrowe, "Dinonysus in *The Iceman Cometh*," *Modern Drama* 4, no. 4 (February 1962): 388.

2

The Nonarrival of Godot: Initiation into the Sacred Void

Albert Camus chose to return to an ancient myth for his definition of the modern hero of the absurd. Punished as all men since Adam have been for aspiring to the knowledge and immortality reserved for gods, Camus's Sisyphus takes up his task in the underworld of repeatedly and eternally rolling a huge stone up a mountain from which it repeatedly and eternally descends. This senseless and futile task becomes an image of bondage more potent, perhaps for contemporary society than the image of the rockbound, suffering Prometheus, one of Robert Brustein's prototypes of the messianic hero in modern drama.[1] Prometheus may rage against the gods with the courage of foresight—he sees the end of his ordeal—but Sisyphus must accept his ordeal as final, only rising above it on the wings of irony and the dry mock. "There is no fate," Camus states "that cannot be surmounted by scorn" and "one must imagine Sisyphus happy."[2]

If Camus has defined the possibilites for the absurd hero in terms of myth, Samuel Beckett has actually created a modern myth. Beckett's classical, absurdist play, *Waiting for Godot*, is not ". . . a burlesque of the biblical myth of redemption," although it may contain such burlesque: rather, ". . . The anti-myth built upon antiheroes rises from mere travesty to the elevated rank of a myth itself; from a work of art, it becomes an almost disassociated mythological symbol in its own right."[3]

The close relationship between myth, "a system of word symbols," and ritual, "a system of object and act symbols,"[4] has been explored both by anthropologists and by those "myth critics" who, following Sir James George Frazer and the Cambridge school of anthropologists, have explored the connections among myth, ritual, and art. Dismissing the debate about which comes first, the ritual or the myth, as irrelevant, anthropologist Clyde Kluckhohn notes that both myth and ritual are symbolic means of manipulating experience that man feels he cannot control. Noting their common psychological basis, Kluckhohn states:

> Ritual is an obsessive repetitive activity—often a symbolic dramatization of the fundamental "needs" of the society, whether "economic," "social," or "sexual." Mythology is the rationalization of those same needs, whether they are all expressed in overt ceremonial or not.[5]

The nonarriving Godot has taken his place beside Sisyphus, Prometheus, and other mythological figures of old, even as the nonacting characters in Beckett's play have provided the ritual basis of the Godot myth.

The two ways of suffering that are dramatized by Aeschylus in his *Prometheus Bound* reappear in *Waiting for Godot* and are seen, as in the earlier drama, to be both contrasting and similar. Like Prometheus bound to his rock, Didi and Gogo are bound to their place of appointment with Godot. Though their bondage may be more self-imposed than that of the rebellious Titan, it holds them just as surely as the adamantine chains that Hephaestus uses to bind him.

> ESTRAGON: Well, shall we go?
> VLADIMIR: Yes, let's go.
> *They do not move.*
>
> (P. 35b)

Pozzo and Lucky's endless peregrinations may again seem more self-imposed than those of Prometheus's fellow-sufferer, Io, who is driven by the gadfly the jealous Hera has sent to punish her for her attractiveness to Zeus, but Pozzo and Lucky are not only tied to each other; they are bound to their endless journey. As in the ancient play, the contrasting forms of suffering in *Godot* are shown to be mere variations on the theme of the bondage of man, whether he is driven to stay or to go, a bondage that in the modern play, unlike the ancient, affords no certain, eventual deliverance.

There are, however, important differences as well as similarities in the sufferings of the four *Godot* characters. Although the play is seemingly lacking in action, its structure is a kind of initiation rite that its four major characters undergo with varying degrees of completion and success. All of them participate in the same rite and are involved in a general crisis of faith, but their resolutions to the crisis differ significantly. Mircea Eliade defines initiation as denoting "a body of ties and oral teachings whose purpose is to produce a decisive alteration in the religious and social status of the person to be initiated."[6] The *Godot* rite, however, is not the kind of puberty rite that Eliade describes "which introduces the candidate into the human community and into the world of spiritual and cultural value."[7] Beckett's drama reflects a world that has little human community and is all but devoid of spiritual and cultural value. Rather, the concern here is with those "specialized initiations" in which the individual attempts to transcend the human condition, ritual in its "metacultural and transhistorical" dimension during which the initiated undergoes "an existential experience—the experience of ritual death and the revelation of the sacred."[8]

The irony of the particular revelation of the sacred in *Waiting for Godot* lies in its location in what seems to be meaninglessness itself, the void. What the four major characters in Beckett's drama are involved in is an initiation rite that leads them to experience the void as sacred and to orient themselves accordingly. Pozzo's initiation begins in act 1 and is apparently completed between the acts so that in act 2 he becomes the shaman or initiatory guide for Vladimir, whose crisis of faith is at the center of the play. Lucky, who is something of an appendage to Pozzo, and Estragon, who is something of an appendage to Vladimir, take their roles in the initiation rite as well.

Pozzo's initiation or ritual death begins in act 1 with the gradual loss of his illusions of purpose and power. When he enters in circus-master fashion, driving Lucky, a rope around his neck, before him, Pozzo presents himself with such pomposity that Didi and Gogo momentarily mistake him for Godot. "I am Pozzo! *(Silence)* Pozzo! *(Silence.)* Does that name mean nothing to you? *(Silence).* I say does that mean nothing to you?" (p. 15b). Informing Didi and Gogo that they await Godot on "his" land, which he beneficently permits, "The road is free to all" (p. 16), he flaunts his many possessions, his watch, pipe, and vaporizer as well as those accessories which Lucky carries and furnishes on demand, such as a coat, whip, stool, and basket of food, chicken, and wine. He is clear, too, about his destination, the fair at which he plans to sell Lucky; and he has the wisdom to discourse on the twilight.

By the end of act 1, however, Pozzo has misplaced his pipe, vaporizer, and watch and has commented on the worn-out condition of both his whip and his memory. Unsure of himself, "I have such need of encouragement!" (p. 25b), he is sympathetic with the tramps as Godot worshipers—"I myself in your situation, if I had an appointment with a Godin . . . Godet . . . Godot . . . anyhow you see who I mean, I'd wait till it was black night before I gave up" (p. 24)—but is also aware of the impending descent of black night that will make Godot's arrival irrelevant. Hanging on desperately, if comically, to an idea of secular time, he denies Vladimir's contention that time has stopped—"Whatever you like, but not that" (p. 24b)—but when he proceeds with assurance to offer his thoughts on the twilight they all inhabit, he soon falters. Combining the lyrical with the prosaic, he ends with an intuition of the gloom of night's sudden descent: "That's how it is on this bitch of an earth" (p. 25b).

All loss need not, of course, be initiatory, but Pozzo's attachment to his possessions makes the loss of some and the failure of others to work akin to the dismemberment ordeals that often accompany initiations, whether in puberty rites or as part of the initiation of a shaman. (Eliade gives numerous examples in which Shamans tell of their dreams of or experience of dismemberment by demons, a dismemberment symbolic of the death to the secular that precedes rebirth into the sacred.[9]) His role as Lucky's master is apparently also part of Pozzo's ordeal, for he sees this former "angel" as a demon. Sobbing, Pozzo complains, "He used to be so kind . . . so helpful . . . and entertaining . . . my good angel . . . and now . . . he's killing me" (p. 23). The nature of the "death" he undergoes at Lucky's hands may be detected during Lucky's "think" speech in which he offers a vision of the wisdom of the ages become incoherent in the face of a universe that is wasting away, the single surety being that man too "wastes and pines wastes and pines" (p. 29). Pozzo's suffering increases during the speech, until he conspires with the others to stop Lucky by grabbing his hat on which he proceeds to trample: "There's an end to his thinking!" (p. 30).

The climactic loss, the descent of "black night," happens between the acts and we only hear about it, Pozzo's blindness and Lucky's muteness, as already accomplished in act 2. The properties that Lucky carried have now turned to sand, as have all the illusions of power or knowledge that had lingered in the former act.

Several critics have associated Pozzo's loss of sight with a concurrent loss of spiritual insight. Richard Schechner, for example, considers Pozzo's epiphany on time to be false. Prodded by Vladimir about when he lost his sight, Pozzo proclaims,

> Have you not done tormenting me with your accursed time! One day, is that not enough for you, one day he went dumb, one day I went blind, one day we'll go deaf, one day we were born, one day we shall die, the same day, the same second, is that not enough for you? (*Calmer.*) They give birth astride of a grave, the light gleams an instant, then it's night once more. (*He jerks the rope.*) On!
>
> (P. 57b)

"The experience of the play," Schechner suggests, "shows that there is plenty of time, too much; waiting means more time than things to fill it."[10] Curtis M. Brooks also finds this second-act discourse on time to be a failure of perception and calls it "anti-mythic." Pozzo, he claims, is lost in profane time, which like him moves "on" but without a direction or sacred center to give it meaning.[11]

On the contrary. The insight to which Pozzo moves may be harrowing but it is not false; rather, it is the true epiphany of the play, a glimpse into the sacred void. Enter Sisyphus!

The Nonarrival of Godot

The theories of Mircea Eliade on time are most helpful here; he relates that religious man from the most primitive to the most sophisticated tends to experience the duration of time in which he lives historically, moment by moment, as profane, and the time of the creation of the world and all its inhabitants, which is a reversible time or "a primordial mythical time made present," as sacred. Religious festivals and rites evoke man's participation in this sacred time, which is transcendental and revelatory of reality.[12]

> Hence religious man lives in two kinds of time, of which the more important, sacred time, appears under the paradoxical aspect of a circular time, reversible and recoverable, a sort of eternal mythical present that is periodically reintegrated by means of rites. This attitude in regard to time suffices to distinguish religious from nonreligious man; the former refuses to live solely in what, in modern terms, is called the historical present; he attempts to regain a sacred time that, from one point of view, can be homologized to eternity.[13]

In the second act Pozzo does, indeed, seem to be lost in profane time. Shorn of his illusions of purpose and power, Pozzo no longer seeks to sell Lucky at a fair,[14] but merely goes "on."

> VLADIMIR: Where do you go from here?
> POZZO: On. . . .
> VLADIMIR: What is there in the bag?
> POZZO: Sand. *(He jerks the rope.)* On!
> VLADIMIR: Don't go yet.
> POZZO: I'm going.
> VLADIMIR: What do you do when you fall far from help?
> POZZO: We wait till we can get up. Then we go on. On!
>
> (P. 57)

Not only does he merely go "on," as Sisyphus does, in futile fashion; his bag, formerly filled with food, contains sand, a good counterpart to Sisyphus's rock. In act 1 he had said that if he had an appointment with Godot, he would wait until "black night" before going on. In act 2 there is no mention by Pozzo of Godot. Black night has come to stay.

Despite total rejection of that eternity which Eliade finds an essential part of the religious experience, a hereafter in which man's suffering has meaning, Pozzo, like Sisyphus, it seems to me, has found a solution to his religious yearnings. Eliade says that the most secular of men revert to the religious quest for the sacred, though they do it in personal terms; and for secular man, too, time has different intensities.[15] Pozzo acts in true mythical fashion when he offers his vision of primal beginnings. And though that vision allows man's life as but a moment between life and death, that moment becomes sacred and hence, paradoxically, endless. As all time becomes "the same day," profane time is destroyed with whatever Godots may wait in the wings. When Pozzo says that "the blind have no notion of time, the things of time are hidden from them too" (p. 55b), he is not, as Brooks claims, denying the blind Tiresias's prophetic vision;[16] he is, rather, declaring secular time to be irrelevant. Like Hamm in Beckett's *Endgame*, who notes that "The end is in the beginning and yet you go on" (p. 69), Pozzo accepts death and nothingness and goes on in the face of it.

Pozzo comes close to Camus's idea of the absurd hero in his ability to go on in the face of an absurd, unknowable world. "The struggle itself toward the heights is enough to fill a man's heart," Camus says; "one must imagine Sisyphus happy."[17] But if Pozzo remains undefeated in the face of the void, passing through his initiation to the "sacred," to what is "real," he does not share Sisyphus's joy in life's futile struggle. Sisyphus retains something of the traditional rebel-victim's victory of mind over matter.[18] But mind—in this instance Lucky—remains an encumbrance to Pozzo, who has given up hope of selling him. Pozzo is doubtless consoled that Lucky is at least dumb—one remembers how he suffered through his "think" speech in act 1—but he does not take kindly to their mutual dependence, still calling him "pig" and "menial." If Estragon can't raise Lucky by pulling on the rope, Pozzo recommends giving "him a taste of his boot, in the face and the privates as far as possible" (p. 56).

As absurd hero and prophet, Pozzo is far more furious than joyful, and we see that fury exhibited in his climactic speech in which he finds Vladimir's questions about time "abominable" (p. 57). But the abominations of time are now Vladimir's, not his. "Have you not done tormenting me with *your* [my italics] accursed time?" (p. 57b). Profane time, Vladimir's, has become meaningless in the light of Pozzo's insight about sacred time as an instant between birth and death, an insight he delivers when *"calmer,"* if not calm.

It is important that Vladimir shares Pozzo's epiphany, and that he is initiated into the mystery of the sacred void, because Pozzo, although he may come closest as a character to Camus's absurd hero, is not Beckett's. The wavering, doubt-ridden, backsliding Estragon and Vladimir are Beckett's anti-heroic heroes, and Pozzo and Lucky, who are far less sympathetic in their master-slave relationship than the tramps in their friendship or "bad marriage," share in that heroism only to the extent that they share in the quest for salvation and, on one level of the play's action, are but parts of a four-sided character.[19]

"Astride of a grave and a difficult birth," Vladimir remarks, picking up Pozzo's birth imagery after Pozzo and Lucky's exit. "Down in the hole, lingeringly, the grave-digger puts on the forceps. We have time to grow old. The air is full of our cries . . ." (pp. 58–58b). Although Vladimir may seem to refute Pozzo's vision,[20] since for him life's fleeting moment seems painfully long, he actually shares it and elaborates on it. As Jacques Dubois suggests, "Beckettian man, like Pascalian man, is torn between two infinities: a very short life in view of his appetite for living and a very long life because of his suffering."[21] Beckett noted in his book on Proust that there are moments of transition in which "the boredom of living is replaced with the suffering of being."[22] Like most initiations, which are transitions, what is involved is not just death, but rebirth.

The death-rebirth agonies of the *Godot* initiation rite involve the four characters in much confusion about time, place, and identity. "So there you are again," Vladimir remarks to Estragon at their opening of the play reunion. "Am I?", Estragon asks (p. 7). Pozzo does not recognize the tramps from meeting to meeting, nor does he know when he went blind, and Didi and Gogo are not sure of the place or time of their appointment with Godot, or of his identity. The various kinds of disorientation that Didi and Gogo and Pozzo and Lucky experience are clearly a part of the mutual religious crisis they are undergoing, but they just as clearly and ironically mark their progress in the initiation rite with which they are unwittingly involved.

Estragon, who seems least aware of what he is doing, where he is, and why, is at the outset really the farthest along of the four. He knows from the beginning that which the others learn by the end: "Nothing to be done" (p. 7). While Vladimir tends to intellectualize and ponder metaphysical questions, Estragon seems to intuit the nature of their predicament more profoundly, even though he may seem, like many a wise fool before him, to be merely slow-witted. Vladimir still works with a traditional sense of justice—if Estragon is beaten nightly, he must have done something to deserve it—but Estragon, in the manner of Camus's absurd hero, is quite convinced of his innocence.[23] When Vladimir suggests they might repent, Estragon goes to the heart of the matter. "Our being born?" he asks (p. 8b). Vladimir responds with that painful laugh which apparently relates to his physical condition, something to do with his bladder, but which, like all that is physical in the play, has its metaphysical dimension.

VLADIMIR: You'd make me laugh if it wasn't prohibited.
ESTRAGON: We've lost our rights?
VLADIMIR: *(distinctly).* We got rid of them.

(P. 13)

Vladimir's is the more acute insight here. Indeed, Estragon's disorientation about time and place is not always a sign of his further progress; Vladimir sometimes catches up or surpasses him. And, as in the case of their repenting being born, they can share the wisdom of a bad joke. The point is that disorientation to profane time and place is not as negative as it seems; it often suggests a reorientation to time and place and an approach to the sacred void into which Pozzo has gazed with his blind eyes.[24]

The initiation in the play involves coming to terms not only with the nothingness (nothing to be done) of the human predicament, but with the nowhereness as well. When Vladimir asks Estragon if he doesn't recognize the place of their meeting in act 2, Estragon responds with fury. "Recognize! What is there to recognize? All my lousy life I've crawled about in the mud! And you talk to me about scenery! *(Looking wildly about him.)* Look at this muck heap! I've never stirred from it!" (p. 39). Slightly later, when Vladimir asks him where they were the evening before, Estragon responds, "How would I know? In another compartment. There's no lack of void" (p. 42). Estragon's inability to recognize their place of meeting is again a measure of his progress; he has already given up scenery as a mere coverup of the void that he has experienced as the essential reality.

Of course, such a perception of place as void seems antimythical in Eliade's terms since sacred place as well as sacred time involves a transcendent reality that gives form to chaos, while Estragon's angry recognition of the void suggests an inversion—the form of chaos is all the shape that there is. Just as Brooks sees Pozzo as lost in profane time, he sees the tramps as lost in profane space. "Vladimir and Estragon," he writes, "are tired pilgrims of the long and dusty way, which ordinarily leads from death, to life, from man to divinity, from time to timelessness. The play derives its power from its ironic implication that the road leads nowhere."[25] The point once again is, however, that the recognition that the road leads nowhere makes of nowhere the sacred center of the void itself; hence nowhere and notime become the very "atemporal mythic moment" that is sacred. Expressing concern with the separateness of chaos and form in art, Beckett has stated that the artist's "task" today is "to find a form that accommodates the mess."[26] "Can you make no use of nothing, nuncle?" the Fool asks Lear, who like the *Godot* tramps undergoes that initiation into nothingness, that acquaintance with himself as unaccommodated man that gives tragic shape, form, and meaning to nothingness.

Just as Estragon in some ways is farther along than Vladimir in the initiation into the sacred void, so Lucky is in some ways further along than Pozzo. Lucky has already, Pozzo tells the tramps in the first act, taught Pozzo all the "beautiful" things he knows; and in his "think" speech, which Pozzo suffers as part of his own initiation, Lucky offers the half-mad babbling that is the result of his own experience of the abyss, the nothingness of the void. Lucky, who embodies the dying certainties of past civilization in act 1, seems in his muteness to embody death itself in act 2,[27] so that Pozzo, who is tied first to the dying and then to Death itself, comes to accept the burden of his own mortality, even though he continues to despise that burden.

Although Pozzo acts in the course of the second act as an initiatory guide, the prophet who announces the doom Estragon has intuited and Vladimir so fears, the tramps are attracted to Lucky's resolution to his religious crisis, the embracing of his slavery. If, as Vladimir suggests when he finds laughter painful, they have not lost their rights but have given them up, then they are more like Lucky in his voluntary slavery than is immediately apparent—Firs on the road rather than left in his dignity to die with the orchard. Estragon, who despairs whenever he is reminded by Vladimir that they must wait for Godot, would prefer the physical bondage of Lucky, who gets the bones, to the existential anguish of his waiting for an uncertain fate. At one point he even seems interested in taking Lucky's place.

> ESTRAGON: *(to Vladimir)* Does he want to replace him?
> VLADIMIR: What?
> ESTRAGON: Does he want someone to take his place or not?
> VLADIMIR: I don't think so.
> ESTRAGON: What?
> VLADIMIR: I don't know.
> ESTRAGON: Ask him.
>
> (P. 23)

And despite his tendency to dominate Estragon, Vladimir would also like to be the secure slave, although he finds he cannot think or dance on command.

> VLADIMIR: Tell me to think.
> ESTRAGON: What?
> VLADIMIR: Say, Think, pig!
> *Silence.*
> VLADIMIR: I can't!
> ESTRAGON: That's enough of that.
> VLADIMIR: Tell me to dance.
> ESTRAGON: I'm going.
>
> (P. 47)

Despite the attractiveness of the slave's role to Didi and Gogo, it is not their choice. Unable to close themselves off, in Lucky's fashion, from the moment of transition in which they seem to dwell, with all its openness to suffering and consciousness, they do not elect his kind of living death, any more than they elect the suicidal death with which they flirt in both acts, the hanging of themselves from the tree. Though they wistfully recall an earlier time when they might have been well enough dressed to ascend the Eiffel Tower and jump, and though Estragon fondly remembers a past suicide attempt in which he was saved from drowning by Vladimir, a time of symbolic rebirth,[28] like Camus's absurd hero the tramps reject that which "engulfs" or "settles" the absurd.[29]

Somewhat less heroic than Camus's absurd hero, however, who rejects death as an escape, Didi and Gogo reject suicide partly because death is as uncertain to them as life. Unsure of their weight—they don't know which one is heavier—they fear that whichever one is heavier will not succeed in hanging himself without breaking the bough. Like so many subsequent Beckett protagonists, all descended from Hamlet with his fears of an unknown hereafter, Didi and Gogo do not, like Pozzo in his epiphany, perceive a great nothingness in death. Haunted by "all the dead voices," who they say "talk about their lives," they surmise that "To have lived is not enough for them," though "To be dead is not enough for them" either (p. 40b).

Nor is Godot enough for the tramps. Although they do not reject Godot in any more final way than they reject suicide, again falling somewhat short of Camus's hero, who considers but rejects both suicide and God, their feelings toward Godot are deeply ambivalent. Vladimir views Godot as someone who will somehow change their lives—"Estragon: And if he comes? Vladimir: We'll be saved" (p. 60b)—and who will punish them if they leave; but he is a figure whose possible arrival terrifies Estragon and whose off-stage actions as described by the messenger toward the end of each act seem as arbitrary as those of the Christian God, whom, with his white beard, he apparently resembles. Like the personal God in Lucky's "think" speech, who loves us dearly, Godot would seem to care—he sends his messenger with vague promises; but, as with Lucky's God and Vladimir's Christ and the two thieves, there are seemingly arbitrary exceptions to that love, which paradoxically comes from "the heights of divine apathia divine athambia divine aphasia" (p. 28b). Lucky's God, like Didi and Gogo's Godot, for reasons unknown, allows man to waste and pine. The failure of Godot as a savior is no doubt also partly a reflection of Estragon and Vladimir's perception of him. They do not quite know what they want from Godot or who he is and thus reduce him in their imagination to a businessman who must consult family, friends, agents, correspondents, books, and bank account before making a decision about how to help them.

Unable to rest in Lucky's stance, nor to make do with Godot, Vladimir comes to a crisis of faith at the play's climax[30] that Estragon experiences before and after him. Led by Pozzo as initiatory guide to the brink of the abyss, Vladimir undergoes the play's central initiation into the sacred void, exploring as part of that experience the mysterious relationship of life to death. Pozzo noted that when he woke up one day "blind as fortune," he wondered if he had awakened. "Sometimes I wonder if I'm not still asleep" (p. 55b). Vladimir picks up his image after he has left.

> VLADIMIR: Was I sleeping, while the others suffered? Am I sleeping now? To-morrow, when I wake, or think I do, what shall I say to today? That with Estragon my friend, at this place, until the fall of night, I waited for Godot? That Pozzo passed, with his carrier, and that he spoke to us? Probably. But in all that what truth will there be? *(Estragon, having struggled with his boots in vain, is dozing off again. Vladimir looks at him.)* He'll know nothing. He'll tell me about the blows he received and I'll give him a carrot. *(Pause.)* Astride of a grave and a difficult birth. Down in the hole, lingeringly, the gravedigger puts on the forceps. We have time to grow old. The air is full of our cries. *(He listens.)* But habit is a great deadener. *(He looks again at Estragon.)* At me too someone is looking, of me too someone is saying, He is sleeping, he knows nothing, let him sleep on. *(Pause.)* I can't go on! *(Pause.)* What have I said?
> (Pp. 58–58b)

Vladimir's epiphany, unlike Pozzo's, is not an angry statement but an exploration of the levels of reality in his world. He has questioned Pozzo's blindness, for unlike Godot's messenger boy, Pozzo seems to see him—"I wonder is he really blind . . . it seemed to me he saw us," (pp. 57b–58)— and to give him the sense of his own reality and identity that he has felt missing from his encounters with Godot's emissary. When Estragon asks him if Pozzo might not have been Godot, Vladimir is no longer sure.

> VLADIMIR: Not at all *(Less sure.)* Not at all! *(Still less sure.)* Not at all!
> (P. 58)

Vladimir questions, in Prospero fashion, the reality of his world, its truth or meaning. Of what does that world consist? A faithful waiting for Godot, blows for Estragon, friendship, death, the alleviation of suffering through habit. Placing Godot in the wings on one side, and death in the wings on the other, Vladimir's initiation involves a vision in which he brings the two face to face. Looking at the now sleeping Estragon, whose nightmares he has refused throughout the play to hear, he concludes his epiphany with a declaration of his own profound ignorance. "At me too someone is looking, of me too someone is saying, he is sleeping, he knows nothing, let him sleep on" (p. 58b). It is as if he has been able, through his initiatory confrontation with death, to move outside of himself and observe himself from another perspective. Unlike Pozzo, however, who can go on in the face of the unknowableness of life, Vladimir says, "I can't go on" (p. 58b). As surely as Oedipus comes to know the deeds he has done and the self that he is, Vladimir comes to know that he will never possess his deeds or know himself—that whether Godot or death comes, he must share the darkness that Pozzo inhabits. But the rebirth that initiation is all about and that Pozzo has experienced, eludes him.

Shortly before Vladimir's crisis of faith, Estragon suggests he cannot go on—"But I can't go on like this" (p. 44)—and he echoes himself and Vladimir toward the play's end when he again says, "I can't go on like this" (p. 60b). Far less devoted to their waiting situation than Vladimir, Estragon has made repeated attempts throughout the play to leave and has questioned the wisdom of their union several times, putting forth the possibility that they were not meant for the same road and noting with dismay that Vladimir sings when absent from his friend. It is Estragon, too, who has belittled Vladimir's faith. "We are not Saints but we have kept our appointment. How many people can boast as much?" Vladimir asks. "Billions" (p. 51b), is Estragon's deflating response. But Vladimir, who has been initiated into the mysteries of nothingness, is drawn back from the abyss into his hopes of salvation by Godot's messenger, and his response to Estragon's final "I can't go on like this" is "That's what you think" (p. 60b). If one were to evaluate Vladimir at this point in terms of Camus's absurd hero, one would have to say that he falters—that he returns to illusions about a transcendental future and to flirtation with suicide, an embrace of the enemy, death; they plan to bring some good rope for the purpose the next day.

As already noted, however, Vladimir is not Camus's hero but Beckett's absurdly antiheroic one. Opting for survival, like Pozzo he will go on; but going on, as Pozzo does, without hope of finding greater meaning in life's fleeting moment is not possible for Vladimir. "What they seek to complete," Michael Robinson writes of Didi and Gogo, "is the arbitrary series begun by birth, to reach that end where time is no more and where their present unreality is changed into certainty of their own identity and existence. What, in fact, they seek is to be reunited with the Self they know must exist outside time in the union of their personal infinity with that of the timeless void."[31] Pozzo may be able to make do with the flicker of life in the timeless void, but Vladimir insists on the Self. "Tell him you saw me" (p. 59), he says, almost attacking the messenger boy with his insistence on his own reality and significance.

Because the images of God are so unsatisfactory in the play, whether they are Lucky's or Didi and Gogo's, one is tempted to agree with those critics who suggest that Beckett knows full well that Godot will never come.[32] Beckett does not, however, deride the now shaky faith of his hero. Rather, he undercuts Pozzo as hero, not only by keeping the master/slave relationship alive between Lucky and him, but also by giving the dead landscape some life, the leaves that appear overnight on the once-dead tree, by providing the agonized Estragon with new boots that fit better, a minor miracle in a world of decay and loss, and above all by sending the messenger boy in with Godot's message of promised future arrival. The stage as microcosm, the "board" (p. 55b) that Pozzo thinks they may be on, is not the "board" for Pozzo because it has a tree; his stage as microcosm is now totally barren. It is, however, the board for Vladimir and Estragon and for the audience who see the tree, who still look to the tree for its promise of the means to suicide or further life, and who relate to the wings from which Godot sends in his messenger and his message of hope.

The Parable of the Door in Franz Kafka's novel *The Trial* may not be the parable of this play, but it offers a useful parallel to the *Godot* situation. Joseph K., condemned to death for unknown crimes, hears the parable from a priest who would instruct him. The door in the parable, which presumably leads to some higher truth or sacred order, is guarded so that the man for whom it is held open may not enter. The guard, however, tells the man who has never entered, just as he closes it, that it was strictly for him. Salvation in Kafka is improbable and remote; the messengers of the higher power are themselves corrupt or seem, like the guard at the door, to withhold salvation rather than offer it. Joseph K., unresigned to Pozzo's vision of life as a flash in the great void, dies like a dog, feeling justly that in his year's "trial" he has not gained much insight. He has not even tried to get past the guard.

Godot's messenger is not corrupt; he is an innocent, who does not understand his master's inclinations, why he is favored over his brother, and he does not recognize Didi and Gogo from day to day. Vladimir's second meeting with him near the play's end, in which he gives the boy's answers for him, suggests Vladimir's increased doubt. He has learned from Pozzo and from his own experience, and if he merely repeated what he now must feel is an all but hopeless litany, an empty ritual of hope deferred in which the words are there, but not the music, then one might say his initiation into the mysteries of death and the void were complete and he could take up Lucky's bags of sand or approach Sisyphus's rock. But Vladimir backs off from the initiation rite he has undergone.

BOY: What am I to tell Mr. Godot, Sir?
VLADIMIR: Tell him . . . *(he hesitates)* . . . tell him you saw me and that . . . *(he hesitates)* . . . that you saw me. *(Pause. Vladimir advances, the Boy recoils. Vladimir halts, the Boy halts. With sudden violence.)* You're sure you saw me, you won't come and tell me to-morrow that you never saw me! *Silence. Vladimir makes a sudden spring forward, the Boy avoids him and exit running.* . . .

(P. 59)

His insistence on the reality of the self and on being perceived[33] is the message Vladimir sends back. The possibility that spring may come again, that the wasteland may be redeemed, that it is significant that one of the thieves was saved, that this is not a Dantesque Inferno ("Estragon: I'm in hell") in which hopeless repetition of suffering is the order, but a purgatorial passage to a renewed and more meaningful existence remains.

The juxtaposition of the two orientations to salvation, Didi and Gogo waiting for Godot and Pozzo and Lucky going on in the face of nothingness, is conflated in Vladimir, who is initiated into the latter but chooses the former. Indeed, what one sees by play's end is that the two attitudes are not as opposite as they seem. They are juxtaposed in Estragon's attitudes as well as in Vladimir's, for Estragon sees himself one moment as a Christ figure, the next as utterly impotent. Having left his boots at the end of act 1 for another person with smaller feet, Estragon shocks Vladimir with his suggestion that, like Christ, he can go barefoot.

>   ESTRAGON: All my life I've compared myself to him.
>   VLADIMIR: But where he lived it was warm, it was dry!
>   ESTRAGON: Yes. and they crucified quick.
>   *Silence.*
>   VLADIMIR: We've nothing more to do here.
>   ESTRAGON: Nor anywhere else.
>
> (P. 34b)

Only a silence separates Estragon's perception of himself as a scapegoat, the counterpart to Lucky, whose dance is the "scapegoat's agony," from his perception of himself as totally ineffectual, lost in profane time and space.

Mircea Eliade begins his book *The Sacred and Profane* by alluding to Rudolf Otto's 1917 publication *Das Heilige (The Sacred)* in which he deals with God as a "terrible *power.*" Numinous experiences for Otto are terrifying because they are inhuman in their otherness and fullness and make man feel his impotence and nothingness.[34] The sense of their own nothingness in the scheme of things, whether that scheme allows us Pozzo's moment in the infinite void, a void which has become more numinous by play's end than the Godot who might save man from it, or whether that scheme allows us Godot, whose own impotence—he does nothing—seems a magnification of their own, is something that Pozzo and Lucky and Vladimir and Estragon share. Nowhere is their unity clearer than when they are all piled up on the ground in act 2 in a helpless heap that demonstrates their shared inability to help each other or themselves.

Still, if one considers the fall of the *Godot* four as part of their initiatory ordeal, one may see some positive aspects in it. They become much like Victor W. Turner's "threshold people," or "liminal personae," who, like neophytes in initiation ceremonies, lack possessions and status or anything "that may distinguish them from their fellow neophytes or initiands."[35] Stripped of his possessions and sight, Pozzo on the ground answers Estragon when he calls out both Abel and then Cain. He has become, Estragon asserts ironically, "all humanity" (p. 54), and, in a sense, all four have so become. United on the ground, the *Godot* characters enter into a new kind of community, in Turner's vocabulary a "communitas," which can be a creative and humanizing transitory condition in which to be.

Then, too, they get up. Rising, clowns that they are, from what Pozzo earlier called this "bitch of an earth" (p. 25b), but Estragon now calls "Sweet mother earth" (p. 53), the four share a tremendous aptitude for survival, if not for salvation. Vladimir and Estragon really only play at suicide as they play at being the tree or being Pozzo and Lucky. Like Pozzo and Lucky, they go "on." The four characters are as resilient as all fools, those who get slapped and bounce back for more.

The two stances, that of going "on" in the face of nothingness and that of going on in terms of standing still or waiting for Godot to transform their lives, come together most clearly in Vladimir, but they are not fully integrated in him. As Robinson says, the tramps fail to unite the self's personal infinity outside of time, Godot's promised transformation of reality, "with that of the timeless void."[36] Or, as Eva Metman notes in her Jungian interpretation of the play, the dependence of the members of the couples on each other and Vladimir's dependence on Godot are stagnating. For Metman, "This inseparability of factors of potential conflict expresses a state of latency in the psyche."[37]

Giving up Godot may be the solution of several critics, but it is not Beckett's solution for the integration of fragmented characters or the fragmented psyche of modern man. If giving up Godot as an illusion were Beckett's solution, Pozzo would be his hero, a Pozzo reintegrated with his intellect, not still tied to it with a rope. That Beckett offers no solution is partly the key to the power of the Godot myth. Taking up Chekhov's dispossessed exiles on the road and Chekhov's ironical nonjudging attitude, Beckett looks at those characters, unaccommodated man exposed to the elements, and finds that they have grown a bit more cruel than those of his mentor (excluding Natasha perhaps); Firs left behind is pathetic; Lucky on the road is both pathetic and vicious. Lopakhin orders the ax to fall but weeps for those he ousts and for himself; he feels as dispossessed by his achievement as those he dispossesses; Pozzo suggests only ill treatment for the slave from whom he has wrested power. But Beckett still provides us characters in *Waiting for Godot* who, like Chekhov's, dream of a redeemed future, that which Godot will bring, one that is related to a more ideal past, a time when Lucky's thinking made sense and when the paradox of a personal God who cares and human suffering was resolved in some sense of justice.

This impulse to look backward and forward in Chekhov and Beckett rather than to the present is correctly perceived by Clayton A. Hubbs in his article "Chekhov and the Contemporary Theatre" as part of the playing out of the ritual drama of the year. "At the back of the plays [Chekhov's] is the ritual of the year drama and behind that the edenic myth of a lost paradise."[38] I have already explored elements of the year drama with its dying-reviving gods in Ibsen's *The Wild Duck* and O'Neill's *The Iceman Cometh* (see chapter 1), and Brooks has shown *Waiting for Godot* to be such a year drama, a battle between winter and spring in which winter remains in the ascendancy. "In the seasonal structure of the play," Hubbs says of *The Three Sisters*, "the action regresses, from spring to winter, from the promise of renewal to death."[39] Hubbs, however, mistakenly thinks that because Chekhov is a secular writer, he does not believe in the reality of his myth. "Chekhov's purpose," he writes, "is to bring about an awareness of myth's absence and the human consequences of the denial of the immediate material world. When that awareness occurs, one assumes that the characters would regain the ability to love and rediscover the 'true myth' of collective communion."[40]

Beckett, however, just like Estragon and Vladimir, does not *not* believe in Godot any more than Chekhov denies the validity of the aspiration of his various characters. While the ritual routines, the little "canters" or vaudeville exchanges of Vladimir and Estragon, may seem merely repetitious and empty of meaning, habit operating as the great deadener, they are rituals nevertheless; and they are done, not only to pass the time, but also to give themselves "the impression we exist" (p. 44b) and to influence Godot's arrival. At the same time that Estragon knows and Pozzo and Vladimir learn that there is nothing to be done, Vladimir and Estragon are not certain and continue to act. Estragon searches for causes in his boot, Vladimir in his hat. When they speak of the dead voices that they attempt to shut out with their conversation, Estragon hears them like the rustling of leaves, which he insists on repetitively in contrast and in conflict with Vladimir who hears them first like wings and sand and then like feathers and ashes (p. 40b). His new, better-fitting boots first appear to Estragon as brown and then "a kind of green" (p. 43b). When they "do the tree," upon which a few leaves have mysteriously appeared, imitating it by standing on one foot, they clearly do it as a ritual incantation to God, as if trying to merge with what little life the tree has in order to make God recognize them. "Do you think God sees me?" (p. 49b), Estragon asks Vladimir, as he staggers about imitating the tree, their desire for recognition and pity becoming desperate.

> VLADIMIR: You must close your eyes.
> *Estragon closes his eyes, staggers worse.*
> ESTRAGON: *(Stopping, brandishing his fists, at the top of his voice).* God have pity on me!
> VALDIMIR: *(vexed).* And me?
> ESTRAGON: On me! On me! Pity! On me!
>
> (P. 49b)

At this point, the staggering Didi and Gogo once again confront the staggering Pozzo and Lucky, and the final series of ritual routines take place, in which the four fall and rise, each couple going "on" in its own way.

The rituals, as in Chekhov, are ineffectual. Just as the Cherry Orchard is not saved and the three sisters do not return to Moscow, so Godot does not arrive. But if they have failed as worshipers, Didi and Gogo have not failed enough.

> VLADIMIR: This is becoming really insignificant.
> ESTRAGON: Not enough.
>
> (P. 44)

From the beginning they have been waiting for Godot to come or night to fall. Night, the void, has fallen once toward the end of act 1 and once toward the end of act 2, has permanently fallen for the blinded Pozzo of act 2, and has been the spiritual environment or condition of their ongoing litany—"Nothing to be done." But if they have progressed toward accepting their lives as a second in the void, the tramps continue to hope for more.

In the final comic ritual routine, Vladimir returns to his role as straight man to Estragon's simpleton. Estragon's trousers have fallen as a result of removing his belt for a suicide attempt, and he is not aware that they are down. In his disorientation to secular space, there is no significant difference at any rate between up and down. Vladimir must remind him.

> VLADIMIR: Pull on your trousers.
> ESTRAGON: What?
> VLADIMIR: Pull on your trousers.
> ESTRAGON: You want me to pull off my trousers?
> VLADIMIR: Pull ON your trousers.
> ESTRAGON: *(realizing his trousers are down).* True. *He pulls up his trousers.*
> VLADIMIR: Well? Shall we go?

ESTRAGON: Yes, let's go.
They do not move.

(P. 60b)

As in act 1, even when night has fallen, Didi and Gogo do not move. The ending of the second act, which simply exchanges the speakers of the ending of act 1—"Estragon: Well, shall we go? Vladimir: Yes, let's go. *They do not move.*" (p. 35b)—is more powerful than the former conclusion, partly because the fallen trousers have left Estragon not only comic in his unawareness of his exposure, but more fully exposed. The dynamics of the couple's inaction have now been explored in more depth than they had been in act 1. Vladimir has undergone his initiation and has experienced a crisis of faith that Estragon, in a more diffuse way, has been undergoing throughout. In the light of that initiation rite, in which nothingness has taken on the shape of the sacred, the black void giving life's mythical moment its luminosity, even as a picture frame sets off the picture it encloses, the rituals the clowns have repeated to fill their time and to worship and summon Godot have become more desperate and doubtful.

I suggested earlier that the key to the power of the Godot myth was partly Beckett's refusal to offer solutions, to tell us whether Godot exists, who he is, or whether he will ever arrive. Significantly, Beckett has noted that the key word in his play is "perhaps."[41] The final lines, together with the characters' immobility, pull together all the strands of the play and ironically demonstrate the contemporary vitality of the Godot myth.

For Didi and Gogo to remain is absurd. The messenger boy has told them that Godot won't come today but will surely come tomorrow. His future arrival may be unsure, but they know he will not arrive today. They must take cover. Their immobility, then, cannot be taken as religious dedication ("They also serve who only stand and wait") so much as for inertia ("Habit is a great deadener") or despair ("I can't go on"). Because, however, the couple return each twilight to wait for Godot, their final stasis, logic aside, does also represent that immobility of waiting which is their form of worship. What we have at the end are two orientations to salvation that the play has explored, life as an atemporal moment in the void and life spent waiting for Godot, integrated in an image of stasis; Didi and Gogo's inability to end their slow crucifixion leaves them suspended in a state of despairing hope. They may not be strong enough to do otherwise, but they do also serve who only stand and wait.

Bound to his rock, Prometheus flings his defiance at Zeus's messengers, comforts the wandering Io as best he can with prophecies of eventual freedom for them both, and boasts that one of his gifts to man was blind hope. As a man-god, he must suffer for his knowledge and gifts, but he asserts himself and he feels free. Pushing his rock up the hill in futile labor, Sisyphus gives up the Promethean gift of blind hope and accepts his suffering as endless, but he finds joy in his scorn of what the gods inflict. By scorning the human condition as absurd, he rises above it, asserts himself, and feels free. Reclaiming the gift of blind hope, Didi and Gogo have given up the right to laugh. Although they, too, assert themselves—"Tell him you saw us"—they are not sure of their own existence or of the nature of Godot.

Why, then, overcome as we are today with a feeling of impotence, do we find Beckett's reflection of our predicament such a potent myth? Unlike Didi and Gogo, of course, we have not given up the right to laugh and we enjoy what Nietzsche called the "discharge of our nausea"[42] as we follow the antics of the four *Godot* clowns; also, despite the inefficacy of the rituals of the play, we cannot help but find in the resilience of these four, both hope for our own survival and a tragicomic assertion of self that, in Kafkaesque fashion, at least keeps the door of salvation open.

Perhaps we do not so much laugh at the *Godot* clowns as for them. As we observe the resilience with which they have handled their own potential despair, whether it be Lucky's persistence in his alleviating role of slave, Pozzo's dogged movement onward with his new, darker vision of reality, or Vladimir and Estragon's tragicomic assertion of self, we see a starkly comic anatomy of the ways in which we may persist in the modern world. And as Vladimir backs off from his initiation into the sacred void, we come to understand that he may be participating, along with Estragon, in some more mysterious initiation rite, a moment of transition in which "the boredom of living is replaced with the suffering of being,"[43] and from that moment, neither of them retreats.

NOTES

1. Brustein, *The Theatre of Revolt*, pp. 18–19.
2. Camus, *The Myth of Sisyphus*, pp. 90–91.
3. Gabor Mihalyi, "Beckett's 'Godot' and the Myth of Alienation," *Modern Drama* 9, no. 3 (December 1966): 329. See also Bert O. States, *The Shape of Paradox: An Essay on "Waiting for Godot,"* pp. 19–20. Discussing Beckett's biblical style, States suggests that ". . . Godot is not (like MacLeish's *J.B.* or Giraudoux's *Judith*) an old biblical myth in modern dress but a new myth, or story about the plight of modern man, in old dress; it is a parable for today, such as might appear in a latter-day Bible aimed at accommodating modern problems of despair and alienation."
4. Clyde Kluckhohn, "Myth and Ritual: A General Theory," in *Myth and Literature: Contemporary Theory and Practice*, ed. John B. Vickery, p. 39.
5. Ibid., pp. 43–44.
6. Mircea Eliade, *Rites and Symbols of Initiation: The Mysteries of Birth and Rebirth*, p. x.

7. Ibid., p. x.
8. Ibid., pp. 128–130.
9. Ibid., pp. 74, 90–91.
10. Richard Schechner, "Godotology: There's Lots of Time in Godot," *Modern Drama* 9, no. 3 (December 1966): 273.
11. Curtis M. Brooks, "The Mythic Pattern in *Waiting for Godot*," *Modern Drama* 9, no. 3 (December 1966): 298.
12. Mircea Eliade, *The Sacred and the Profane: The Nature of Religion*, p. 68.
13. Ibid., p. 70. In the Judeo-Christian tradition, Eliade explains, God does manifest his presence in historical moments that are not reversible, but here, too, historical time will be abolished with the future arrival of the messiah (Judaism) or the second coming (Christianity) (pp. 110–13).
14. In the original French version of *Waiting for Godot*, the name of the fair at which Pozzo plans to sell Lucky in act 1 is *Saint-Sauveur*. The implication here is that in the second act Pozzo no longer seeks religious salvation in any traditional sense.
15. Eliade, *The Sacred and the Profane*, p. 71.
16. Brooks, "The Mythic Pattern in *Waiting for Godot*," p. 298.
17. Camus, *The Myth of Sisyphus*, p. 91.
18. Steven J. Rosen, *Samuel Beckett and the Pessimistic Tradition*, p. 47.
19. Several critics discuss the four characters as if, at least on one level, they are one. See, for example, Martin Esslin, *The Theatre of the Absurd*, p. 67, or Frederick Busi, *The Transformations of Godot*, p. 95. Busi discusses the play as a monodrama in which the four characters are Godot and have arrived.
20. Schechner, "Godotology," p. 273.
21. Jacques Dubois, "Beckett and Ionesco: The Tragic Awareness of Pascal and the Ironic Awareness of Flaubert," *Modern Drama* 9, no. 3 (December 1966): 290.
22. Samuel Beckett, *Proust*, p. 8.
23. Camus, *The Myth of Sisyphus*, p. 39. Speaking of the absurd hero, Camus writes, "He feels innocent. To tell the truth, that is all he feels—his irreparable innocence."
24. Bert O. States, in the *The Shape of Paradox*, senses Beckett's mythical use of time in his discussion of Lucky's "think" speech. "I would argue, however," he writes, "that the impulse in a work to transcend the limits of finite time and space, in the right conditions, eventuates in myth and that we have the basics of such conditions in *Godot*; . . . this pell-mell madness [Lucky's speech] functions very much like amnesia in the Beckett universe: it releases the character from bondage to a sensuous and temporal world. Does it not, in fact, create the same liberty of inference, or free association, that we have in Shakespeare when 'mad' characters like Lear are set loose from society to conjure impossible nightmare worlds based crudely on the world of social fact? And could we not say that in such moments Shakespeare verges on the mythical?" (pp. 43–44).
Oddly enough, States refutes his own point later in his otherwise fine interpretation of the play, when he discusses memory as a means to grace, whether in a "divinely ordained" world or a "humanistic" one, finding the cases of amnesia in the play to be an indication of "grace withheld" (p. 101).
25. Brooks, "The Mythic Pattern in *Waiting for Godot*," p. 295.
26. Quoted by David H. Hesla in his *The Shape of Chaos: An Interpretation of the Art of Samuel Beckett*, p. 7.
27. Sigmund Freud identifies muteness with death in his essay "The Theme of the Three Caskets," in *The Standard Edition of the Complete Psychological Works of Sigmund Freud*, 24 vols, trans. and ed. James Strachey, 12:301.
28. Water dreams, says Freud, often suggest birth, and dreams that involve rescue from water suggest giving birth (Sigmund Freud, *The Interpretation of Dreams*, pp. 435–37, 459).
29. Camus, *The Myth of Sisyphus*, pp. 40–41.

30. I take issue with those critics who deny the play any kind of Aristotelian structure or climax. Ramon Cormier and Janis L. Pallister, for example, in *Waiting for Death: The Philosophical Significance of Beckett's En Attendant Godot,* suggest that the play lacks conventional form. "His antiplay," they say of Beckett's *Godot,* "a dyptych containing a play-within-a-play, has no characterization and no traditional plot" (p. 3). If one grasps the play's ritual structure, the initiation rite in which the characters are involved, one may, it seems to me, see how the play, despite its actionless appearance, is actually structured, in part, in quite traditional ways.

31. Michael Robinson, *The Long Sonata of the Dead: A Study of Samuel Beckett,* p. 244.

32. Gunther Anders, for example, says Beckett derides his characters' belief in Godot; Anders suggests that the play may deal with religion but is not itself religious ("Being without Time: On Beckett's Play *Waiting for Godot,*" in *Samuel Beckett: A Collection of Critical Essays,* ed. Martin Esslin, p. 145).

33. Beckett's interest in George Berkeley and his dictum that "To be is to be perceived," has apparently been a major influence on his art. See Rosen, *Samuel Beckett and the Pessimistic Tradition,* pp. 166–68.

34. Eliade, *The Sacred and the Profane,* p. 10.

35. Victor Turner, *The Ritual Process: Structure and Anti-Structure,* p. 95.

36. Robinson, *The Long Sonata of the Dead,* p. 244.

37. Eva Metman, "Reflections on Samuel Beckett's Plays," in *Samuel Beckett: A Collection of Critical Essays,* ed. Martin Esslin, p. 132.

38. Clayton A. Hubbs, "Chekhov and the Contemporary Theatre," *Modern Drama* 24, no. 3 (September 1981): 360.

39. Ibid., p. 361.

40. Ibid., p. 364.

41. An interview with Beckett quoted by Alec Reid in *All I Can Manage, More Than I Could: An Approach to the Plays of Samuel Beckett,* p. 11.

42. Nietzsche, *The Birth of Tragedy,* p. 60. Neitzsche here defines the comic as the "artistic discharge of the nausea of absurdity."

43. Beckett, *Proust,* p. 8.

3

Farcical False Arrivals: The Dying-Reviving God

The nonarrival of Godot in Samuel Beckett's *Waiting for Godot* leaves the battle between winter and spring unresolved. Godot's character remains ambiguous—whether he will bring salvation or damnation if and when he comes remains a question. And juxtaposed with Didi and Gogo, who will continue to wait in fear and hope for an answer to that question, is Pozzo. Still attached to Lucky, the now silenced bearer of the wisdom of the ages (bags of sand), Pozzo moves "on" in an atemporal mythic instant whose light, paradoxically, is a mere flicker in the darkness of the great void.

The arrival of Godot in a variety of other modern dramas does not, however, signal the victory of spring. Numerous twentieth-century plays written before and after *Waiting for Godot* retain the rhythms of ritual renewal that Beckett has foregone, but they retain those rhythms only to mock them. The ironical treatment of such rituals of renewal in Ibsen's *The Wild Duck* and O'Neill's *The Iceman Cometh* has already been explored. Eugene O'Neill's statement that the subject behind the important art of his day was "the death of the Old God and the failure of science and materialism to give any satisfactory new One for the surviving primitive religious instinct to find a meaning for life in, and to comfort his fears of death with"[1] leads, as well, to more recent dramas that still focus on the failure of new arriving gods, plays that expose their arriving Godots as false messiahs.

In his one-act drama *The American Dream* (1960), Edward Albee offers an American Godot as well as a perfect parody of the ritual of the dying-and-reviving God that Frazer explored in *The Golden Bough*. In that ritual, as seen above in chapter 1, an old king-god, with whom the tribe identifies its well-being, is sacrificed as a scapegoat in the belief that such a sacrifice will take away the sins of the tribe. Renewal is achieved as his soul is transferred to a new king-god, possibly one before whom he has fallen in battle; or renewal involves the death and resurrection of a single figure whose rebirth insures the continuance and well-being of the people. In Albee's play, death and resurrection is played out in terms of identical twins.

For Mommy and Daddy in Albee's *The American Dream,* salvation lies in a particularly American concept, that of getting satisfaction. Daddy complains about not getting the plumbing fixed and of the late arrival of Mrs. Barker.

> DADDY: come in, You're late. But, of course, we expected you to be late; we were saying that we expected you to be late.
> MOMMY: Daddy, don't be rude! We were saying that you just can't get satisfaction these days, and we were talking about you, of course. Won't you come in?[2]

Daddy's complaints, however, are mainly to please Mommy in order to gain peace. When Mommy discusses his impotence—"Daddy doesn't want to sleep with anyone. Daddy's been sick"—he agrees: "I don't even want to sleep in the apartment," he assures Grandma. "I just want to get everything over with" (p. 70).

Mommy, however, is still very much caught up in the quest for satisfaction, which she sees in terms of status and appearances. She tells Daddy about a beige hat she bought that the hated chairman of her women's club, who turns out to be Mrs. Barker, informed her on the street was wheat-colored. Returning to the store, Mommy demanded a beige hat and was perfectly satisfied, after making a scene, when they gave her the same hat, which this time they assured her was beige. Daddy is a little slow in response to the story, but he finally catches on that for Mommy appearances can provide satisfaction.

> DADDY: *(clearing his throat)* I would imagine that it was the same hat they tried to sell you before.
> MOMMY: *(With a little laugh)* Well, of course it was!
> DADDY: That's the way things are today; you just can't get satisfaction; you just try.
> MOMMY: Well, I got satisfaction.
> DADDY: That's right, Mommy. *You did* get satisfaction, didn't you?
> (P. 61)

The incident of the hat that Mommy relates foreshadows the main action of the play, the arrival of the American Dream. An identical twin (same hat) to the child that has failed to give Mommy and Daddy satisfaction, the young man whom Grandma recognizes and names the American Dream, will provide the satisfaction that his unfortunate brother has not produced. What the play continues to reveal in its ongoing use of caricature and "metaphysical cliché"[3] is how completely this satisfaction, too, will lie in appearances and how identical the twins really are.

Mrs. Barker, it seems, had visited the couple years ago, providing them with a "bumble" from the Bye-Bye Adoption Service. As Grandma recalls the incident to Mrs. Barker, who can't figure out why she has come there, she describes the gradual dismemberment of the baby with whose natural urges and humanity Mommy and Daddy could not cope. Not only did the baby cry "its heart out," but when "it only had eyes for its Daddy," Mommy "gouged those eyes right out of its head" (p. 99). Finding later that "it began to develop an interest in its you-know-what" they "cut its hands off at the wrists" but only after "they cut off its you-know-what" (p. 100). After further crimes and dismembering punishments, the baby has the nerve to die, which of course means Mommy and Daddy are out some money and want satisfaction.

What Albee presents here is a parody of a sparagmos,[4] the ritual dismembering of the scapegoat, whose body is scattered over the earth to make the crops grow. And what follows with the arrival of the American Dream is a parody of the rebirth aspect of the rite, in which the body is ritually reassembled with the suggestion of rebirth attending the reassembling of such figures as Dionysus, Hypolitus, or Pentheus. Here the reassembled god is the beautiful, Hollywood-style young man, whom Grandma sees as the solution to the plot complications of the play.

The American Dream, it turns out, is willing to do anything for money, including removing the burden of Mommy's demands from Daddy, servicing her incestuous desires, and generally providing the superficial satisfaction the family requires. Circling and poking the young man, Mommy finds him "much better than the other one" (p. 125) and joins the others, all but the now absent Grandma, who watches from the wings, in a drink to satisfaction. A mere shell, this arriving Godot is devoid enough of all feelings to provide a satirically happy ending, although Grandma cuts the play off while it's still a comedy and "everybody's got what he thinks he wants" (p. 127).

Were it not for the young man's confession to Grandma of his sense of loss, the play would merely parody the dying-reviving god ritual, showing in comic fashion how the new god is but a hollow shell, a lifeless hat that will take on any color one wishes. In those terms the play would show that the American Dream is hollow—dead. When the young man, however, relates to Grandma the series of psychic losses he has experienced after being separated from his twin when very young, losses that parallel, in true Corsican-brother fashion, the physical losses suffered by his twin at the hands of Mommy and Daddy, he seems still to feel those losses, which he claims have left him a feelingless shell.

YOUNG MAN: . . . How can I put it to you? All right; like this; Once . . . it was as if all at once my heart . . . became numb . . . almost as though I . . . almost as though . . . just like that . . . it had been wrenched from my body . . . and from that time I have been unable to love. Once . . . I was asleep at the time . . . I awoke, and my eyes were burning. And since that time I have been unable to see anything, *anything*, with pity, with affection . . . with anything but . . . cool disinterest. And my groin . . . even there . . . since one time . . . one specific agony . . . since then I have not been able to *love* anyone with my body. And even my hands . . . I cannot touch another person and feel love. And there is more . . . there are more losses, but it all comes down to this: I no longer have the capacity to feel anything. . . .

(Pp. 114–15)

Some critics have complained that the speech is unduly sentimental, undermining the play's otherwise farcical and satirical thrust and leaving us with an ambiguous American Dream.[5] If the American Dream is without feelings, how can he speak so poignantly of his sense of loss? And why should he care whether Grandma is "old enough to understand"?

But the paradoxical nature of the American Dream, who bemoans his losses while asserting that he can no longer feel, is what the play is about. If he can touch Grandma, who is significantly of "pioneer stock," the carrier of vital American ideals, with his sense of loss, and the audience as well, then the dream, though it may not be well, is still alive. Projecting himself in his speech as a victim rather than a perpetrator of the corruption he now embraces as the only means for survival, the American Dream conveys a sense of that meaning and vitality he once possessed. Absurd and ambiguous, the American Dream is man made into robot, but he is a suffering, a nostalgic robot, a contradiction in terms.

This Godot, whose survival depends on his ability to service and save Mommy in her terms, is, as he confesses, a false savior who is himself lost. Then, too, in the somewhat less comic *The Sandbox* (1959), which Albee interrupted the writing of *The American Dream* to create, but which seems to occur later in time, Grandma, Albee's half-cynical, half-idealistic voice in *the American Dream,* is buried in a sandbox; and the American Dream serves here as her angel of death. While Grandma appears to escape at the conclusion of *The American Dream,* using her winnings in a cake contest to go off on her own, the implication in the earlier play is that, as in *Waiting for Godot,* there is no place to go. As fellow victim with the Young Man of Mommy and Daddy, Grandma becomes his victim as well in *The Sandbox,* finding that she cannot move. Godot was to save Didi and Gogo from death or hell, but with his nonarrival he left them instead in a state of paralysis. *The Sandbox*'s psychically mutilated but angelic looking Godot, who does calisthenics througout the play, brings with his arrival the paralysis of death. Once prostituted, the American Dream must play his role and help bury the source of his own life, "pioneer stock."

The affection the two feel for each other—Grandma acclaims her Angel of Death's performance, and he kisses her—reveals them united, bowing to the ethic of his survival at any cost. Wise though she may be, Grandma has acted, in *The American Dream*, as "the midwife who brings about the stunted birth willed in their different ways by the others."[6] Now she accepts the consequences of her deed with grace and relief. Albee has suggested that she dies at the end of *The American Dream*. In *The Sandbox*, we see her accept that death.

While the disorientation of the characters in *Waiting for Godot* may be part of a process in which secular time and place lose their meaning and the characters progress toward reorienting themselves in terms of the sacred void, the disorientation of the characters in *The American Dream* cannot be seen as part of a progress. Mommy and Daddy cannot figure out why they asked Mrs. Barker to come and Mrs. Barker cannot figure out why she has. When Daddy is sent off to break Grandma's TV, he can't find it; he can't even find Grandma's room. And when Mommy goes off to get the fainting Mrs. Barker a glass of water, she can't find the water. When Mrs. Barker goes off to get her water in the kitchen, she can't find Mommy and Daddy.

While Mommy and Daddy are lost in their own apartment (stress is put on the fact that this is an apartment, not a house), Grandma, who has packed up all that is valuable in her boxes, is the only character who knows what is going on. Standing partly for the evicted elderly and partly for the old pioneer values that her daughter and Mrs. Barker, who is her public counterpart,[7] have rejected, Grandma fakes senility but is the only sensible one. The "age of deformity" that Grandma accuses the others of living in can be understood only in terms of Grandma's values, and there is not only no place left for Grandma in the apartment, there is also no place left for her in the world—hence her death in *The Sandbox* at the hands of the angelic shell.

In Eugène Ionesco's drama *The Chairs* (1951), a play that preceded Albee's two short plays by several years and *Waiting for Godot* by three, the playwright uses similar kinds of caricature and symbolic cliché for similar satirical ends. The arriving Godot in *The Chairs* is an orator who is to sum up the meaning of the ninety-four-year-old Old Man's life and that of his wife by delivering a message to the assembled multitudes who are making their way to the couple's island retreat. While Godot arrives in this play, the multitudes are missing; the old man and his wife bring on more and more chairs as they welcome numerous nonarriving guests and proceed to converse with those who are blatantly missing from the stage. Missing, too, is the message; the orator, like Lucky in the second act of *Godot,* is mute, deaf as well as dumb in this case. In a subsequent edition of the drama, the orator turns to the blackboard as a means of communication, but his message, though brief, is even more garbled and incoherent than Lucky's first act "think" speech. "ANGELFOOD," he first writes on the board in capital letters and then "NNAA NNM NWN-WNW V." When he fails to get a response he erases what he has written and writes, "ΛADIEU ΛDIEU ΛPΛ."[8] Like Lucky, he refers to God and the angels. The couple, who have committed suicide, confident that the meaning of their lives will be revealed in the orator's speech, are absent at play's end, and the orator himself leaves in barely disguised disgust after his efforts to communicate fail to elicit a response.

Despite this Godot's presence, then, we are left with absence. If the American Dream was a suffering robot, a false, Hollywood-style messiah bringing empty satisfaction rather than salvation, then the orator, at least on one level, is an equally false messiah as well as being "a 'conceited' nineteenth century poet, created by a twentieth century 'poet' disillusioned with reason."[9]

Just as Albee's play, however, involves more than social protest, providing in its parody of the dying-and-reviving god ritual a poignantly farcical exploration of contemporary family life, so Ionesco's play involves far more than admonitions on the limits of man's rational faculty. Ionesco's experiments with the dislocation of language and his use of caricature, like Albee's use of them after him, are grounded in psychological insights and ritual parodies that afford the audience a complex experience of modern spiritual dilemmas.

By providing false messiahs, Ionesco and Albee do not release us from waiting for Godot; by debunking false solutions, they do not destroy but enhance the mystery. As Martin Esslin says, when speaking of Ionesco, "We live in a world that has lost its metaphysical dimension, and therefore all mystery. But to restore the sense of mystery we must learn to see the most commonplace in its final horror." Quoting Ionesco, Esslin continues:

> "To feel the absurdity of the common place, and of language—its falseness—is already to have gone beyond it. To go beyond it we must first of all bury ourselves in it. What is comical is the unusual in its pure state; nothing seems more surprising to me than that which is banal; the surreal is here, within grasp of our hands, in our everyday conversation."[10]

The surreal in *The Chairs* is revealed in a combination of banality and senility. While it was Mommy, Daddy, and Mrs. Barker who were confused about what was going on and were literally as well as symbolically lost in Mommy and Daddy's apartment, Grandma in that play knew what was going on. The ancient couple in *The Chairs*, however, operate in clouds of senility; they remember their past together, for example, in often opposite terms.

> OLD WOMAN: [*to the Photo-engraver*]: We had one son . . . of course, he's still alive . . . he's gone away . . . it's a common story . . . or, rather, unusual . . .
> (P. 134)

> OLD MAN: Alas, no . . . no, we've never had a child . . . I'd hoped for a son . . . Semiramis, too . . . we did everything . . . and my poor Semiramis is so maternal, too . . .
> (P. 134)

Separated from each other by the numerous chairs they bring on, they do not even unite in death, each jumping out a separate window into the darkness below, thus frustrating the Old Man's desire "that we might rot together" (p. 158).

> OLD MAN: . . . Our corpses will fall far from each other, and we will rot in an aquatic solitude. . . .
> (P. 158)

The Old Man is overwhelmed with hope, however, when first the Emperor (invisible) and then the orator, a real character, arrive. Echoed by his separated wife, the Old Man greets the Emperor as if he indeed were Godot, the long awaited one, and he tells him of his suffering and his plans to save mankind through the orator's articulation of his message. The Old Man will sacrifice himself as an old king-god in order that his message on the meaning of life may be articulated by the new king-god, the orator. To underline the Old Man's inevitable failure, a failure made more ironical by his failure to realize it, the Old Man is unable to make either the Emperor or the orator see him or recognize his existence.

> OLD MAN: Your Majesty! . . . I'm over here! . . . Your Majesty! Can you hear me? Can you see me? Please tell his majesty that I'm here! Your Majesty! Your Majesty! ! ! I'm here, your most faithful servant! . . .
> (P. 148)

When he addresses the orator as "friend," the orator looks in the other direction and subsequently in all directions, but never at the Old Man or the Old Woman.

One is reminded of Vladimir's desperate assertion of self to the mes-

Farcical False Arrivals 61

senger boy who does not recognize him from day to day. But one is prepared, too, for the failure of the Godot/orator, whose ability to speak is supposed not only to save humanity but to save the Old Man himself from what he feels is his homeless or orphaned state.

> OLD MAN: [*sobbing, his mouth wide open like a baby*]: I'm an orphan . . . dworfan.
>
> (P. 118)

The Old Man and Old Woman have dwelt at some length on their arrival eighty years ago in Paris from which they were excluded, a city that, according to the Old Woman, "never existed" (p. 116) and according to the Old Man must have existed "because it collapsed . . . it was the city of light, but it has been extinguished, extinguished, for four hundred thousand years . . . nothing remains of it today, except a song." To complete the contradictions about their arrival/nonarrival in Paris/non-Paris the surviving song is, "Paris will always be Paris" (p. 116).

The Old Woman sees a solution in art, the creation of words. "It's in speaking that ideas come to us, words" she tells her husband, "and then we, in our own words, we find perhaps everything, the city too, the garden, and then we are orphans no longer" (pp. 120–21). But how can the self-conscious, posing, artificial orator, who refuses so much as to glance at the old couple, be the saving, creating artist, the father who will provide a home for his children?

Not only is such a father missing from the play, according to Marian Tolpin, but so is the mother. Tolpin discusses Ionesco's use of "primary process modes of thought," which appear much as they do in dreams but which the playwright integrates into a "work with a philosophic view of men which the dream never contains."[11] What she finds beneath the view of man's isolation is "a disguised version of an infantile separation trauma."[12] The emperor and orator, whose attention the couple fail to get, are "both caricatures of God and the parent."[13]

> The deaf-mute orator serves as a nodal point for a condensation of the psychic material of *The Chairs* because he is totally unaware of the old couple's existence. He cannot be moved or touched by their eager welcome, their entreaties, their trust, or their death. As such he is the God of the Absurd world. Concealed beneath the presentation is the parent-figure who does not respond to the pleas of the Old Man and Old Woman who are the trusting infants who count on him for fulfillment. Yet, in his turn, the Orator is also the desperate pleader who cannot get a response from the insensate chairs; he is also the helpless infant for whom there is no object to hear his pleas.[14]

The essential dramatization here is that of separation from the mother. According to Tolpin, Paris and the garden from which the couple were excluded are images of the mother, and the memory of that loss is what starts the Old Man bemoaning his orphaned, motherless state. The Old Woman also is both lost child and a caricature of a mother whose name, Semiramis, "is the Assyrian-Babylonian counterpart of the Great Mother."[15] This primal and son-destroying mother, who is not in some ways unlike Albee's castrating Mommy, admires her husband one moment, only to belittle him the next for his lack of ambition and success. The Old Woman's story of her son who abandoned her and the Old Man's story of his abandonment of his dying mother actually suggest the mother's abandonment of the child.[16]

The Old Woman as a combination of mother, wife, and whore (Semiramis flirts shamelessly with a Photo-engraver, exposing her underclothes, a breast, and herself as a prostitute) is a familiar figure in absurdist drama. She appeared in Albee's play and will appear again in the plays of Harold Pinter. All mothers betray their sons to death in *Waiting for Godot,* giving birth "astride of a grave," and the seemingly helpless Winnie of Beckett's *Happy Days,* buried first to her waist and then to her neck in a mound of earth, torments her withdrawn husband (his revenge) with the kind of patronizing, demanding love that results in their mutual sense of isolation within their relationship.

As seen in chapter 2, despite their different final orientations, Pozzo and Lucky resemble Didi and Gogo in their sense of helplessness and smallness, whether it be before Godot or the great void. Albee's Grandma has combatted that sense of helplessness bravely, but she avoids her own inevitable end in *The American Dream* only by suggesting a comic ending, and she has become a helpless victim of Godot in *The Sandbox.* There remains, then, in the false arrivals of *The American Dream* and *The Chairs* a kind of equation of Godot with death, not unlike their possible equation in *Waiting for Godot* in which Vladimir's separation in his mind of the two, "We are waiting for Godot to come— . . . or for night to fall" (p. 51b), does not prevent Estragon from hiding in terror when he thinks that the savior approaches.

If, however, the Old Man and Old Woman die in separation from the truth and from each other, like Didi and Gogo they maintain their illusions. They believe that a street will be named after them, and unlike the disappearing city of Paris, they feel that they will leave traces behind.

OLD MAN: We will leave some traces, for we are people and not cities.
(p. 158)

One may discount such illusions more easily than one may discount those of Didi and Gogo because there are signs of Godot's existence in *Waiting for Godot,* and his absence is more enigmatic than the orator's

Farcical False Arrivals

presence. But if the Old Man's ideas have clearly not redeemed him from his orphaned state or created the city of Paris, one cannot forget the momentary arrival that the couple experience in their memories of exclusion.

The story of their arrival/nonarrival in Paris is the story of their lives, which the Old Woman has made the Old Man repeat each night for the seventy-five years of their marriage. It is their myth, which they relive in the ritual retelling of it.

And what of its contradictions? They arrive, but are cold and wet and are kept out. Even the gate of the garden is closed. They recall the place as Paris, which both did and did not exist, but which one needed to reach by going through the garden.

The ensuing laughter of the couple provides a resolution to these contradictions. They laugh until they cry, and then mysteriously an adjective (idiotic) becomes a noun (the idiot) and they do arrive.[17]

> OLD MAN: [*while the Old Woman begins to laugh softly, senilely, then progressively in great bursts, the Old Man laughs, too, as he continues*]: Then at last we arrived, we laughed till we cried, the story was so idiotic . . . the idiot arrived full speed, bare-bellied, the idiot was pot-bellied . . . he arrived with a trunk chock full of rice; the rice spilled out on the ground . . . the idiot on the ground too, belly to ground . . . then at last we laughed, we laughed, we laughed, the idiotic belly, bare with rice on the ground, the trunk, the story of sick from rice belly to ground, bare-bellied, all with rice, at last we laughed, the idiot at last arrived all bare, we laughed . . .
>
> (Pp. 116–17)

The rice, which the bare-bellied, pot-bellied idiot spilled on the ground, and the idiot who is himself spilled on the ground, become one with the laughing couple in a fertility rite that opens the gates and creates the city and the arrival. The translation does not quite capture the full nature of the fertility rite. In the French version the entire passage is filled with words that mean laughter or that have the sound of *ri* (from *rire*—to laugh) or that rhyme with *ri*. Paris itself, the city/noncity to which they seek entrance, is used as a pun, since it means by laughter. Arrival, rice, and laughter become indistinguishable because of the similar sounds of the words: *"On arri. . . .:"* (we arrived), *"on a ri"* (we laughed), and *"le riz"* (the rice).[18] The trunk in which the idiot carries the rice (*"la malle"*) also merges in sound with the idea of being sick from rice (*"mal de riz"*), which has evolved in turn from being sick with laughter—*Alors, on a ri, on avait mal au ventre, l'histoire était si drôle. . .* " (p. 130). The idiot, naked on the ground, who is pot-bellied and moves "belly to ground" and who is born from the story—"The story was idiotic . . . the idiot arrived full speed"—becomes the personification of the fertility rite in which his bare belly is the trunk of rice (he is pregnant with it) that aches with laughter and spills onto the ground. The stomach full of laughter becomes the stomach on the ground, which becomes the trunk full of rice, which becomes the rice spread on the ground. The emphasis on the nakedness of the idiot or the nakedness of his belly and the mutual rising laughter of the couple as the Old Man finishes the story suggests a sexual climax—"*On a . . . arri . . . ah! . . . arri . . . ah! . . . arri . . . va . . . ri*" (p. 131)—so that the spilling of the rice may indicate the spilling of semen as well. Paris will no doubt "always be Paris," then, as long as one can laugh.

The suggestion is that only the fool arrives, and through their fooling, their creation of words that the Old Woman later claims may be delivering, the couple also arrive. Speaking, the Old Woman later insists, is easy once you begin.

> OLD WOMAN: It's easy once you begin, like life and death . . . it's enough to have your mind made up. It's in speaking that ideas come to us, words, and then we, in our own words, we find perhaps everything, the city too, the garden, and then we are orphans no longer.
> (Pp. 120–21)

Only the fools of farce can overcome the tragedy of helplessness and separation, and for that mythical moment each night the Old Man and Old Woman do just that. They overcome secular time, enter into and make perfect nonsensical sense of their plight, find their sacred space and time, and are home. The moment, of course, does not last. The spilled rice, with its positive connotations of fertility, becomes something the Old Man has lost along with his mother. The sacred gives way to the secular, and the found are lost once more.

Such loss is central to Sam Shepard's Pulitzer Prize–winning 1979 drama, *Buried Child*. In his play, Shepard returns to the theme of the death of the American Dream, and like Albee, he offers a parody of vegetation rites. An arid field behind a family's house gives up not only the murdered victim of this ostensibly happy American family, but enough vegetation to cover the murderer, the sleeping grandfather, who, with a dying voice, recognizes a returning grandson as his heir. The exhuming of the corpse of the illegitimate child of the grandmother, drowned and buried by the betrayed grandfather in an attempt to keep up appearances, taken in couterpoint with the returning grandson, whom the grandmother recalls as an ideal baby or angel, but whom nobody until the end of the play has recognized at all, suggests another parody of a dying-reviving god rite. The social satire here, however, is unfocused, and an Artaudian sense of horror predominates. What would seem to be largely a personal nightmare ends up, in Shepard's play, despite his humor, producing a melodramatic effect.

Albee's and Ionesco's farcical treatments of their false messiahs may lack some of the tragic effect that Ibsen and O'Neill mixed with their comic treatment of similarly false arrivals in *The Wild Duck* and *The Iceman Cometh*, but their vision is far more collective and mythic than Shepard's. Indeed, the liberating strain of the tragic is not totally absent, and the comic offers its own kind of liberation. Grandma's witty understanding of the false renewal she helps to bring about and the old couple's ritual reenactment of their arrival-nonarrival in Paris provide us with touchstones, lacking in Shepard's play, for those authentic renewals which the characters in these dramas fail to achieve.

NOTES

1. Eugene O'Neill, quoted by Brustein in *The Theatre of Revolt*, p. 329.
2. Edward Albee, *The American Dream* in *The American Dream and The Zoo Story: Two Plays by Edward Albee* (New York: A Signet Book, New American Library, 1961), p. 75. All subsequent quotations from the *The American Dream* are from this edition.
3. Anne Paolucci, *From Tension to Tonic: The Plays of Edward Albee*, p. 45.
4. Whitney Balliett calls the dismemberment "Sophoclean," "Off Broadway," *The New Yorker*, Feb. 4, 1961, p. 63.
5. Ruby Cohn, *Edward Albee*, pp. 14–15.
6. Paolucci, *From Tension to Tonic*, p. 81.
7. Ibid., p. 86.
8. Eugène Ionesco, *The Chairs* in *Four Plays by Eugène Ionesco*, trans. Donald M. Allen (New York: Grove Press, 1958), pp. 159–60. All subsequent quotations from *The Chairs* are from this edition.
9. Marian Tolpin, M.D., "Eugène Ionesco's *The Chairs* and the Theater of the Absurd," *American Imago* 25, no. 2 (Summer 1968): 128.
10. Esslin, *The Theatre of the Absurd*, p. 93.
11. Tolpin, "Eugène Ionesco's *The Chairs*," pp. 120–21.
12. Ibid., p. 122.
13. Ibid., p. 124.
14. Ibid., p. 127.
15. Ibid., pp. 130–132.
16. Ibid., p. 135.
17. A student pointed out to me this significant grammatical transformation.
18. Eugène Ionesco, *Les Chaises* in *Théatre D'Eugène Ionesco I* (Paris: Gallimard, 1962), pp. 130–31. All subsequent quotations from *Les Chaises* are from this edition.

4

Another False Arrival and Several Unhappy Birthdays

Joseph K., the protagonist of Franz Kafka's *The Trial,* is taken to his death on the evening before his thirty-first birthday, one year after his arrest, which took place on his thirtieth birthday. As he walks with his two executioners to the place of execution, he stops struggling, not wishing to act as if he has not learned anything in the year of his agony. He has, in fact, not learned nearly as much as we have watching him seek ways to escape his doom and deny his guilt. We see, too, at the end, that he has not the courage to take his own life, an action his executioners seem to expect of him, and that he must instead die "like a dog."

The absent birthday party in *The Trial* captures the tone of several modern dramas in which the playwrights employ absent or present birthday parties as symbolic or structural devices with which they explore Pozzo's agonized cry in *Waiting for Godot,* "They give birth astride of a grave, the light gleams an instant, then it's night once more" (p. 57). In Henrik Ibsen's *The Wild Duck,* Hedvig kills herself on the morning of her birthday; in Eugene O'Neill's *The Iceman Cometh,* with its numerous parallels to the Ibsen play, Harry Hope's birthday party is an express failure, and in Harold Pinter's *The Birthday Party,* the entire play revolves around the horrors of a birthday party that is imposed on the drama's central character, Stanley. In these plays, as in others in which birthday parties play a significant role—such as Anton Chekhov's *The Three Sisters,* Tennessee Williams's *A Streetcar Named Desire,* Günter Grass's *The Wicked Cooks,* and Samuel Beckett's *Krapp's Last Tape* and *All That Fall*—the ritual rhythms of renewal are mocked, and any Godots who arrive are false messiahs much like the ones discussed in *The Wild Duck, The Iceman Cometh, The American Dream* and *The Chairs.*

Stanley's resurrection as a new god in Pinter's *The Birthday Party* is as false as the American Dream's arrival as a savior in Albee's play. Here, as in the Ibsen and O'Neill plays, Pinter uses the ritual of a birthday party to crystallize the seasonal nature of the drama of the dying-and-reviving god with whom man associates the death and rebirth of vegetation (Frazer) or the death and rebirth of the world itself (Eliade). "The cosmos is conceived as a living unity that is born, develops, and dies on the last day of the year, to be reborn on New Year's day."[1]

Like Ibsen and O'Neill, too, Pinter does not limit himself to the caricature and farce of Albee and Ionesco: instead he combines the comic and the tragic in ways in which the latter takes over from the former. "I think I'm aware of comedy more than I ever was before; a big kind of comedy that doesn't stay funny very long," O'Neill wrote when speaking of *The Iceman Cometh*,[2] an idea echoed later by Harold Pinter, who suggested that everything, including tragedy, was funny, though at some point tragedy "is *no longer* funny. It is funny and then it becomes no longer funny."[3]

In Pinter's drama *The Birthday Party* (1957), as in *The Wild Duck* and *The Iceman Cometh*, a closed world or retreat is invaded by an outside, menacing force that brings damnation in the guise of cheer and salvation. If Godot does not arrive, Monty/Godot sends in his messengers to act for him. Once again, too, the menace revolves around a birthday celebration, which moves ironically toward an equation between birth and death. And once again the treatment of the play's ironies is comic, after which tragedy takes over. More bitterly satirical than the former plays, *The Birthday Party*'s scapegoat is sacrificed, not as part of misguided idealism and the cruel demands of nature (Hedvig) and not as part of the idealistic demands of humanity (Parritt), but because of the malevolent demands of the human power structure for conformity.

Like the bums who inhabit Hope's saloon, Pinter's protagonist, Stanley Webber, is hiding out from life. His haven is Meg and Petey's seaside boarding house at which he is the only guest, nonpaying at that. Though Stanley comforts himself with the past, his memory of his artistic success—he apparently had at least one concert during which his "unique touch" on the piano was recognized—he has fewer illusions about the future than Hope's inmates, content to live a half-life in hiding from the powers who had "carved" him up and "shuttered" him out from subsequent concerts and success.

The birthday party is again a death party, but here the passive Stanley is the designated and reluctant celebrant, the scapegoat who denies that it is his birthday. Stanley is fully aware of the dangers of death involved in any real birth or rebirth in his life. Stress is put on his constant sleeping and on his annoyance with Meg's attempts to waken him; the prospects of a birth celebration, with its implications of awakening, send him into a possessed state as he beats the toy drum Meg gives him because she cannot afford a piano.

Other than the fact that they have been sent by Monty, we know little of the background of Goldberg and McCann, the men who perpetrate the celebration and the destruction of Stanley; neither do we know why Stanley must be destroyed or "reborn," an equation in the play. Crucial details given, however, do suggest that Stanley has in some way bucked the system, that his crime is his "unique touch" and his refusal, as he puts it, to "crawl down on my bended knees" before the powers that be. The henchmen of these powers, Goldberg and McCann, the cliché-ridden Jew and recently defrocked priest, are presented as caricatures of corrupt power and materialism, who masquerade under the middle-class values that they protest as their own. Typical of Goldberg's amusingly false sentimentality, staged partly for the ladies at the party, is his response to Meg's toast to Stanley:

> Well, I want to say first that I've never been so touched to the heart as by the toast we've just heard. How often, in this day and age, do you come across real, true warmth? Once in a lifetime. Until a few minutes ago, ladies and gentlemen, I, like all of you, was asking the same question. What's happened to the love, the bonhomie, the unashamed expression of affection of the day before yesterday, that our mums taught us in the nursery?[4]

If Hope's birthday party in O'Neill's drama was blighted by the self-deceptive good will of Hickey, Stanley's party is bathed in the menace and horror of Goldberg's and McCann's elaborate and deliberate hypocrisy. McCann's careful and seemingly motiveless tearing up of a newspaper into equal strips serves as a reminder of the carving up Stanley tells Meg he experienced after his one successful concert and is an ominous prelude, as well, to the spiritual tearing asunder of the scapegoat that follows. As the sins of the tribe are mockingly heaped upon him, Stanley is readied for the sacrifice.

> GOLDBERG: Where is your lechery leading you?
> MCCANN: You'll pay for this.
> GOLDBERG: You stuff yourself with dry toast.
> MCCANN: You contaminate womankind.
> GOLDBERG: Why don't you pay the rent?
> MCCANN: Mother defiler.
> GOLDBERG: Why do you pick your nose?
> MCCANN: I demand justice!
>
> (P. 54)

In Kafka's *The Trial*, Joseph K. is never accused of a specific crime. Because McCann and Goldberg accuse Stanley of such a variety of crimes, and because many of the accusations are contradictory—he is asked why he never married and why he left his wife—the effect is

Another False Arrival and Several Unhappy Birthdays

similar. Like Joseph K., Stanley is to play the scapegoat's role, taking on the several guilts of the tribe.

Richard Schechner finds the accusations to be a somewhat meaningless ritual,[5] while Edward Malpas suggests that at least some of the accusations reflect "the subjective sufferings of the tormentors," Goldberg's racial sufferings, McCann's national ones.[6]

MCCANN: You betrayed our land.
GOLDBERG: You betray our breed.

(P. 55)

In another interpretation, Lois G. Gorden insists on the incestuous, Oedipal nature of Stanley's guilt, alluded to by Goldberg and McCann, who accuse him of defiling his mother, and reenacted in his flirtation with the motherly, seductive Meg.[7]

The two men do undoubtedly project the guilt for their own sufferings onto Stanley, and Stanley does, indeed, suffer, like Gregers and Hickey, from severe Oedipal conflict. One gets an impression of a weak father who did not make it to his son's successful concert—"My father nearly came down to hear me" (p. 23)—and one sees his surrogate father, Petey, who senses Stanley's victimization, easily intimidated by the threatening Goldberg and McCann. Stanley's relationship to the hovering, maternal Meg is alternately flirtations—he calls her a "succulent old washing bag" (p. 19)—and hostile—he even tries to strangle her at the party.

Pinter, however, does not seem to share Ibsen's or O'Neill's particular kind of interest in the psychology of his characters. *The Birthday Party* contains nothing like Relling's diagnosis of Gregers or like Hickey's and Parritt's long, revealing confessions. Because of their cruel and hypocritical behavior and the broad and contradictory nature of Goldberg and McCann's accusations, we cannot trust them as accurate and must rather, working on textual clues, see Stanley as a victim of the forces of a malicious Godot, who insists on submission and conformity.

That conformity is what is demanded is made quite clear when McCann and Goldberg suggest, in a litany whose rhythms are similar to the one in which they heaped the sins of the tribe on him, the nature of Stanley's rebirth. Offering to repair his glasses, which they have broken, Goldberg and McCann will give him new vision; they will "renew" his "season ticket."

GOLDBERG: We'll make a man of you.
MCCANN: And a woman.
GOLDBERG: You'll be re-orientated.
MCCANN: You'll be rich.
GOLDBERG: You'll be adjusted.

MCCANN: You'll be our pride and joy.
GOLDBERG: You'll be a mensch.
MCCANN: You'll be a success.
GOLDBERG: You'll be integrated.
MCCANN: You'll give orders.
GOLDBERG: You'll make decisions.
MCCANN: You'll be a magnate.
GOLDBERG: A statesman.
MCCANN: You'll own yachts.
GOLDBERG: Animals
MCCANN: Animals

(P. 88)

Stanley's reaction to his newly created nonidentity is similar to the inarticulate mumbling of the deaf and dumb orator at the end of *The Chairs*. Goldberg and McCann march Stanley off to Monty, remade, clean-shaven, dressed in striped trousers, black jacket, white collar, and bowler, but unable to see or speak—a walking robot.

Just as Hickey's promise of rebirth brought a living death to the occupants of Harry's saloon, so Goldberg and McCann's promise of rebirth brings a living death to Stanley. The sacrificial rite, then, is a parody of those rituals which patterned tragic drama of old, and the play stands, in part, as a bitterly comic comment on the ongoing cyclic nature of life in which all that is most brutal and false in society is renewed at the expense of the most pathetic of rebels. The ironies are greatly heightened, too, by Meg's blindness to the sacrifice that has taken place before her very eyes: the next days she dwells on the joyful party at which she was the "belle of the ball."

But it is one thing for the orator of *The Chairs* to offer his incoherent mutterings to the absent crowd and quite another for an audience to see Stanley reduced to incoherence before their eyes. And it is one thing for the handsome young man in *The American Dream* to say that he is empty inside and quite another to see the elaborately dressed Stanley turned into a manikin. The farce of Ionesco and Albee gives way in Pinter to horror. Though the tragic overtones may not be as intense as those in Ibsen's and O'Neill's dramas, they are present.

At the same time that the play's satire is heightened by Meg's unawareness of its action, the tragic implications emerge through Petey's awareness of Stanley's victimization as well as through Stanley's awakening and agony. As Goldberg and McCann make preparations to take Stanley away, Petey insists that a doctor is needed and even orders the men to leave Stanley alone, but he is easily defeated by Goldberg's insidious invitation to come along. The terror of Stanley's removal is further driven home as Petey attempts to resume reading the paper and McCann's torn strips fall out to the ground: Stanley's remains.

The tragic dimension of the play's action is conveyed, as well, by the doubt and suffering of Monty's agents. McCann is full of anxious questions about the job, which Goldberg evades in a comic speech that masks his emptyness.

> GOLDBERG: The main issue is a singular issue and quite distinct from your previous work. Certain elements, however, might well approximate in points of procedure to some of your other activities. All is dependent on the attitude of our subject. At all events, McCann, I can assure you that the assignment will be carried out and the mission accomplished with no excessive aggravation to you or myself. Satisfied?
>
> (P. 32)

And Goldberg himself ends one series of clichés about his success in life with half-statements that reveal his own despair.

> AND DON'T GO NEAR THE WATER. AND YOU'LL FIND—THAT WHAT I SAY IS TRUE.
> BECAUSE I BELIEVE THAT THE WORLD . . . *(Vacant)* . . .
> Because I believe that the world . . . *(Desperate)* . . .
> BECAUSE I BELIEVE THAT THE WORLD . . . *(Lost.)* . . .
>
> (P. 80)

The suffering of the men saves them from being mere caricatures and, together with Stanley's weak defiance and Petey's impotent awareness, suggests the possibility of a ritual renewal beyond the one ostensibly enacted. Monty as new god is not satisfactory, and the play, on one level, becomes an invocation to a new god of meaning and comfort to appear.

Although Pinter has less interest in psychological explanations in his play than Ibsen and O'Neill, he does use Stanley's Oedipal conflict symbolically. The game of blindman's buff played at the birthday celebration, which is reminiscent of the similar game played by Mrs. Soerby with her guests in *The Wild Duck*, is a comic variation in both plays on the search for truth and self that Oedipus undertakes in Sophocles' tragedy *Oedipus The King*. While the heroic Oedipus blinds himself when he arrives at insight, the antiheroic Stanley is symbolically blinded by Goldberg and McCann, who break the glasses without which he cannot see. The effect is not that which Lois Gorden suggests, a kind of purging of Oedipal desires,[8] for Pinter replaces the articulate, self-punishing Oedipus with the inarticulate, victimized Stanley, a man victimized by other lost victims of Monty's system.

Stanley's attempt, when brutalized at the party, to strangle Meg and rape the visiting Lulu evokes echoes from the ancient play. When

Oedipus feels the fates closing in on him, he strikes out in anger, threatening Tiresias and Creon; and when he arrives at the knowledge of his identity, he runs inside, intent on strangling the already dead Jocasta. Roger Pierce has suggested that when Stanley tries to strangle Meg he is assisting at his own birth, after which he feels free to approach Lulu, whom he has previously responded to in a very minimal way.[9] His fury, however, may well be over the way the women desert him at the party, Meg taking an interest in McCann, Lulu in Goldberg. Whichever explanation one adopts, one cannot help seeing something of a "primal scene" in which this modern version of Oedipus strikes out in rage and in vain while the competing men destroy him. The play, however, both evokes symbols of the Sophoclean tragedy and undermines the tragic effect as Stanley hides from the doom that Oedipus goes forward to meet.

Like Ibsen's and O'Neill's dramas before his, Pinter's play would seem to be a variation on Pozzo's insight that life is a gleam of light in the dark void. The playwrights use the birthday party ritual in each case more to satirize than to celebrate renewal. Just as Old Ekdal and Larry Slade attain some tragic insight, which is akin to Pozzo's second-act perception of life as a second's flicker in the void, so awareness is minimal in Pinter's absurdist play. Here the victories of two Hemingway-style killers seem more related to the power-hungry first-act Pozzo than to the disillusioned second-act one, leaving us without the half-revived hope of the other plays.

Tragic awareness of the truth, then, is minimal in these three plays with their false arrivals and their characters who cling to illusion. The protagonists in *The Wild Duck, The Iceman Cometh,* and *The Birthday Party* are not seeking renewal in their birthday celebrations. Gregers thrusts the truth of Hedvig's birth on a reluctant Hjalmar, Hickey robs his friends of hope on Harry Hope's birthday, and Goldberg and McCann impose a living death on their reluctant celebrant, Stanley. Most of the characters in these plays prefer their half-lives to the "sacred" truths that are imposed on them, while the minor characters, who are reborn in terms of those truths, suffer tragically either in death (Hedvig and Parritt) or life (Old Ekdal, Larry). The predominant tone is one that mocks renewal, the final effect—nonrenewal.

The truth in these plays, however, is in each case delivered by a false messiah, a self-deceived Godot who suffers from the illusions from which he would rid the others. In three plays by Samuel Beckett in which birthdays are used symbolically, *All That Fall* (1957), *Endgame* (1957), and *Krapp's Last Tape* (1958), though there is still little cause for celebration, no truth is imposed by false Godots. Here, instead, the characters make some attempt to use the birthday to confront some truth.

Mr. Rooney, Hamm, and Krapp are all would-be artists, who seek to overcome their despair and to find a shape to "accommodate the mess."[10] As artists, they do not so much await Godot as act as their own creators of their own worlds. In *All That Fall,* Mrs. Rooney has set out to meet her husband's train as a surprise for him on what may be his one-hundredth birthday: "Was I a hundred today? *(Pause.)* Am I a hundred, Maddy?"[11] She is treated on their way home to an account by her husband of the train's delayed arrival, which he refers to as his composition. "Where was I in my composition?" (p. 81). Hamm returns several times during *Endgame* to an account of a particular Christmas Eve, the eve of Christ's birthday, which he calls his chronicle, and Krapp, who has failed as a novelist, "Seventeen copies sold of which eleven at trade price to free circulating libraries beyond the seas,"[12] still has the artist's concern for recording the truth; witness his reenactment on his sixty-ninth birthday of his annual ritual of listening to a past birthday tape and recording a new one to contain his reflections on the past year.

Each would-be artist in these "birthday" plays struggles with the child in himself. Hedvig and Parritt died as rejected children in *The Wild Duck* and *The Iceman Cometh,* and Stanley is reduced to a living death in *The Birthday Party* as Meg's drum-beating child. In the Beckett birthday plays, however, the protagonists, Mr. Rooney, Hamm, and Krapp, appear not to be victimized children so much as victimizers of them. "Did you ever wish to kill a child? *(Pause.)* Nip some young doom in the bud" (p. 74), Mr. Rooney inquires of his wife. He confesses to her that he has had such a desire; he had been tempted to kill the boy, Jerry, who leads the blindman home at night from the train. And what Mr. Rooney leaves out of his "composition" about the train's delay is revealed by his potential victim, Jerry, to be a child who has fallen from the train to his death beneath its wheels. The strong suggestion is that Mr. Rooney has followed his inclination and has killed the child.

"If he could have his child with him. . .", Hamm says in the final moments of *Endgame,* referring to events in his chronicle. Set on Christmas Eve, Hamm's chronicle involves the pleas of a father to save his child, to provide shelter for him. Hamm imagines his response to those pleas.

> You don't want to abandon Him? You want him to bloom while you are withering? Be there to solace your last million last moments? *(Pause.)* He doesn't realize, all he knows is hunger, and cold, and death to crown it all. But you! You ought to know what the earth is like, nowadays. Oh I put him before his responsibilities![13]

While both Mr. Rooney and Hamm are ambivalent about their own deaths, their hostility to the child is a measure of their desire to see the death of life itself. T. S. Eliot's Magi arrive at Christ's birth unsure of whether they were led there to witness a birth or a death. When the speaker in Eliot's poem says, "I should be glad of another death," he seems to sense the new life that is to come with the death and resurrection of Christ. Unable to believe in such a new life or to accept Pozzo's bleak perception of "birth astride of a grave," such characters as Mr. Rooney, who probably has imposed death, and Hamm, who at play's end stoically prepares for his own, are not glad of another death as the promise of new life but as a release from the pain of living. Their cruelties to children, whether real or imaginary, are a measure of their own suffering; they are as much victimized children as the victimizers of them. As Mrs. Rooney says to explain the cry of a beaten wife on the way home, "Her poor husband is in constant pain and beats her unmercifully" (p. 78).

Krapp does not, like Mr. Rooney and Hamm, express hostility toward children, but he has withdrawn from life and love and any chance of paternity into what has turned out to be a sterile art. The hostility that he does express is toward his mother, whose death he recalls waiting for with impatience. "There I sat, in the biting wind, wishing she were gone" (p. 19). With the death of each parent, he has given up his role as a lover. On the tape he listens to on his sixty-ninth birthday, his thirty-nine-year-old self has been listening to an earlier tape when he was twenty seven or twenty nine, at which point he planned "for a less ... *(hesitate)* ... engrossing sexual life" (p. 16), but he has also noted his father's death. Similarly, the thirty-nine year old Krapp makes his "farewell to love" at the time of his mother's death.[14]

Krapp's anger at his mother would seem to be like that basic anger which Mr. Rooney and Hamm express at life itself, whether it be toward the mother who gives life or the child who carries that life on. But Krapp would actually like to be the child whom Dan Rooney and Hamm would destroy, not the vulnerable grown child, but the child who enjoys the safety of the fetal state. Tossing aside his new birthday tape, on which he has begun to reflect bitterly about the year he has just passed, Krapp returns, as he has twice before in the play, to his thirty-nine-year-old farewell-to-love tape. Here he recalls the girl in the punt, who has just agreed with him that "it was hopeless and no good going on," across whom he lay down, his face "in her breasts," and his hand on her. "We lay there without moving. But under us all moved, and moved us, gently, up and down, and from side to side" (p. 27). Because they have decided to part, the moment is a farewell to love, not a fulfillment of it. It is more a momentary return to the womb in which one is irresponsible, carried, than a sexual communion, though it partakes of both; in *Myth and Reality* Mircea Eliade suggests that man dwells on his beginnings because they provide him with a model and a source of renewal. "The return to origins," he writes, "gives the hope of rebirth." In Eliade's terms, Krapp is seeking the sacred moment of origin; he is attempting to arrest secular time, to determine what is significant, sacred, and worth retaining.

What we are left with at the end of the play is the inefficacy of the ritual. Krapp's life, released from the womb, has not been fulfilling. Like his book, Krapp has failed. He still drinks too much, gives in, despite a condition of ongoing constipation, to his penchant for bananas, and has not achieved artistic success. While the young thirty-nine-year-old voice on the tape does not wish to go back with the fire in him now, the sixty-nine-year-old Krapp has nowhere else to go but back. As the listening part of his birthday ritual takes over from the recording part, and he gives up his new tape for the old, his return to the past does not sustain and renew him; it engulfs him. The irony is, of course, that Krapp's failure to live creatively and fully is prophetically and clearly contained in the "primal" tape to which he returns.

Trapped in space and lost in time, Krapp grieves on as do many others in Beckett's dramatic world. "Ah yesterday," is the lament of Hamm's mother, Nell, in *Endgame*, who like Krapp can hardly deal with the present. For Clov, however, yesterday is that "bloody awful day, long ago, before this bloody awful day" (pp. 43–44). There is no sacred, redeeming past in the memory from which one may escape or from which one may gain sustenance with which to go on. And Hamm, who was not present at whatever has befallen the earth in *Endgame*, must invent a yesterday, a past—hence his chronicle.

Like the girl Mrs. Rooney tells of, for whose fatal condition a doctor could find no cause until he realized she "had never been really born" (p. 84), Krapp, Mr. Rooney, and Hamm have not been properly born; hence they seek consolation in regression (Krapp) and murderous aggression (Hamm and Mr. Rooney). What they lack, along with most of Beckett's characters, is that sense of identity and wholeness which would enable them to celebrate their births. Like Estragon in *Waiting for Godot*, who complains amid the diversion of Pozzo's and Lucky's antics that "nothing happens," Mr. Rooney responds to Mrs. Rooney's questions about the delayed train with the words "I have never known anything to happen" (p. 73). Hamm wistfully wonders if he might not end his story and "begin another" (p. 69), but he is unable to do so. Death, an ending, would be a happening for any of them, and might give rise to a new birth.

Hence, though Hamm and Mr. Rooney seem to struggle with the children outside of themselves, the men are struggling with the improperly born child within. It is that improperly born, unwhole child that Hamm and Mr. Rooney would see the end of, while Krapp would return to an embryonic state of bliss, never to emerge into the cruel and lonely world he inhabits. Hamm's father, Nagg, recalls the time when he and his wife moved their crying baby out of earshot and wishes for the day when Hamm will call to him as he did "when you were a tiny boy, and were frightened, in the dark, and I was your only hope" (p. 56). Beckett's characters, however, all share that helpless position. And they are all out of earshot.

In Eva Metman's Jungian interpretation of some of Beckett's plays, the child "is an image of wholeness: the child is unbroken and entirely itself."[15] Hamm's and Mr. Rooney's fantasies of infanticide, in her view, reflect their fear of life. Out of fear, Metman suggests, Mr. Rooney would kill the child in himself. It seems to me, however, that Hamm's and Mr. Rooney's desire to kill the child in themselves, which seems so cruel when expressed in their aggressive fantasies, is part of their attempt to find that wholeness which might come with maturity.

The child as wholeness and selfhood appears more clearly in *Endgame*. Metman astutely perceives that an "inner liberation is heralded by the advent of—may we say—a child-god." While Metman sees the Godot in *Waiting for Godot* as the traditional God that keeps Estragon and Vladimir from allowing an inner truth to emerge into consciousness, the boy that Clov sights toward the end of *Endgame* is an "image of the self" and "corresponds to the solemn change towards merciless reality in Hamm and ruthless acceptance of freedom in Clov." Metman admits that Beckett stops short of the confrontation between Clov and the boy that might herald a new cycle, but she finds a tendency in Beckett's plays to move toward "images of wholeness."[16]

Krapp regretfully recalls the ball he played with and gave to a dog at the moment of his mother's death, but during the play he discards his present tape. Hamm, thinking Clov gone and himself alone, discards the few possessions that might maintain him in life a bit longer. Jerry, Mr. Rooney's guide to and from the train, returns an object to him that according to his wife "looks like a kind of ball. And yet it is not a ball" (p. 89). What is dramatized in these three plays, then, is Krapp's nostalgia for what he has given up, Hamm's dignified resignation to a death that is ironically undermined by Clov's presence, and the return of the ball of life to Mr. Rooney, whether he would have it or not.

The Beckett characters' aptitude for survival, based as it is on a deep-seated ambivalence about life and death, prevents them from attaining either a release in death or that salvation which might come with death and rebirth. There is, however, something tragic about Hamm at the conclusion of *Endgame*, when he "turns the process of dying into an act of dying . . . ,"[17] which places him with Old Ekdal and Larry Slade in terms of facing and accepting life in the terrible terms that the blind

Pozzo has set forth. The boy, who remains outside, may be the arriving Godot (when Hamm claimed God to be a bastard that doesn't exist, Clov had noted, "Not yet."), and Hamm prevents Clov from destroying the boy with the gaff. "If he exists he'll die there or he'll come here. And if he doesn't . . ." (p. 78). What is over is Hamm's cycle—he returns to his Christmas Eve narrative.

> If he could have his child with him. . . .
> *(Pause.)*
> It was the moment I was waiting for.
> *(Pause.)*
> You don't want to abandon him? You want him to bloom while you are wilting? Be there to solace your last million last moments?
> *(Pause.)*
> He doesn't realize, all he knows is hunger, and cold, and death to crown it all. But you! You ought to know what the earth is like nowadays. Oh I put him before his responsibilities!
>
> (P. 83)

The implication here is that the father's responsibility and therefore Hamm's responsibility is to reject the boy. To do otherwise in this barren world would be a selfish act involving the sustaining of a life only to derive solace in one's own "last million last moments." Hamm's night must now fall, and he meets that fall by discarding his last possessions and rejecting new life in his now completed chronicle. What other life exists outside he leaves to take its own course.

The conclusion of *Endgame* is not unlike the conclusion of Beckett's *Act Without Words I*. Tormented by a teasing, invisible force who offers and then withdraws the means to life and to death, the silent protagonist of the mime refuses at the end to respond. Although his refusal may be taken as despair, it may also be taken for rebellion. Stanley Gontarski not only interprets the ending as a rebellion but as a birth as well, both of existential man and of the existential artist. "As he refuses the summons of the outside force," Gontarski contends, "as he refuses to act predictably, in his own self-interest, as he refuses the struggle for the most elemental of man's needs, Man, in a frenzy of inactivity, is born."[18]

Hamm's final refusal of the means to survival suggests such a birth of self, a birth in which, as in Pozzo's vision of "birth astride of a grave" and as in the mime, "birth and death coincide."[19] But the birth of Hamm as an artist has to do not only with the completing of his chronicle, in which, even as he discards the props that sustain him, he also rejects life, but in the release of Clov. If Clov is the sleeping child in the chronicle, then despite the implication in that work of art that Hamm has rejected the father's plea to take in the child, Hamm has taken him in. Susan Maughlin has suggested that Clov, like the chronicle, is Hamm's creation, a character such as the ones in Pirandello's *Six Characters in Search of an Author* and one that Hamm, with much pain and ambivalence, finally completes or releases. Clov's failure to leave the scene is not, Maughlin suggests, a sign of his subjection to Hamm to whom he no longer responds at the end, but to Beckett. He "cannot leave the world of the play—the only area he can live in."[20]

Why, then, does Hamm end his chronicle with the judgment of death, if he has given birth to the character of Clov? Is not he much like O'Neill's Larry Slade, pronouncing judgment on life, sending Parritt to his death, but experiencing through the judgment a new commitment to life? Somewhat more triumphant in his final stance than Larry, Hamm's tragic moment is complicated by Clov's presence, which unlike Parritt's final departure, tends to undermine Hamm's dark celebration of himself. Clov may remain, as Maughlin suggests, because he is subject to Beckett's world, but the fact that his eyes are fixed on Hamm until the end suggests a multitude of ironies and questions. At any moment Clov could make himself known to Hamm, return the discarded means to survival to him, and they could begin again—not anew—but continuing the old, not the cycle of death and rebirth, but the repetition of what has already been a kind of endless waiting for Godot. Again the power of Beckett's drama lies in its irresolution, though *Endgame* would seem, beneath its apparent increase in bleakness from *Godot*, to move more in the direction of the celebration of freedom and rebirth than the former play.

Krapp, who has rejected life in a manner related to Hamm's rejection of it, is unable, like Hamm, to face that death "which crowns it all." His discarding of his present birthday tape is not the deliberate act of Hamm's release of objects but a desperate flight from the present, and his return to the old tape is a hopeless regression into the past. Unable to accept his death, he seeks in anguish for the source of life in the past.

Mr. Rooney's main accomplishment on his birthday may be the tears that he, unlike Krapp, is able to shed. As they pause on their journey home and hear the strands of "Death and the Maiden" played by an old woman, Dan admits to Maddy, though "violently," that he is crying. But no sooner has he cried than he joins Maddy in "wild laughter" over the text of the next day's sermon, "The Lord upholdeth all that fall and raiseth up all those that he bowed down" (p. 88). Like Semiramis and the Old Man in *The Chairs*, who laughed together at their arrival/nonarrival in Paris, Maddy and Dan come together and briefly laugh at their unsaved condition, a paradoxically saving moment. Another source of celebration lies in Mrs. Rooney alone. Although she has actually given birth astride of a grave (she bemoans the loss of her daughter Mimi), her

Another False Arrival and Several Unhappy Birthdays   79

irrepressible hunger for and love of life, despite adverse physical conditions and terrible emotional deprivation, offset Mr. Rooney's despair. While Dan dreams of "another home on other roads" (p. 77) and notes their struggle with language as if it were a struggle with death, Mrs. Rooney is reminded by an *"urgent baa"* of the ongoing, living language of nature, and she reminds Mr. Rooney and us of it.

> MRS. ROONEY: Oh, the pretty little woolly lamb, crying to suck its mother! Theirs [their language] has not changed, since Arcady.
> (P. 81)

The child who fell or was pushed from the train is dead. The child of nature and, given the Christian symbolism of Jesus as Lamb of God, the child of God lives.

Despite, then, the antagonism to life, and to children as a sign of life, which is expressed by Hamm in his chronicle set significantly on the eve of Christ's birthday, by Dan on his birthday, and by Krapp in his nostalgic regression to a childlike state on his birthday, the plays continue to celebrate life with a stunning ambivalence. In the sufferings of Pat Rooney, Hamm, and Krapp, one still hears the universal language of the lamb crying for its mother as well as the sounds of laughter that they emit over the predicaments they suffer. Godots though they would be, artist-shapers of their own worlds, sacrificers of the sacrificial lambs (the boy on the train, the boy whose father would have Hamm give him shelter) and of all unborn children (farewell to love), Dan, Hamm, and Krapp are much, in their suffering, like the sacrificed children of Ibsen's, O'Neill's, and Pinter's birthday parties; they are themselves the children—the sacrificial lambs.

As creators or shapers of their own worlds, Dan, Hamm, and Krapp have failed due largely to their solipsistic tendencies, which have led them to withdraw from life. Dan Rooney contemplates retirement from his office and considers his blindness "a great fillip. If I could go deaf and dumb I think I might pant on to be a hundred" (p. 75), he suggests before realizing he might already be a hundred. Hamm has withheld light and life from others, and Krapp has withdrawn from love and from life. As in the case of Pinter's Stanley, however, there is finally no place to hide. Hence Dan describes himself on the train feeling caged like a wild beast, a description that also holds for his condition off the train and for the imprisoned Krapp as well. Only Hamm, who follows more in the footsteps of Old Ekdal and Larry Slade, has the strength at last to confront death, and in so doing he returns, at some level, from his retreat to life. One feels in the final moments of *Endgame* that what Clov witnesses along with the audience is that brief second between birth and death of which Pozzo speaks. As Hamm gives birth to himself and to his creation, Clov, the child who lingers on the outer reaches of his kingdom becomes a potentiality.

NOTES

1. Eliade, *The Sacred and The Profane*, p. 73.
2. Eugene O'Neill, quoted by Arthur Gelb and Barbara Gelb, *O'Neill*, p. 488.
3. Harold Pinter, quoted by Arnold P. Hinchliffe, *Harold Pinter*, p. 41.
4. Harold Pinter, *The Birthday Party* in *The Birthday Party and The Room: Two Plays by Harold Pinter* (New York: Grove Press, 1960), p. 59. All subsequent quotations from *The Birthday Party* are from this edition.
5. Richard Schechner, "Puzzling Pinter," *Tulane Drama Review* 11, no. 2 (Winter 1966): 178.
6. Edward Malpas, "A Critical Analysis of the Stage Plays of Harold Pinter," p. 96.
7. Lois G. Gorden, *Stratagems to Uncover Nakedness: The Dramas of Harold Pinter*, p. 21.
8. Ibid., p. 21.
9. Roger Pierce, personal correspondence, 28 October 1968.
10. Hesla, *The Shape of Chaos*, p. 7.
11. Samuel Beckett, *All That Fall* in *Krapp's Last Tape and Other Dramatic Pieces* (New York: Grove Press, 1970), p. 75. All subsequent quotations from *All That Fall* are from this edition.
12. Samuel Beckett, *Krapp's Last Tape* in *Krapp's Last Tape and Other Dramatic Pieces* (New York: Grove Press, 1970), p. 25. All subsequent quotations from *Krapp's Last Tape* are from this edition.
13. Samuel Beckett, *Endgame* (New York: Grove Press, 1958), p. 83. All subsequent quotations from *Endgame* are from this edition.
14. Don Nigro, "In Search of Lost Krapp," p. 2. "The Death of the cursed progenitor and the beginning or end of self as progenitor and lover appear to be for Beckett ritual events related in mythological time, as in the story 'First Love,' where the narrator associated his doomed marriage with the death of his father."
15. Metman, "Reflections," p. 137.
16. Ibid., pp. 134, 135.
17. Ibid., p. 134.
18. Stanley Gontarski, "Birth Astride of a Grave," *Journal of Beckett Studies*, Winter 1976, pp. 37, 39.
19. Ibid., p. 37.
20. Susan Maughlin, "The Play within the Play in *Endgame*," pp. 4, 9. In Maughlin's theory, Hamm's pain killer runs out as he completes his creation of Clov; the creative process is a kind of pain killer, and one suffers as one releases one's creation into life, p. 5.

5

Exorcising Godot: Possession and Self-Possession in Genet's *The Maids* and Pinter's *Old Times*

> SOLANGE: The orchestra is playing brilliantly. The attendant is raising the red velvet curtain. He bows. Madame is descending the stairs. Her furs brush against the green plants. Madame steps into the car. Monsieur is whispering sweet nothings in her ear. She would like to smile, but she is dead. . . .[1]

> KATE: *(To Anna.)* But I remember you. I remember you dead.
> *Pause.*
> I remember you lying dead. . . . When you woke my eyes were above you, staring down at you. You tried to do my little trick, one of my tricks you had borrowed, my little slow smile, my little slow shy smile, my bend of the head, my half closing of the eyes, that we knew so well, but it didn't work, the grin only split the dirt at the sides of your mouth and stuck. You stuck in your grin.[2]

Madame, in Jean Genet's one-act play *The Maids* (1947), would like to smile, Solange says in the drama's final speech, but she can't because she is dead. Anna, in Harold Pinter's *Old Times* (1972), would also like to smile, Kate says toward the end of that play, but she, too, is dead and unable to arrange it.

Madame is not literally dead in *The Maids*. Claire has taken the poisoned tea the two maids have prepared for their mistress. Taking Madame's part, as she has done in some of the fantasies the two maids have enacted from the outset of the play, the fantasy becomes a kind of reality with Claire as Madame dying in her place. Nor is Anna literally dead at the conclusion of *Old Times*. Kate's roommate of twenty years ago has come to visit Kate and Deeley in their country home, though even before her arrival she has been somewhat mysteriously present and merely turns into the action as it progresses. Near the end of the play

Kate declares her dead and gone, but she is still on stage, silent and reclining on a divan at the final curtain.

Still, a kind of death does take place in each case, one that is symbolized by the arrested smiles. Claire and Solange have been possessed by Madame in a double sense. They have felt more like her slaves than her maids, and she has so invaded their consciousness that her spirit, like that of some evil Godot, has possessed them as well. "It is not The Absence of Godot which supplies Genet's existential predicament, but rather His pervasive Presence. Not insufficient Being, but Being so absolute it negates isolation, surrounds, oppresses."[3] Anna has not controlled Kate's life for many years, although it would seem from their reminiscences about old times that she had dominated Kate in their shared past. During her visit she attempts to reassert her hold on Kate, a hold that her presence on stage before her so-called arrival suggests has been latent over the years. By playing maid and mistress, Solange and Claire act out the invasion of their spirits by Madame, though in the past they have never played out their fantasy of killing Madame to the end. By remembering and bringing the past to life, Anna, Kate, and Deeley act out the invasion of Kate's spirit by Anna. And in both cases, despite Madame's and Anna's continued physical life, there is a final and decisive exorcism of their influence.

Even though Solange and Claire, the sister-maids, appear to be far more rebellious than Pozzo's Lucky, mocking their mistress through their imitations, while Lucky cries at the thought of separation from his cruel master, they are actually just as firmly tied to their mistress as Lucky is literally tied to his master. As inextricably bound to one another, as well, just as Estragon and Vladimir are, Claire and Solange play out their fantasy games with a similar religious intensity. To complete the parallels of bondage between the two plays, there is the absent Monsieur, who like the absent Godot may be said to project a constraining presence as well.[4]

The Godot to be exorcised here, however, is not Monsieur but Madame, whose basic indifference to the maids is what makes their captivity so unbearable. Madame's kindness—she gives the maids her clothing and concerns herself casually with their happiness—is self-centered and patronizing.

> MADAME: When you needed anything, I saw that you got it. With my old gowns alone you both could have dressed like princesses. Besides . . . *(She goes to the closet and takes out the dresses)* of what use will they be to me? I'm through with finery and all that goes with it.
> (P. 69)

When Monsieur, who has been questioned by the police on false charges made by the maids, is freed and Madame needs her finery again, she reclaims her gowns with the same self-centered indifference with which she gave them.

Unaware of the suffering that she inflicts on her maids, Madame is nevertheless instinctively aware of the hostility behind their seeming subservience.

> MADAME: I'm not tired. You treat me like an invalid. You're always ready to coddle me and pamper me as if I were dying. Thank God, I've got my wits about me. I'm ready for the fight. *(She looks at SOLANGE and feeling that she has hurt her, adds with a smile)* Come, come, don't make such a face. *(With sudden violence)* All right, it's true! There are times when you're so sweet that I simply can't stand it. It crushes me, stifles me! And those flowers which are there for the very opposite of celebration!
>
> (P. 68)

That which is the opposite of celebration for Madame is, of course, a true celebration for Claire and Solange. To kill Madame with kindness is a reflection of the danger they see in her kindness and is their only weapon, a possible means to their own release.

In his study of the play, Jean-Paul Sartre has pointed out that there is some question about the fantasized death of Madame. The Black Mass that the maids play out nightly is to end with Madame's murder, but they are always interrupted before it takes place. In fantasy? In reality? "And besides, what would there have been 'at the very end'? The true murder of the fake Madame? The fake murder of Claire? Perhaps they don't even know themselves."[5]

As in *Waiting for Godot,* the characters are tied to each other in dependency relationships that suggest their lack of wholeness. The maids despise themselves and each other, even as Madame despises them.

> SOLANGE: She loves us the way she loves her armchair. Not even that much! Like her bidet, rather. Like her pink enamel toilet-seat. And we, can't love one another. Filth . . .
> CLAIRE: Ah! . . .
> SOLANGE: . . . doesn't love filth. . . .
>
> (P. 52)

Their love-hate relationship with each other is another version of their love-hate relationship with Madame. As in the white-black conflict in Genet's *The Blacks,* there is no release from slavery, only an alternation of dominance and subservience in which the subservient long to overthrow the dominant only to become him or her. Pozzo had learned all he knew from "his Lucky" to whom at some earlier point he had apparently been subservient.

Here, then, is the mysterious paradox of power in which the possessor/possessed relationship seethes with ambivalence. The problem, as clearly revealed in *The Blacks,* is that an authentic whole self can't emerge when the rebel is beset with envy. How can one exorcise the master or mistress if one's whole desire is to become him or her?

Sacrificing Madame would not suffice for the maids, who must find a solution for their self-hatred, the love-hate relationship with each other, and their love-hate relationship with Madame. Instead, Genet finds the perfect solution for the needed exorcism in the suicide of Claire that she commits at the end of the drama while playing the part of Madame. On the psychological level of the play's action, Claire satisfies both her self-hatred and her hatred of Madame by killing herself in the role of Madame, releasing Solange, who is playing the role of Claire, to a renewed existence in which she will symbolically survive. "Solange, you will contain me within you" (p. 96), Claire informs her reluctant partner in the sacrificial rite.

On a metaphysical as well as psychological level, the suicide as fantasized murder works as an exorcism. What the maids need to destroy is not Madame, who is herself not particularly real, but "Madameness," the very idea of their mistress.[6] Just as Estragon wonders not only if Godot will come, who he is, and whether he exists, wondering as well about his own existence, so Claire and Solange are unsure about their own reality and the line between illusion and reality. Much of their role playing, like the playing of Estragon and Vladimir, involves a kind of religious search for meaning, a search, in this case, through illusion for the reality they lack. The maids employ illusion-filled ritual in order to transcend an unacceptable reality.

Sartre finds the playing of Madame by the maids to be an "actual incantation."

> We shall see later on that by imitating the gestures of his superior, the domestic treacherously draws him into himself and becomes saturated with him. There is nothing surprising in this, since Madame herself is a fake Madame who plays at distinctions and at her passion for Monsieur and who dreams of drawing into herself the soul of a whore who follows her pimp to jail.[7]

The object of such incantation is to draw Madame into themselves so that Madameness may finally be banished.

By taking Madame's place in death, Claire adopts the role of the ritual scapegoat. Although it was the king who must die in countless rituals designed to insure the fertility and renewal of the kingdom, Frazer recounts how often a common criminal replaced the king, one who might be treated briefly with the honors due his master before being asked to make the ultimate sacrifice.[8] Solange, who is to contain Claire even as Claire contains Madame in Claire's death scene, wears in her final fantasy "the red garb of criminals" (p. 92). In their combined guise of criminal/scapegoat, the maids feel that they can attain that understanding for which they have longed—"Madame now sees my loneliness—at last!" (p. 92), Solange exalts—and that stature which in their eyes has been reserved for Madame and Monsieur. The criminal combines with the mistress, dying not for the renewal of the old kingdom but for the new in which the exorcism of Madameness leaves the maids triumphant and liberated.

The English version of the play, based as it is on an earlier manuscript of the play than the one Genet has designated as definitive (see note 1), gives a slightly different emphasis to this triumph and liberation than the final version does. In both versions Solange has a long tirade just before the final suicide-murder in which she imagines herself assuring the inspector of police who will be handling her case (she assumes she will be hanged for the murder of Claire-Madame) that she has "scaled the fiercest heights" (p. 92). Despite her outpouring of words, Solange speaks of her future silence on the matter; like Iago, Solange as Claire will refuse to speak. "It would be a fine thing if masters could pierce the shadows where servants live. . . . That my child is our darkness, ours" (p. 93). Exultant, Solange steps out on the balcony and imagines an audience of others on balconies watching her procession to death. The servants who will accompany her are those who will have attended Claire's funeral. Claire's funeral and her own hanging merge in her mind, and she imagines herself merging with Claire amidst a new community of crowned servants. "Now we are Mademoiselle Solange Lemercier, that Lemercier woman," Solange announces, then breaking down; "Claire . . . we're raving!" (p. 95).

At this point in both versions Claire insists on turning the fantasy into reality or into her imagined reality by drinking the poisoned tea. The earlier version, then, allows Solange to complete her tirade in a final triumphant speech in which she imagines the smile frozen on the dead face of Madame.

> Madame is dead. Her two maids are alive; they've just risen up, free, from Madame's icy form. All the maids were present at her side—not they themselves, but rather the hellish agony of their names. And all that remains of them to float about Madame's airy corpse is the delicate perfume of the holy maidens which they were in secret. We are beautiful, joyous, drunk and free!
>
> (P. 100)

This speech, however, was not present in the first one-act version of the play,[9] and is also not present in the last and definitive version. Instead, Clair maintains the note of triumph, and Solange's ecstatic final tirade is replaced by her submission to Claire and their sacrificial act.

> CLAIRE: Tu es lâche. Obéis-moi. Nous sommes tout au bord, Solange. Nous irons jusqu'à la fin. Tu seras seule pour assumer nos deux existences. Il te faudra beaucoup de force. Personne ne saura au bagne que je t'accompagne en cachette. Et surtout, quand tu seras condamnée, n'oublie pas que tu me portes en toi. Précieusement. Nous serons belles, libres et joyeuses. . . .[10]

> CLAIRE: You are a coward. Obey me. We are at the very edge, Solange. We will go to the end. You alone will assume our two identities. You will need a lot of strength. No one will know in jail that I am secretly with you. And above all, when you are condemned, don't forget that you will be carrying me within you. Preciously. We will be beautiful, free and joyous. . . .
>
> (My translation)

As Claire drinks the poisoned tea, the play ends with Solange turning to the audience, remaining still, and crossing her hands as if she were in handcuffs, *"les mains croisées comme par les menottes"* (p. 93).

Genet sharpens the irony in this final version, in which he puts the emphasis less on the maids' mutual triumph than on their mutual sacrifice. To be free and joyous, the maids must be sacrificed; their salvation is achieved only in submission to death. One is reminded, then, at the very end, that the cost of exorcism is death.

As in August Strindberg's *Miss Julie*, death alone offers a release from social boundaries that enslave both the master and servant. In that play, however, the servant Jean remains, cringing before his master's ringing bell, while it is Miss Julie, the master's daughter, who finds some triumph and promise of wholeness in a death in which the last (she considers herself to be last since her seduction by Jean or her seduction of him) shall be first. Claire's death in the role of Madame suggests the attainment of a similar grace. It is a gesture that not only allows Madame, in Solange's words and wishful world, to understand the maids' loneliness but also relieves that loneliness as the servants, again in Solange's mind, become a new triumphant community.

One may be tempted to dismiss Claire's death as mere self-punishment: "Solange and Claire," according to Philip Thody, "have no alternative value to offer. They would like to possess Madame's qualities themselves, and although their fury at being unable to do so may express itself in dreams of murder, they finally punish only themselves."[11] Thody, however, misses the value Genet assigns to the ritual that his maids enact. Influenced by the theories of Antonin Artaud, Genet's plays, as Robert Brustein perceives, "take the form of liberated dreams, organized into rites. Through the open exaltation of crime, eroticism, and savagery, he hopes to exorcise his own, as well as the spectator's, cruelty."[12] As a rite of exorcism, Claire's murder/suicide becomes one of those Artaudian "signals through the flames" that suggests the level of reality that sacrifice may confer.

Madame herself is irrelevant. Her arrival and behavior suggest the false arrivals of Albee's empty American Dream or Ionesco's mute orator. To exorcise her spirit, which is real in its influence, is, however, another matter. Violence, in this case the sacrifice of Claire, is Genet's way to reality, the sacred reality or transcendent one that frees all maids from all madames.

Moving through Pirandellian levels of illusion, the characters in Genet's dramatic world can orient themselves to reality only through death. The indifference with which Madame rejects her maids is akin to the indifference with which the author of Pirandello's *Six Characters In Search of An Author* (1922) has rejected his characters, and in both cases the response to that indifference/rejection is a compulsive playing out of roles that lead to death. In Pirandello's play, in which Godot as Author is absent, the death of the children is the inevitable and senseless outcome of an authorless or godless world, but that death convinces the actors and directors for whom the characters perform of the characters' reality and makes the director question his own. In *The Maids,* however, in which Godot is all too present, Claire chooses death as an exorcism as the means to convince herself and Solange of their reality or even as a doorway to that reality. The Six Characters reenact their drama compulsively in order to find its shape and meaning, a meaning that the children's deaths do not furnish, although they do establish the reality of the searching characters. Solange and Claire also reenact their fantasy compulsively in order to find its meaning; and as they feel their way to the suicide/murder, they approach that sense of freedom and community which comes with the exorcism of Madame/Godot.

Perhaps Genet is not so far away from Beckett after all. The void still looms as the essential reality, indeed as the sacred reality that Pozzo has discovered and Vladimir has approached in his failed rite of initiation. Jean Gitenet describes Genet's drama as a "leap into the void"[13] a void that embodies the sacred reality that Beckett makes of it in *Godot.*

As Gitenet points out, Genet's sacred world "takes root in the profane world that it rejects"[14] but is a movement toward emptiness. Genet's definition of drama is much like Pozzo's idea of life: "They give birth astride of a grave, the light gleams an instant, then it's night once more." Genet writes, "What of drama? If it has, in the author, its brilliant origin, it is up to him to capture the lightning and to organize, from the flash that lights up the emptiness, a verbal architecture—that is, a grammatical and ceremonial structure—artfully indicating that an appearance which shows up influences is torn from emptiness."[15] This statement reveals an awareness on Genet's part that Claire's suicidal, sacred act is but another illusion, a lightning flash that "lights up the emptiness." In Nietzschean terms it is a flash from an Apollonian dream world in which art consoles with illusion, an illusion that, however, is that lightning flash which illuminates the void, the Dionysian chaotic ground of being.

The exorcism of Madame/Godot through Claire's suicide/murder, the leap into the void, which seems so much more decisive in action than the withdrawal from the void that Didi and Gogo enact in *Godot,* remains something of an illusion itself and may be compared to the waiting of the two tramps in *Godot.* Although there is no mention of God in Genet's definitive version of the drama, in the earlier version upon which the English translation is based, Claire and Solange have postulated a watching God. It is for this God that they enact their ceremony, a power beyond that of Madame for whom their rite is an offering, another Godot for whom they choose not to wait, but for whom they make their leap into the void and that makes that leap not just an Apollonian illusion but an act of faith. Even in the more existential, definitive version, one feels the deity in its very absence; the blasphemous use of ritual invokes a rejected God. Like Beckett, Genet glances both at the sacred void and at that watching Godot who does not arrive.[16]

More deeply influenced by Beckett than by Genet, Harold Pinter's drama nevertheless shares Genet's greater conclusiveness; in his plays Godot arrives. The more blatant cruelties of Pinter's early dramas—the beating death in *The Room,* Stanley's victimization in *The Birthday Party*—are muted but very present in the later plays; and if the exorcism in *Old Times* merely freezes the smile on Anna's face, one experiences it still as both a death and a liberation of sorts.

In Pinter's surreal drama the rhetorical debates and frenzy of Genet's dreamlike stage are replaced with a subdued, subtextual action that only gradually rises to the surface in what remains symbolic violence. Kate and Deeley draw their subtextual swords in the opening dialogue, but they use them somewhat playfully as they discuss the imminent arrival of Kate's ex-roommate, Anna.

> DEELEY: Did you *think* of her as your best friend?
> KATE: She was my only friend.
> DEELEY: Your best and only.
> KATE: My one and only.
> *Pause*

If you have only one of something you can't say it's the best of anything.
DEELEY: Because you have nothing to compare it with?
KATE: Mmmm.
DEELEY: *(Smiling.)* She was incomparable.
KATE: Oh, I'm sure she wasn't.

(P. 9)

Kate's ambivalent attitude toward Anna emerges here as she spars with her husband, but just as Solange and Claire had a love-hate relationship with Madame and with each other, so Kate has very mixed feelings not just about Anna but about Deeley as well. As in *The Maids*, the action is centered on a triangle in which the symbolic exorcism of one of its members fundamentally changes the relationship of the two who remain.

Although the struggle, like that in *The Maids*, involves dominance and independence, the element of class struggle that colors the action in Genet's play is absent. Deeley, Kate, and Anna are all middle class and middle aged, and the power struggle is played out in terms of the dynamics of marriage and friendship.

In *Old Times*, Kate, like Pinter's heroine Ruth in *The Homecoming*, appears as an Aphrodite-like creature of the water. More at peace than Ruth, who thirsted for the water of life in the arid desert of her American existence, Kate lives by the sea; here she enjoys walks by it, walks in the rain, and long, sensuous baths. "Sometimes I walk to the sea. There aren't many people. It's a long beach" (p. 20), Kate affirms. "She likes taking long walks. All that. You know. Raincoat on. Off down the lane, hands deep in pockets. All that kind of thing" (p. 24), her husband Deeley explains to Anna, Kate's visiting roommate of twenty years past. Speaking later of Kate's behavior in the bath, Deeley describes it as "both thorough and, I must say it, sensuous" (p. 53).

Kate's full kind of sensuality and self-possession is what attracts and repels Deeley and Anna, whose battle for possession of Kate structures the play.[17] Deeley's and Anna's depictions of Kate as a creature of the water are tinged with a hostility based on their sense of exclusion from Kate's world, her winds, her silence, her sea. Kate, they insist, is a dreamer, one who floats like the water. Her face itself has floated from his touch, Deeley complains, causing Kate to insist, "My head is quite fixed. I have it on" (p. 24).

When Anna patronizes Kate as a creature of silence and the sea—"How wise you were to choose this part of the world, and how sensible and courageous of you both to stay permanently in such a silence" (p. 19)—Deeley disassociates himself from Kate's world. It is Kate, not he, who stays, Deeley insists. He is a restless traveler of the globe, familiar with Anna's milieu, a volcanic island.

> DEELEY: You live on a very different coast.
> ANNA: Oh, very different. I live on a volcanic island.
> DEELEY: I know it.
> ANNA: Oh, do you?
> DEELEY: I've been there.
>
> (P. 22)

Speaking of his courtship with Kate, Deeley explains that Kate's winds were really never his.

Anna matches Deeley's memory of his courtship of Kate with her memory of hearing of their marriage. Her clichéd "My heart leapt with joy" (p. 36) both echoes and at the same time undermines her description of Kate's leap or jump into love with Deeley, a leap this time in terms of water. "Some people," Anna explains, "throw a stone into a river to see if the water's too cold for jumping, others, a few others, will always wait for the ripples before they will jump." She is sure that Kate would test the very depths before jumping: "But in this case she did jump and I knew therefore she had fallen in love truly and was glad" (pp. 36, 37).

Kate fully understands Anna's and Deeley's patronizing. As they sing snatches of old songs to and about her, she complains that they speak as if she were dead. And sensing the nature of the life-and-death struggle beneath the chatter, Kate emerges from her bath and her comparatively passive and silent state to defend herself from them—in terms of water: "The water's very soft here. Much softer than London. . . . That's one reason I like living in the country. Everything's softer. The water, the light, the shapes, the sounds. There aren't such edges here. And living close to the sea too. You can't say where it begins or ends. That appeals to me. I don't care for harsh lines. I deplore that kind of urgency" (p. 59).

It is Anna's and Deeley's urgency, their edges, their possessiveness, that Kate rejects. Although attracted now to one, now to the other, Kate's final rejection of both is not, as some critics have suggested, a measure of her coldness or detachment[18] so much as it is a measure of her emerging selfhood and her renewal. The smoldering, possessive Anna, at least on one level of the play's action, is not the opposite of the floating, dreamy Kate but is rather her double, another part of Kate's self who makes a claim and must be exorcised. According to Kate, Anna not only stole her underwear but also attempted to steal her smile (p. 72). And Deeley adds to the evidence by suggesting that on their first meeting Anna had pretended to be Kate: "Did it pretty well. Wearing your underwear she was too, at the time. . . . She thought she was you, said little, so little.

Maybe she was you. Maybe it was you, having coffee with me, saying little, so little" (p. 69).

Rather than being surprised at the disclosure of Deeley's and Anna's alleged past relationship, Kate proceeds to tell Deeley how Anna fell in love with him, clearly speaking here for herself. And when Anna asserts her separate identity by agreeing that it was she, not Kate, who was with Deeley, Kate turns on her with a speech of annihilation. In a play in which memories are used as weapons[19]—"There are things I remember which may never have happened but as I recall them so they take place" (p. 32), Anna says in a key line—Kate remembers Anna dead, her face covered with dirt. Whether Kate is destroying her former roommate, that roommate's lesbian hold on her, or but another part of herself that dwelt in a more envious, grasping past, the destruction is initiatory for Kate and renewing.

By rejecting Kate's subsequent efforts to dirty his face—"He would not let me dirty his face, or smudge it, he wouldn't let me" (p. 73)—Deeley, it seems, has lost the possibility of rebirth that Kate, in her ritual role of Earth Mother, has offered. Failing to see that her earth offer is "sexually forthcoming," Deeley suggests "a wedding instead, and a change of environment" (p. 73), but because of his failure to grasp the nature of Kate's gesture, "neither mattered" (p. 73).

The doubling in Pinter's play is somewhat more subtle than it is in Genet's, in which the sisters perceive their likeness to one another clearly. "And me, I'm sick of seeing my image thrown back at me like a bad smell" (p. 61), Claire exclaims to Solange. Their similar efforts to dominate one another are reflected in their role playing in which they take turns at playing Madame. But even when not role playing, they continue to attempt to dominate each other, even as they feel dominated by their other double, Madame. "No. I shall have my crown," Claire tells her older sister. "I shall be the poisoner that you failed to be. It's my turn now to dominate you!" (P. 61).

In *The Maids*, the sister-doubles are reconciled through the suicide-murder of Claire-Madame. Imbibing Madame by playing at being her, Claire involves her sister in the arresting of Madame's smile, a symbol of her kindness that is the heart of her tyranny. "It's easy to be kind, and smiling, and sweet—ah! that sweetness of hers!—when you're beautiful and rich" (p. 52), Solange exclaims. Because Solange is persuaded to enter into the rite of exorcism that Claire's suicide accomplishes, she will be rid of Madame but will contain Claire. Freedom in Genet's play leads to a sense of new community.

In *Old Times* there is a similar identification that Kate makes with Anna before the final exorcism. Excluding Deeley, Kate seems to move into the past and a time when Anna ran her baths, chose her clothes, and provided her with friends. "Would you like me to ask someone over?" (p. 45), Anna asks Kate, though she is visiting her in her married home; she then proceeds to suggest a variety of men as if Deeley did not exist and she and Kate were back in London. Kate seems to need to go back in time and to feel Anna's influence again before she can take steps to remove that influence entirely.

Deeley, however, fails to play the role Kate assigns him in the exorcisim that she initiates, and hence *Old Times* lacks the reconciliation of doubles that is dramatized in *The Maids*. Deeley fails to meet Kate's challenge because he is much too much like Anna, possessive, restless, and frightened. Kate attempts such a reconciliation in her memory—she tells of how after Anna's removal from her room she brought Deeley in. "When I brought him into the room your body of course had gone" (p. 72), she informs the reclining Anna. But Deeley's failure to accept her proffered earth is his failure to join Kate in the burial of false relationships symbolized by Anna's smile. Anna has served as a double for Deeley as well as for Kate, just as Madame served as a double for the sister-maids, but Deeley's sobs at the play's end testify to his banishment with Anna rather than his reconciliation with Kate. The death of the one relationship results in the death of the other.

Kate's annihilation of her possessive, homosexual self leaves her less divided, more whole, and finally self-possessed. Deeley's inability to suffer the death of the Anna in him excludes him from such a victory. Unlike Solange, who through the exorcism of Madame by Claire will contain Claire and enjoy a new sense of community before she joins Claire in death, Kate will have no one with whom to share her newfound selfhood. Her exorcism of Anna rids her of Deeley as well, and whatever celebration she attains is entirely based on her possession of self.

In the world of Pinter's play, Godot is no longer some malign outside force, such as Monty in *The Birthday Party*, who sends his henchmen in for the kill. Although Anna is part emissary from other worlds, the London of Kate's youth, a volcanic island, she is patently also an emissary from Kate's unconscious, a dream figure tempting Kate to a kind of regression that involves servitude—she is to be possessed. Hence, the uncanny effect of Anna's presence and exorcism may be related to Freud's indentification of the uncanny with the emerging of the repressed.[20]

Godot, then, in *Old Times*, is largely an inner force, a past self. The effect, however, is still far from merely psychological. Despite the absense of the political-social arena in which all of Genet's plays take place, the exorcism of Godot in Pinter's *Old Times* has mythical resonance, and the ritual of exorcism acquires quite naturally the kind of universal significance that Genet strives so self-consciously to attain in *The Maids*.

Kate's refusal of enslavement to others or to the more grasping part of herself becomes mythic as her association with earth and water aligns her with the forces of life and she acquires some of the archetypal ambiance of an Earth Mother. Anna must be buried—"You stuck in your grin"—and so must Deeley if he is to be reborn. If not, he must be discarded. Indeed, Kate has the cruelty of a survivor fighting for her life; but cruelty is also a part of her Earth Mother role in which she seems to act as part of the force of nature itself—its servant, but no man's and no woman's.

The decisive movement toward liberation in *The Maids* and *Old Times* is, of course, foreign to Beckett's dramatic world. The gradual reduction of life in that world in which the earth slowly swallows its inhabitants (*Happy Days*), and those inhabitants sometimes swallow their fellow sufferers (Pozzo's inhumane treatment of Lucky, Hamm's withholding of light from Mother Peg), renders the characters essentially passive before their suffering. They can't go because they are waiting for Godot. Lucky may be "possessed" by Pozzo, but he has no wish to change his condition; on the contrary, he doesn't put down the bags he carries, Pozzo explains, in an attempt to convince his master to keep him. Pozzo even gains the sympathy of Didi and Gogo, who are initially appalled by the way Pozzo treats Lucky but are later equally appalled by the sufferings Pozzo claims to endure as a master. And Pozzo's claim that he learned all he knows from Lucky suggests a possible earlier reversal of their roles.

Although power struggles are at the center of Beckett's dramas as well as Genet's and Pinter's, those struggles are suffered, in Chekhovian fashion, by both the dominant and dominated in Beckett's plays. There is no question of exorcism of Godot, whose absence, not presence, is a source of agony. And there is no question of exorcising Pozzo/Godot to deliver Lucky because Lucky has gone beyond being possessed by Pozzo to being his possession. To the extent that the pair, like Kate and Anna, appear to be a single character, one of whom dominates the other, Pozzo is actually and ironically more possessed by Lucky as a possession than the reverse; Lucky's "think" speech is a torment to him as well as to Didi and Gogo. But there is no release from its incoherence or its insistence on the wasting and pining that, amid that incoherence, are man's lot. In the insight that accompanies his acquired blindness, Pozzo no longer seeks to rid himself of his possession/legacy, to sell him at the fair. He has accepted Lucky as a burden, and they move "on" together.

This is not to suggest that the truth of Beckett's fictive world is foreign to Genet's and Pinter's. The more violent movement through exorcism to self-possession that forms the basis of action in *The Maids* and *Old Times* expresses by its very violence a reaction to the agonies of fragmentation that beset Beckett's drama. Claire's suicide/murder, accompanied as it is by Solange's gesture of submission in handcuffs, leaves the audience with the burden of their mutual sacrifice just as Kate's hard-won self-possession leaves the audience with a sense of her state of somewhat terrifying isolation.

Still, the false smiles have been arrested, and the false Godots have been expelled.

NOTES

1. Jean Genet, *The Maids* in *The Maids and Deathwatch: Two Plays by Jean Genet*, trans. Bernard Frechtman (New York: Grove Press, 1961), p. 99. All subsequent references to *The Maids* are from this edition.

This quotation and several others that I use in the following chapter are from the Frechtman translation, which is the only one available in English. It should be noted, however, that Frechtman has not based his translation on what has become the definitive French version of the play, and that the version of the play that he translated is substantially different from the definitive one.

Genet had originally written a longer version of the play called *La Tragédie des Confidentes* for Louis Jouvet, but Jouvet had suggested reduction to one act. This one-act version, according to Odette Aslan in *Jean Genet,* went into rehearsal in 1946 and after some modification in the early stages of rehearsal was sent out for publication. Claire Saint-Léon, who attempts to rectify some critical confusions about the several texts of the play and has had the opportunity to study several manuscript versions of it, has suggested in "*Les Bonnes* de Jean Genet: quelle Version Faut-il Jouer?" that the definitive text did not emerge until the end of the rehearsal period and the actual production of the play in the spring of 1947, a text that is quite different from the initial one published in May of 1947 in the journal *L'Arbalète,* no. 12. Some critics have ascribed the differences to changes demanded by Jouvet in rehearsal, but Saint-Léon suggests that they are basically Genet's own additions and are based on his growing distaste for realism and the sharpening of his poetic sensibility, which led to the elimination of several speeches (p. 515).

The main point is that the script that was published in the spring of 1947 in the journal *L'Arbalète,* no. 12, and that was translated into English, is the one that several critics have mistakenly come to regard as the definitive one. See, for example, the discussion of *The Maids* in Joseph H. McMahon's *The Imagination of Jean Genet*, pp. 150-55, in which he considers the earlier edition to be the revised version. When the two versions were published together in 1954 by Jean Pauvert under the title *Les Bonnes, Piéce en un acte, les deux versions précédées d'une lettre de l'auteur,* Genet's letter to Pauvert explained that the order of the versions had been misunderstood; here he designates the version that came out of final rehearsals in 1947 as the one that he approves and the version that had been translated into English as an earlier one.

Some of the significant changes in the definitive edition are: the removal of Solange's final tirade, shifting the emphasis back to Claire's final act and Solange's submission to it, the removal of all references to a watching God, and a slightly different characterization of Madame, who is less self-involved than in the former version, more generally concerned about Monsieur, and more insightful about her human condition and her own imprisonment in her role as Madame.

2. Harold Pinter, *Old Times* (New York: Grove Press, 1971), pp. 71-72. All subsequent references to *Old Times* are from this edition.

3. N. Joseph Calarco, *Tragic Being: Apollo and Dionysus in Western Drama*, p. 170.

Christopher Innes in *Holy Theatre* discusses Frantz Fanon's contention that the aim of ritual in Genet's drama is "not an external change in power structure, but the creation of a new identity for the oppressed by the violent exorcisim of an alien presence that dominates them through spiritual possession," p. 155.

4. Jean-Paul Sartre, Introduction, *The Maids and Deathwatch*, p. 15.

5. Ibid., p. 24.

6. Lewis Cetta, *Profane Play, Ritual, and Jean Genet: A Study of His Dramas*, p. 40. Cetta points out that for Genet "illusion is a deeper reality than reality," p. 39.

7. Sartre, Introduction, *The Maids*, p. 21.

8. Frazer, *The Golden Bough*, p. 667.

9. This first version may be found in the Bibliothèque de l'Arsenal and is much like the English version except for the absence of Solange's final tirade (see Claire Saint-Leon, "*Les Bonnes* de Jean Genet," p. 513)

10. Jean Genet, *Les Bonnes & Comment Jouer Les Bonnes* (Paris: L'Arbalète, Marc Barbezat, 1963), pp. 91–92.

11. Philip Thody, *Jean Genet: A Study of his Novels and plays*, p. 167.

12. Brustein, *The Theatre of Revolt*, p. 378.

13. Jean Gitenet, "Profane and Sacred Reality in Jean Genet's Theatre," trans. Janie Vanpée, in *Genet: A Collection of Critical Essays*, ed. Peter Brooks and Joseph Halpern, p. 176. "Therefore DEATH, guarantee of the sacred and negation of the profane, seems to be for Genet, the supreme point, pivot of the absurd from which all objectification of dramatic character (dialogues, acting, and staging) takes on sense *and* non-sense" (p. 177).

14. Ibid., p. 172.

15. Quoted by Gitenet in ibid., p. 175.

16. In his discussion of *The Maids*, Christopher Innes suggests, mistakenly I think, that the maids' attempt in the third repetition of their sacrificial ceremony is "not the murder of a God-surrogate but of God himself. . . ." In Innes's interpretation, Claire becomes a willing image of Christ. "The consecration is a desecration, self-annihilation is achieved by destroying God" (pp. 156–57).

17. For a discussion of the possessiveness of Anna and Deeley, see Lucina Paquet Gabbard, *The Dream Structure of Pinter's Plays*, p. 247; Alan Hughes, "'They Can't Take That Away From Me': Myth and Memory in Pinter's *Old Times*," *Modern Drama* 17, no. 4 (December 1974): 467–76; and Robert Skloot, "Putting Out the Light: Staging the Theme of Pinter's *Old Times*," *Quarterly Journal of Speech* 61, no. 3 (October 1975): 265–70.

18. Gabbard in *The Dream Structure of Pinter's Plays* mistakenly, I think, describes Kate as narcissistic (pp. 235, 244) and Anna as altruistic (p. 245); while Francis Gillen, "All These Bits and Pieces': Fragmentations and Choice in Pinter's Plays," *Modern Drama* 17, no. 4 (December 1974): 485, mistakenly discusses Kate as cold and detached.

19. See Hughes, "'They Can't Take That Away From Me,'" for a good discussion of memories as weapons in *Old Times*.

20. Sigmund Freud, "The Uncanny," *The Standard Edition of the Complete Psychological Works of Sigmund Freud*, 24 vols., trans. and ed. James Strachey (London: The Hogarth Press, 1938), 17:176.

6

In Search of Godot

The search of Pirandello's Six Characters for an author anticipates the kind of search for Godot that structures several modern plays. Although the hero's quest for fulfillment is as old as literature, the quest for wholeness that Pirandello captures in his seminal *Six Characters in Search of an Author* (1922) anticipates that particularly modern feeling of fragmentation which dominates *Waiting for Godot* with its world bereft of God. Pirandello's Six Characters, however, will not wait; they are driven to replay their sordid, melodramatic story before an audience in hopes that they will find that Godot who, unlike their initial creator, will accept them and hence give meaning to their lives.

While Godot is the author the Six Characters seek in the director and actors for whom they perform in Pirandello's play, he is an ideal place in Eugène Ionesco's drama *The Killer* (1957), a recipe for soup in Günter Grass's play *The Wicked Cooks* (1957). And nobody waits for him in these plays.

At the outset of *The Killer,* considered by many critics to be one of Ionesco's most important plays,[1] Bérenger stumbles almost by accident on a paradise that offers the salvation he has craved. ". . . I knew that somewhere in our dark and dismal city," Ionesco's protagonist tells the city's architect, "in all its mournful, dusty, dirty districts, there was one that was bright and beautiful, this neighborhood beyond compare with its sunny streets and avenues bathed in lights . . . this radiant city within a city which you've built. . . ."[2] When he discovers that this paradise, to which he had hoped to move, has been ruined by a killer who is systematically killing off its inhabitants by showing them a picture of a colonel and then drowning them in an ornamental pool, he vows to track the killer down in order to return the paradise to its ideal state. His search for the killer, then, in so far as it is a search for his own redemption, is a search for Godot.

The cooks in Grass's play are all in pursuit of the Count's soup recipe, which, in the cook's world, is invaluable; all the customers want it. "Everybody calls it the gray soup," Vasco tells the Count from whom he demands the recipe, "and they come back into the kitchen in their black suits with their blond ladies and nice smell, and they say to me: 'Cook it for us Vasco!' Well, what am I supposed to do? Am I gonna admit I can't? I'm a bad cook? Ask the Count, if you please. He knows how to make it. He made it two, three times, and the customers went wild."[3] But the soup comes to stand for more than wordly success—it is in some way a sacred soup, one that bestows grace. To have the recipe for such soup is to have the key to that grace, to come into communion with Godot. Such a recipe will come, the cooks believe, only to those who seek it.

In *The Killer* the inevitable failure of the search is suggested from the outset. The paradise that so impresses Bérenger is conspicuously absent. In the absence of scenery, Bérenger, who keeps harping on the reality of the radiant city, becomes ridiculous. "Your radiant city is *real*," he exclaims, going over to examine nonexistent grass and "rose-pink flowers" that the architect explains "really are roses," but that Bérenger must verify: "'Real' roses?" (p. 12), he inquires.

Lest one think that Bérenger has stumbled unwittingly into *Our Town*, one soon sees that his guide, the district's architect, is very unlike the friendly Stage Manager who helps the audience grasp the reality they cannot see in Wilder's drama. Ionesco caricatures the architect with such obvious satire that Bérenger's inability to see him as he is or to see through him makes Bérenger's almost willful blindness a key to his failure as a searcher.

As Bérenger expatiates about his need for a new setting and a new life, the architect continually responds in bureaucratic terms. He assures Bérenger that he has built the city under orders from the City Council—"I don't allow myself any personal initiative" (p. 11)—and proceeds to discourse on its technical perfections. Without rain, the flowers and grass, for example, are watered from below. Bérenger feels that he has arrived by a marvelous accident—he took the wrong tram—but the architect has expected him and has his correct age in a file; he even classifies Bérenger's enthusiasm.

BÉRENGER: I'm sorry, I get carried away.
ARCHITECT: That's characteristic of you. You're one of those poetic personalities. As they exist, I suppose they must be necessary.
(P. 19)

Bérenger's confessions of his past raptures and despairs and his new hopes are registered by the architect, who becomes involved with office work but assures him that he will listen to him with one ear and observe him with one eye. (Significantly, the killer, whom Bérenger confronts in the play's final moments, has only one eye.) The promise of the "radiant" district, Bérenger confesses, is like the moments in his life in which he has emerged from the damp grayness he usually inhabits to moments in which he feels so light that he can fly and so filled with rapture that he is sure of his immortality; although these moments take place in silence and isolation, he explains, he never feels empty or alone. But since the architect conducts his bureaucratic business in counterpoint to Bérenger's outpouring, his emotional flights are ironically grounded in the architect's cold indifference.

Although Bérenger refuses to be put off by the architect's bureaucratic responses, maintaining a Chaplinesque zeal and innocence in the face of the cool responses he receives, he cannot fail to respond to the stone that is thrown at him nor the architect's tale of the killer who is gratuitously destroying the district (the French title of the play is *Tueur Sans Gages,* "killer without pay"). At the same time that Bérenger recounts his fall from grace in the past, his descent from spring into winter that produced a "chaotic vacuum" or void inside him, overcoming him with a sense of "tragic" and "intolerable separation" (p. 24), he reenacts that loss with the architect. Shocked by the tale of the killer, he is made even more desolate by the news of the death of Dany, the architect's secretary, who ignores the architect's warning of danger, quits her job, and is promptly dispatched by the killer.

Bérenger's newly experienced sense of separation and tragic loss is clearly based on the loss of illusion. The city of his dreams, upon which he thinks he has stumbled, is absent from the stage. Its architect, who doubles as a police superintendent and physician, is the epitome of an unfeeling civil service that he both serves and embodies. Dany, who is the victim of the system she tries to leave as well as a victim of the killer, has not only ignored Bérenger's rhapsodic proposal of marriage, she has totally ignored Bérenger, so that when he bemoans the loss of city and fiancée, Bérenger bemoans that which was not his to lose.

One can only surmise, then, as Bérenger suffers his alleged losses, that he has never had anything but the illusion of radiance and fullness in his life. Like the old couple in Ionesco's *The Chairs,* the fullest moments of Bérenger's life have contained only an illusion of communion and community. He praises the architect who reduces him to a file card, even as the ancient couple praised the invisible emperor who refused to acknowledge their existence and the orator who was on stage but who could not, as a deaf mute, deliver the Old Man's message to an absent multitude.

No less than Vladimir and Estragon, Bérenger is faced with what Richard Coe calls "the void at the center of things."[4] Essentially acting on Beckett's empty stage, Pozzo's Board, he tries, with the touching innocence of Beckett's two tramps, to keep up his hopes. His admiration for his guide, by whose callousness he refuses to be put off, reminds one of Didi and Gogo's shaky but persistent faith in Godot, whom they imagine as a businessman who must consult his associates, bank account, and so on before making any decisions about coming to their aid. Bérenger shares with the tramps and Kafka's Joseph K. the need to place his trust in figures whom he hopes will save him from the void but who seem to be inextricably bound up with inhumane systems that foster that void.

Bérenger, however, unlike the indecisive *Godot* tramps, will wait no longer. By the end of act 1, he exits insisting, "It can't go on! We must do something! We must, we must, we must!" (p. 42). It is no more reasonable to him than to Ionesco himself that man, who is already tragically mortal, should permit unnecessary killing and should become almost a willing victim of the forces of evil in life. "It is already puzzling," Ionesco notes when speaking about why he writes, "to be squeezed between birth and death, but to be forced to kill and be killed is inadmissible."[5] Bérenger, who projects his creator's outrage, is baffled by the architect's cool acceptance of life's misery and of the killer who seems to epitomize the evil that causes that misery. He is equally baffled by the seeming willingness of the killer's victims to look at a picture that they know is a trap. The killer, then, comes to symbolize both death itself and that in the social fabric which contributes to what Ionesco sees as this "inadmissible" killing and being killed that hastens man's doom. The translator of *The Killer,* who uses City Council for Ionesco's *La Municipalité* (the group that ordered the architect to build the ideal city) and Civil Service for Ionesco's *Administration* does not quite capture the suggestiveness of the French words. Both *La Municipalité* and *Administration* are more encompassing in France as bodies that order and control one's life than their English or American counterparts. Given the time that Ionesco was writing and the fact that he was a Romanian in exile, one cannot help but speculate, too, on the degree to which he was thinking of the Stalinist tyranny. Bérenger's quest to bring the killer to justice has clearly both social and metaphysical dimensions, although he sets out as innocently as Oedipus "to find the killer."

The play does not lead as unfailingly as *Oedipus Rex* does to the location of the killer in the self, although Bérenger's final attitude before the killer contains some of that archetypal truth. The killer is rather everywhere and nowhere in this drama, a many-headed but invisible monster, whom Bérenger only recognizes at the end but whom the audience can detect every step of the way. Like Vladimir, Bérenger undergoes an initiation rite that is too overwhelming for him to assimilate or possess.

The architect/superintendent/physician's complicity with the killer lies partly in his indifference; he is the civil servant who will not act, and the lethal nature of his power is dramatized in Dany's death. Dany will only be safe, he assures her, if she stays in the Service. Hearing of her death, the architect solidifies his position. "She was in the Civil Service! He doesn't attack the Service! But no, she wanted her 'liberty'! That'll teach her. She's found it now, her liberty. I was expecting this . . ." (p. 41). The architect admits that she might have achieved safety in flight, but Dany, like Bérenger, apparently desired liberty without knowing how to pursue it.

To be safe from the killer, one must, it appears, be a slave to the government; one must inhabit the living death of a brave new world, be protected by *1984*'s Big Brother, or carry Lucky's bags of sand. Leonard Pronko notes that the city is deathlike in its closed, empty aspects, and life is "so mechanized that no spontaneity can remain . . . The happy city is in reality the terminus, the depot of the street car that is life, for all the lines lead here we are told. And, conveniently, right outside the walls of the city there is a cemetery."[6]

Ionesco connects the architect directly with the killer as he notes that the briefcase the architect carries in act 1 is *"rather thick and heavy, like the one Edouard has in Act II"* (p. 10). Edouard's briefcase contains all the killer's plans, pictures of the colonel, the spoils he has taken from the victims, and the killer's identity on his card. Then, too, the architect has constructed a city that is a "mirage," beautiful but uninhabitable. He, too, has lured his victims with a picture.

Bérenger, who fails to recognize the architect as the killer, also fails to recognize his adversary in Edouard. Waiting for Bérenger in the darkness of his friend's apartment as if for his next victim, Edouard is established as suspicious because he insists he got in with keys that Bérenger gave him, a gift Bérenger cannot recall. He zealously guards his briefcase, with all of the killer's paraphernalia, although he insists, when it falls open to reveal the incriminating contents, that he has no knowledge of them. "I'm not always looking inside my briefcase," he explains (p. 66). Bérenger's sickly friend, whose cough makes him partially the victim of the damp and dirty environment that Bérenger inhabits and to which he now returns, finally recalls that the killer once sent him all of these items before he put his fantasies into effect, and that the whole matter had slipped his mind.

Although the briefcase does contain the calling card and address of the killer, suggesting his separate identity, Edouard's guilty behavior, combined with his knowledge of and indifference to the killer's activities, suggest his complicity. Perplexed by the architect's indifference, Bérenger is horrified by that of his friend. "Your indifference makes me sick," he announces to Edouard, "and I don't mind saying it to your face"

(p. 64). In the surreal, nightmarish atmosphere of the play, Edouard's complicity, like that of the architect, is suggestive of the killer's presence in them. Since the architect and Edouard have identical briefcases, both apparently bulging with the same evidence of guilt, it is particularly ironical and horrifying that Edouard, who conveniently forgets the briefcase, and Bérenger rush off to tell the architect, in his function as superintendent of the police, of the killer's identity and plans.

This proliferation of killers, like the proliferation of chairs in *The Chairs,* continues throughout the play. In the former play, that proliferation suggests, as Ionesco himself has suggested,[7] the weight of nothingness. But as the couple are separated by a space filled with unoccupied furniture, they flee that nothingness through separate windows with their illusions intact; they do not recognize it as such. In *The Killer,* the proliferation of killers again suggests the threat of the void or nothingness; unlike *The Chairs,* however, the form of the killer changes continuously and Bérenger does confront him in one of his forms at the end.

If the architect is one form that the killer takes, holding out a false image of light that covers the void, and Edouard is another form the killer takes, sickly, one arm shriveled, seeking to hide in the gray, heavy, and damp world in which he seems to have taken root, the killer seems to reside, too, in the very texture of life, be it that of the empty radiant district or the full but equally empty district in which Bérenger lives. One gets a sense of the death-within-life nature of that district at the opening of act 2 before Bérenger returns to his home and encounters Edouard.

The Concierge, who dominates the scene and who will appear as Mother Peep in act 3, presides over this interlude with a senseless series of clichés. (The Concierge in France is an authority figure who controls who may be admitted to the apartments she oversees.) The song she sings about the "stinking weather" (the life of the city is heard mostly through voices and sound effects in this scene) confounds the hot and the cold: "When it's cold it's not hot,/When it's hot it's because it's cold," but concludes with the essential coldness that death insures; "cold as cold, and that's your lot!" (p. 44). The Concierge laments the "dog's life" that people lead, in which "we all end up in the same place, a hole in the ground" (p. 45), but she proceeds to beat her dog "Treasure" mercilessly throughout the scene. Richard Coe points out that Ionesco often uses a Concierge figure as a symbol of the decaying bourgeoisie,[8] and here, although she seems harmless enough at one level, she certainly is one of Ionesco's "inadmissible" types that helps deaden life before the onset of death.

The voices of two Old Men add to the amusing deadness as they note the passing away of "surprising people" (p. 49), and the general inhumanity of life is expressed in the absurd suggestion of a VOICE FROM THE STREET that the time wasted urinating by "our fifty-eight delivery boys" can be diminished by their taking turns; "They can make water in turn once a month for four and a half hours without interruption. That will save all the coming and going, which sends up our costs. After all, camels store up water" (p. 51).

When the killer emerges again as Mother Peep in act 3, she looks like the Concierge and no doubt in performance is often played by the same actress. Here the killer takes the form of an absurd political tyrant, keeper of the "public" geese. (The association with Hitler's goose step is clear, and one of the meanings of *piper* in French, from which the translator derives Mother Peep, is to trick, to deceive, to lure or dupe.) As Bérenger tries to drag Edouard along to report their findings, they come upon Mother Peep in action, and Bérenger notes the resemblance to his Concierge; Edouard denies it, although he seems to know all about her even as he knew about the killer. Bérenger is held back by the tired Edouard, and while they hunt for the briefcase he has left behind, we are inundated with Mother Peep's nonsense slogans in which she promises "to disalienate man" by alienating him (p. 77) and to change everything, which means "changing nothing" (p. 76). Here Ionesco vents the despair that emerges in his memoirs and interviews about the nature of politics and the changelessness of the most promising revolutionaries. "War shall change its name to peace and everything will be altered, thanks to me and my geese" (p. 77), Mother Peep promises. Ionesco interweaves the dreadful nonsense of her rally with Bérenger's increasingly desperate search for the briefacase with its evidence and Edouard's attraction to the rally; "Long live Mother Peep" (p. 78), he soon shouts with the others.

The ensuing comic routine with a series of briefcases that resemble Edouard's but fail to contain the lost evidence, contributes to the nightmarish atmosphere in which Bérenger's search appears increasingly fruitless. The Man who drunkenly denounces Mother Peep and calls for a hero who will stand up against his age has a briefcase of half-empty wine bottles. Bérenger and Edouard attack a little Old Man seeking the Danube in Paris, but his briefcase proves to be empty. When Mother Peep and her geese liquidate the drunken Man, *"Punch and Judy Style"* (p. 83), Mother Peep's briefcase, which also resembles Edouard's, opens and reveals the goose game. "We are all going to die. That's the only alienation that counts!" (p. 83), Edouard exclaims over the melee. Even more than the scene with the Concierge, this scene explores the various kinds of death that make up Bérenger's life, hamper his search, and are part of his initiation into the void.

What Bérenger witnesses but fails to grasp is his own tragicomic

In Search of Godot   103

demise as the Man who will not do the goose step or play the goose game. He misses, too, the irony of the Old Man's empty briefcase, which is no less and no more meaningful than the full one Edouard must now return to find in Bérenger's apartment, where, as the Old Man deduces, he has no doubt left it.

As Bérenger plunges further along into his nightmare, still not noticing that Man has been effectively canceled out and seeking to warn the Superintendent, he is hindered by a surreal traffic jam involving military trucks in which giant policemen impede rather than abet his progress toward the Prefecture. It is, of course, about as logical for him to find relief from the killer in his journey as it is for the Old Man to find the Danube in Paris, and he even notes, after checking his watch, that time has stopped. He thinks he recognizes the Superintendent's voice in one of the policemen but is uncertain; his perception of the pervasiveness of the killer is still something felt or intuited but is not fully conscious. The policeman/Superintendent/killer's directions are aimed at all present: "To the left! To the right! Straight on! Straight Back! Forward!" (p. 87). Hence, space as well as time is effectively canceled, and the *"scene of general chaos"* (p. 87) is an image of the void at the center.

Noticing that the police all seem to have the same voice, Bérenger is further dismayed when another image of Man, a soldier with a bunch of carnations, is manhandled by the police, his flowers tossed aside. As Bérenger tries to identify himself as a good citizen in search of justice, he is greeted by their seemingly senseless hostility; the Second Policeman disappears, proclaiming his hate; traffic and wall then also disappear, leaving Bérenger alone to face the killer in his final form—or formlessness.

Bérenger now inhabits the *Godot* twilight, moving in a *"limitless half-light"* (p. 94) and not making any progress. "It's as though I wasn't moving at all" (p. 95), he notes. Insisting that he's not afraid, he exposes the nature of his own alienation, the void within, as he says, "I've always been alone . . . and yet I love the human race, but at a distance" (p. 95). Bérenger seems to sense his own duplicity here—the inauthenticity of his action; "Fact is, I *am doing* something . . ." (p. 96), he affirms, and then gilds his motives with the sentimental attitude that he must avenge the death of his financée, with whom, of course, he has not had any relationship. "I must have revenge for Dany. I must stop the rot" (p. 96), he insists, tempted to flee but going forward in comic Hamlet fashion for his supposed revenge. Ironically, however, when Bérenger decides that one murder more or less won't matter and he will return the next day, the killer appears.

In his confrontation with the puny, one-eyed, bedraggled killer, who laughs derisively at all he says, or is possibly not even present—*"Bérenger could be talking to himself . . ."* (p. 98)—Bérenger must finally confront the force that has pervaded the play, stalked him at every turn, and is partially within. Aware that he could overcome the killer, Bérenger chooses instead to try to understand him. As in *Hamlet*, revenge is not his pervasive motive; his desire is to understand the mystery of life and death. On one level, Bérenger's defeat is related to that of all the characters in *The Rhinoceros* (1960) who succumb to rhinoceritis partly from a kind of tolerance of and fascination with the evil it represents. The Bérenger of that play maintains his humanity because he is a rather natural nonconformist, something of a drunk like the Man of *The Killer*, whereas the Bérenger of *The Killer* succumbs partly through his efforts to be a good citizen and because of his touching faith in reason. He insists that the killer tell him "why" he kills.

The silence of the killer, punctuated only by his chuckles, forces Bérenger to look into himself for the killer's motives. "I suppose you don't believe in happiness. You think happiness is impossible in this world?" (p. 99) Bérenger conjectures, voicing his own doubts about its possibility. He proceeds to surmise that the killer hates uniforms as symbols "of an abuse of power" (p. 101), women, all humanity, or that he wishes to save man from the fear of death. Béringer insists that he cannot hate the killer because if he does he hates himself, and no clichés about brotherhood can withhold the underlying truth that he does indeed hate himself. As the killer scorns religion, pity, love, money, and reason, all gives way in Bérenger as well to that hate which his platitudes mask. "You filthy dirty moronic imbecile" (p. 108), he shouts at him, threatening death but then giving in to a sense of futility. "Oh God! There's nothing we can do. What can we do. What can we do . . ." (p. 109), he stammers as he succumbs on bended knee to the victor.

Lest one miss the full significance of Bérenger's defeat, Ionesco explains it in the initial stage directions for the play.

> Bérenger's speech to the killer at the end of the play is one short act in itself. The text should be interpreted in such a way as to bring out the gradual breaking-down of Bérenger, his falling apart and the vacuity of his own rather commonplace morality, which collapses like a leaking balloon. In fact Bérenger finds within himself, in spite of himself and against his own will, arguments in favour of the killer.
>
> (P. 9)

Bérenger's search for a lost paradise is a search for a Godot that will deliver him from the misery of his life, even as Vladimir and Estragon hope Godot will deliver them from the misery of their lives. The sacred overtones of the search are clear in the play, as Bérenger identifies his search for a new life and setting with a search for a redeeming meaning. What he needs, he tells the architect, is "a background that would answer some profound need inside . . . the projection, the continuation of the universe inside you" (p. 19). Bérenger wants the inner light that he has experienced only a few times in his life to become an environment in which he can reside for more than a few redeeming moments.

Mircea Eliade points out the religious nature of the symbolism Ionesco uses as he discusses the efforts of the playwright to transcend time and place. For Ionesco, images of light and flight stand in opposition to those of grayness and weight and are associated with deliverance from gravity, a sense of immortality, and a feeling of oneness with the universe. Although Eliade is well aware that Ionesco's own search for light, which he projects in *The Killer,* is part of a search for his happy childhood in La Chapelle Anthenaise, which had seemed so filled with light, he points out that such nostalgia becomes more than a romantic return to a personal paradise, partaking of the mystic's search for the sacred.[10] "Whatever his previous ideological conditioning," Eliade notes about Ionesco and others who experience light as he does, "the light produces a break in the subject's existence, revealing to him—or making clearer than before—the world of spirit, of the sacred and of true freedom."[11]

Rosette C. Lamont remarks that Ionesco chooses Jung over Freud because of Jung's greater openness to religion,[12] and Alexandre Rainof points to Ionesco's use of Jung in understanding how his personal longings may be expressed in art as universal archetypes. "For him [Ionesco], visual metaphors become dream transpositions on stage, manifestations of given archetypes, profoundly personal and individual, *ergo* non-mechanical and at the same time universally graspable."[13]

> This belief in the presence of a collective unconscious means, in as far as Ionesco is concerned, that the path which he has chosen, away from a verbal language and logical exposition, is the right one, the most valid and the most universal from the standpoint of achieving a real communication. Mircea Eliade's influence, and the friendship Ionesco claims to have established with him, would be, of course, particularly relevant to this orientation of Ionesco's theater in terms of both "sacred time," "sacred space," and a Shamanic ritual with Edenic overtones.[14]

Ionesco does speak of his artistic aims in a way that fulfills to perfection Eliade's writings on man's essentially religious quest to return to his beginnings as the source of renewal.

> I am in fact seeking a world which has recovered its virginity; I would like to repossess the paradisiacal light of my childhood, the glory of the first day, an untarnished glory, and of an intact universe which would appear before me as though it were new born. It is as though I wanted to witness the event of creation before the Fall, looking for it within myself, as if attempting to sum up the stream of history, or

within my characters who are other incarnations of myself, or who are like those others who resemble me in their quest, conscious or not, of an absolute light.[15]

Indeed, the search for "a world which has recovered its virginity" dominates Ionesco's thinking so that the arrival of Godot is less important to him than the transformed world that will result with that arrival. Ionesco's identification with Israel and the Jewish people is partly based on his sympathy for their suffering and their yearning for the arrival of a messiah, but he sees that arrival in terms of the "ideal city" that will result.

> If it weren't for the Jews, people would not believe in, would not hope for the coming, the return of a Messiah who will bring salvation. We keep on hoping, knowing that the Messiah is behind the door; we hope that some day he will open it and that the world will know abundant joy. We all hope in the Ideal City, that is to say, we all hope the New Jerusalem will rise out of the desert wastelands and from out of death. We hope for the tranfiguration of the world, and we will have this hope as long as this myth that comes to us from the Jews endures.[16]

As Germain Brée perceives, "It is in spatial terms" that Ionesco "defines a range of emotions through which he responds to the world,"[17] a statement that illuminates the playwright's use of place rather than person as Godot in *The Killer*.

Ionesco's world in *The Killer*, however, may be even more Freudian than Jungian, in that the search for Godot as "ideal city" appears, at least on an unconscious level, to be a kind of search for death. One witnesses the almost suicidal movement in this play that Thomas R. Whitaker posits for several of Ibsen's dramas, an unconscious "quest for absence."[18] As Bérenger moves through the labyrinth of his life, it is death that he confronts at every trun, death that he finds at the center, and death before which he bows at the end. Like his creator's, his desire for a paradise that embodies the perfection of life before the fall would seem to be a desire for the womb; in Freudian terms it is a desire for that final stasis which lies beyond the pleasure principle, the death that precedes even what life there is in the womb.

In O'Neill's *The Iceman Cometh* and in Beckett's *Waiting for Godot* we have seen the yearning for salvation shading into a yearning for death—"Would that Hickey or Death would come"—"We are waiting for Godot to come—or for night to fall." The ambivalence of the characters in each play toward the savior figure, whether he be Hickey as false messiah or Godot as absent messiah, relates to a profound ambivalence about life itself. In his discussion of postmodern literature, Ahab Hassan has remarked on the closeness of parody and nihilism to a yearning for transcendence; he points out that when writers such as West, Burroughs, and Barth are being most negative, "they almost declare themselves, thereby, waiters upon transcendence."[19] Such literature, Hassan declares, "moves in nihilist play or mystic transcendence toward the vanishing point."[20] In *The Killer* this almost unconscious movement of Bérenger toward death at the same time that he consciously pursues salvation is a reversal of the nihilist writers who consciously would seem to pursue oblivion but unconsciously are seeking Godot.

Self-conscious artist that he is, Ionesco recognizes this connection of the death instinct with a yearning for the transcendent and has suggested that Freud's discovery late in his life of a death instinct relates to the "'Nirvana instinct.'"[21] The killer, however, before whom Bérenger bows at the end of *The Killer,* is far from a figure of peace. He is vacuous, ugly, absurd, and possibly even not there. He is what lies at the core of the Civil Service in the guise of the architect/policeman, he is at the core of Bérenger's friendship with Edouard, and he is at the core of Mother Peep's politics; and if he is not there, he is also at the core of Bérenger himself. The structure of Ionesco's play is very much like that of Strindberg's *The Ghost Sonata,* in which a character as naive and foolishly heroic as Bérenger, though younger, seeks to possess happiness in a house that he learns is filled with falseness and death. But unlike Arkenholtz's initiation, which ends with a vision of a transcendent peace beyond, Bérenger suffers a defeat with no such vision. And even though time and space lose their secular qualities as he approaches the killer, the void that is so suggested does not have that quality of sacredness which Pozzo's void assumes with its denial of secular time and space. Bérenger is not initiated into a sacred void; he does not wear one of the thousand faces of Joseph Campbell's archetypal heroes who must return from the initiation experience with new knowledge. Bérenger is initiated, but he is defeated by the rite, swallowed up by the void.

Beneath the complexity of Bérenger's peregrinations in *The Killer,* the death instinct may dominate; death rather than Godot may be life's paramount force, the killer being but an image of the absurdity at the heart of that void which is life. Ionesco's characters, who seem so actively to pursue Godot, may in reality be essentially passive, drawn unconsciously to that final meeting with death which they so fear but secretly seek. "The organism must live in order to die in the proper manner, to die the right death. We must have the arabesque of plot in order to reach the end. We must have metonymy in order to reach metaphor,"[22] Peter Brook asserts, using Freud's theories on the death instinct to account for the movement of plot in literature.

The desire to end, however, is, as Brook suggests, a way of seeking meaning in which the beginning follows the end;[23] in some way, then, the desire for the end is a desire for one's origins, for a homecoming. When Bérenger confronts his own shallowness and emptyness in *The Killer*, the metaphor is not complete, for this is not the homecoming of which he has dreamed. The wholeness for which Bérenger has longed is not achieved, a wholeness that relates more to Freud's Eros searching, like Plato's Androgyne, for "a lost primal unity which was split asunder,"[24] than to the seeking of death as emptyness. Bérenger remains a passive victim as he meets death, not a hero who masters it. He is vanquished by an end that does not allow him his beginning.

Although Ionesco has lent Bérenger his own craving for the sacred, he has shown him to be too blind and superficial to find it. "It is because they have not mapped out a road to follow," Ionesco writes, "that my characters wander in the dark, the absurd, in incomprehension and anguish."[25] Mistaking a dead district for paradise at the outset, Bérenger is hardly able to map out a road to follow. "Totalitarianism is not only hell, but also the dream of paradise . . . ,"[26] says the Czech expatriate, Milan Kundera in an interview with Philip Roth about his novel *The Book of Laughter and Forgetting*. Kundera, who like Ionesco is in exile from the political tyranny of his country, not only refers to Ionesco in his novel but also Illuminates Ionesco's writing in it. ". . . Hell is already contained in the dream of paradise and if we wish to understand the essence of hell we must examine the essence of the paradise from which it originated."[27] As already seen, the "radiant city" is just such a paradise, and Bérenger has been taken in by it.

Because Bérenger wants so much to believe that this paradise is the embodiment of the one he has dreamed he might inhabit, he has failed to see its dangers. He is like the Bérenger of Ionesco's later play *The Stroll in The Air* (1963); when he finds he can fly, this latter Bérenger looks down upon the earth from a new perspective only to discover a terrible hellish void, not the paradise of which he has dreamed. In Kundera's novel two young American students reporting in class on Ionesco's play *The Rhinoceros* rise through the ceiling with their teacher as Rhinoceros-angels, an image that suggests the dehumanization that may result from fanatic flights as well as from animal descents. For Kundera, the enthusiasm of fanatics "ready to hang anyone not sharing their joy" is no less pernicious than the "absolute skepticism" of their more obviously devilish counterparts.[28]

The key to Bérenger's failure to find Godot may well lie in his inability to love people except at a distance. The dehumanization that is so rampant in Ionesco's dramas, in which characters are interchangeable *(The Bald Soprano)*, in which they turn into animals *(The Rhinoceros)*, or in which language becomes menacingly meaningless *(The Lesson)*, is overcome only in his *Story Number 1* and *Story Number 2 for children under three years of age*. Here a loving father teaches his daughter Josette how to use language nonsensically and creatively so that together they break through or open the walls that so isolate Bérenger in *The Killer*.[29]

Godot, then, as "ideal city" remains absent in *The Killer*, much as he is absent in *Waiting for Godot*, and Bérenger's search has brought him face to face with a more terrifying void than the one Pozzo is able to navigate. Yet Bérenger's search has affirmed values greater than the ones he so shallowly proclaims before the killer, a kind of courage and idealism with which he stands up as best he can to the negative forces within and without. Like Vladimir, who insists at the end of *Waiting for Godot* that the messenger boy tell Godot he saw him, that he exists, Ionesco, through his Bérenger, accomplishes the main goal of his writing. Ionesco writes, he says, "to allow others to share in the astonishment, the dazzlement of existing, in the miracle of this world of ours, and to shout to God and to other men our anguish, letting it be known that we existed. All the rest is secondary."[30]

In Günter Grass's *The Wicked Cooks* (1957), the search for Godot is somewhat more fruitful. In this play, which Martin Esslin describes as "an ambitious attempt to transmute a religious subject into poetic tragicomedy,"[31] one character, the Count, has the recipe for the Godot soup the other cooks seek; and by the end of the play another character, Vasco, attains it.

Despite the greater access to Godot in the world that Grass creates in this drama, however, it is a world no less absurd than those created by Ionesco or Beckett in their plays. As in Ionesco's world, objects seem to have a life of their own, so that the distinction between the human and the inhuman is blurred. Rather than the proliferation of chairs or briefcases that Ionesco uses to produce the weight of that nothingness which Beckett achieves through the increasing reduction of properties, Grass creates a world in which objects and people merge in fantastic and sometimes frightening ways. In Grass's play, cooks emerge, for example, from such objects as an egg, a salt cone, or snowflakes, while the coveted soup recipe is intangible and attained only through mysterious means. "In *The Wicked Cooks*, the sequence—from the readily visualized to the shapeless—reaches a height where the object itself, the soup recipe, disappears as the vehicle of resistance, dissolves into the abstract and the secret, and therefore can find answer and resistance only in a greater secret, the mystery of death."[32]

Once again, Godot/God and death are mingled as they have been in so many of the plays so far considered. The soup itself is called the "gray soup" by the customers. Denying at first that the soup has a name, the Count, who is actually a commoner named Herbert Schymanski, proceeds to give it several; "November soup, Phoenix Soup," and "Gray Eminence" (p. 202) are the names he throws out. These names suggest winter, the death and rebirth associated with the Phoenix bird, who, consumed periodically by fire, rises from its own ashes, and the "very special ashes" (p. 206) that the Count tells Vasco this cabbage soup contains.

The Count, who senses terrible danger in the possession of the coveted recipe, must finally pay for it with his life. Although Petri, the chief of one faction of cooks who is trying to procure the recipe, claims the role of victim for the cooks, since without the recipe they are losing their reputation, the Count confesses in a letter to an absent friend his own sense of victimhood. "How wild they are" (p. 197), he says in his letter, regretting that he ever ventured from the role of customer to that of cook. Tempted to give the cooks the recipe, he refuses, he says, out of fear. "The way they appear takes my breath away, and it costs me an effort to remain calm" (p. 198). The Count fears that they will dehumanize him—"First they've taken away the glasses from the nearsighted, next they'll expropriate the possessive pronouns. They'll force me to wear a glass tie so they can look into my heart, so they can read what's there—for I will not speak!" (p. 198).

As Ionesco's play, *The Wicked Cooks* bristles with political overtones. One senses the Count's fear as the fear of tyranny, whether it be the fascist tyranny of Grass's youth, the Communist tyranny of East Germany, or the capitalist tyranny with which the Count would seem to contend.

The power-hungry cooks are apparently unworthy of the recipe, and indeed, when the Count reneges on a bargain to give it to them in return for Vasco's girlfriend Martha, his fear of them is confirmed. The Count and Martha are pushed to the wall, the cooks threatening them from an actual wall that surrounds the Count's house, and the couple commit suicide. Having lived for a time with Martha in happiness, the Count claims that he can no longer remember the recipe. "I've told all of you often enough," he claims, "it is not a recipe, it's an experience, a living knowledge, continuous change—you ought to be aware that no cook has ever succeeded in cooking the same soup twice" (p. 281). The few months with Martha, he explains, have made "this experience superfluous," and he has forgotten it.

The grace that accompanies the recipe is not something that can be taken or even given but must in some mysterious way be achieved. And the possession of the recipe is no protection as the Count and Martha's suicide takes on the aspect of a Christ-like sacrifice. The couple cannot operate in the cooks' terms, and the cost is their lives.

But the Count and Martha do not die in vain. Although their double suicide is somewhat reminiscent of the ancient couple's suicide in *The Chairs*, since both couples embrace their deaths calmly and willingly, there are significant differences. Ionesco's couple die under the illusion that their lives have been meaningful and that this meaning will be passed on as a message by the orator they have hired for the purpose. Separated from each other by the absent crowd and the chairs, the couple fail to unite in death; and rather than receiving a message of meaning, the audience gets a message of meaninglessness from the mute orator. The Count and Martha, on the other hand, have developed a loving relationship that does bring them together, both in life and death, so that the forgetting of the recipe, life's meaning, is like the giving up of the elderly couple's illusion that life's meaning can be passed on in any formulaic way.

As the cooks peer over the wall that encloses the Count's house and garden, they see a loving couple washing each other's feet and the cook Stach remarks, "I call that love!" (p. 275). The couple enjoy an Eden-esque paradise in which soup is now made of flowers.

> KLETTERER: But the garden does look nice. A bit too many flowers, no vegetables.
> BENNY: You don't understand that. They live on roses.
> STACH: Their menu is something like this: *(He sits down on the wall)* First, pansy soup with primrose on the side.
>
> (P. 176)

The cooks make fun of the couple, but Vasco, the antihero descendant of the explorer, regards them wistfully and begins to penetrate the nature of their relationship. In his own search for grace, he has ignored, mistreated, and given up Martha, but he now sees her in a new light. Noticing her hair, her neck, and then her hands and fingers, he imagines their special touch. Detecting Vasco's growing insight, the Count bequeaths the task of finishing the painting of his wall to him. Vasco now understands that there is no recipe to be had from the Count, and fondling one of Martha's big shoes, he contemplates her Ruth-like role as the faithful bringer of new life. (*Schuster* means "shoemaker"; as the owner of the restaurant and the power that demands the recipe for the soup, he is denied by the barefoot Count and Martha.) After the shots ring out signifying the couple's death, an enlightened Vasco runs off, and though they are aware that the recipe is not something they can take from him, the others nevertheless follow in hot pursuit. The recipe, Grün says, is "an excuse for running. Nobody wants it any more. It's not a matter of the Soup, of course" (p. 288). Contemplating a dead goldfish, they reason that no cook can bring it back to life, that death cannot be overcome, and then, despite that wisdom, they exit, running. "There he goes," Petri says of Grün. "But in my legs, too, something is getting ready to strike out for a hypothetical goal!" (p. 289).

The Count has recognized Vasco as his possible successor or disciple early in the play. Insisting that he is no Count, but a mere commoner, he encourages Vasco to think about his name. "That's who you are. The great explorer, the man who refuses to believe that the continents are numbered and the seas have been named" (p. 199). (The English translation has Vasco using poor grammer and slang, neither of which he employs in the original. Like the Count, Vasco is a commoner but also a thinker.)

Although Vasco is a cook, he operates alone, eschewing the "organization men" in their collective struggles for the recipe. Afraid to operate outside of the system, he is terrified when he loses his cook's hat while confronting the Count on a bridge, and he is similarly afraid to go to his aunt's deathbed lest he have to remove his hat again "and not be a cook for five minutes" (p. 209).

Being a cook is an ambivalent business at best. Grün, one of Petri's crew of cooks, sings at the outset of the drama of the cooks as "a wicked white bouquet / blooming in the dark of night," and Stach, another of the cooks, joins in singing of how they stir the night "as though the night were soup" (p. 196). The five singing cooks then transmute the simile into a metaphor. "The night, it is the soup! / The night, it is the soup!" (p. 197), they sing as they exit.

Grass portrays the cooks as self-consciously wicked in their whiteness. Vasco's panic when he loses a part of his uniform—his hat—has to do with the tyranny of his profession, which insists on conformity. The cooks do not possess the recipe for the Gray Soup of Grace; the night is their soup, the darkness, which they stir up and in which they move and bloom. When Vasco says he fears to see his aunt die, lest he have to remove his hat, he is suggesting that there is the danger of death for himself in nonconformity. Like Dany in *The Killer*, who meets her death when she leaves the Civil Service, Vasco, the explorer, faces terrible danger as he continues to operate outside of the system.

But when Vasco does go to his dying aunt, confronting time in her confused cuckoo clock and her impending death, his search for Godot is not satisfied. His aunt offers a conventional Christian solution, chiding him for going to St. Anthony to pray for something he has lost (his hat) rather than relating to the Virgin Mary. She insists that he remove his hat—"and I always thought, when a cook takes his hat off, he's a Christian" (p. 214) she remarks—but she finds that he looks as wicked with it off as with it on. Despite her conventional religious stance, the aunt wonders about Stephan, his wickedness, his questions, his habit of biting his fingernails.

Leaving his hat in his aunt's room, Vasco flees to another in which he contemplates his identity; his real name is Stephan—it is the Count who has recognized him as the explorer, Vasco. Remembering bitterly how his father, who was a cook, had apprenticed him to Petri, he fears Petri's discovery of his lost hat, a fear that conjures his chief and the other cooks up from the various objects in the room. Taunting him about his lost hat and threatening him with a spoonful of a terrible brew they concoct, the cooks are reminiscent of Goldberg and McCann taunting Stanley in Pinter's *The Birthday Party*. They seem to know what he has done and what he thinks. One cook, Petri assures Vasco, cannot make soup "out of the cloudy night" (p. 219), though five might be able to do so. "Never ever alone at night," Vasco recalls is Petri's teaching. When Martha disperses the cooks, whose presence now seems to have been a mere nightmare, Vasco remarks again on the cuckoo clock's long calls. "It's so hard not to count along and simply to believe how late it is" (p. 226), Vasco laments. His initiation well underway, Vasco feels his movement toward death, not realizing yet that he will find no transcendence without it.

Several of the rituals that structure the plays explored appear in this one. Although Vasco's quest-initiation is central, sacrificial rites abound. In act 4, for example, there is the fall of Petri and the rise of Kletterer (*Kletterer* means "climber" in German), chief of a rival group of cooks who apparently lack what little restraint Petri and his group have used in their mad pursuit of the recipe. As with Frazer's dying gods, impotence is a sure sign of decline, and Petri's decline is humorously illustrated when he discovers that his trumpet, with which he rules and conjures up the cooks, is bent out of shape. Although it is soon fixed, Kletterer appears and takes it away, bringing it later to the cooks' gathering as a sure sign of his new power. The new king/god is in control.

Actually, however, neither king/god is in control. The power struggle, as well as the ritual renewal, is parodied, much as it is in Albee's *The American Dream*, in which the new god, the American Dream, is revealed as hollow and impotent. Whether Grass is satirizing capitalism, communism, or fascism in his portrayal of rivalry among the cooks,[33] he is certainly portraying the absurdity of the antics of any power-hungry, tyrannical group and of all people as they move in such groups.

Going beyond satire, however, Grass continues Vasco's initiation in act 4 as the antihero witnesses the Count's predicament. Once again, there is a birthday party. The cooks tell the laundress, Mrs. Kuhlwasser, that they need her drying room for the celebration. The goal of the party is, of course, to procure the recipe from the Count, and the shift in power from Petri to Kletterer is but one aspect of the events at it. In the background is the absent Schuster, owner of the restaurant where Petri's cooks work, whose demands for food and for the sacred recipe are much like the impossible and absurd demands of the Dumb Waiter in Pinter's *The Dumb Waiter*. In the foreground is the alleged birthday party, which, like Pinter's in his *The Birthday Party*, becomes a sacrificial rite. While the Count is harassed and threatened, his collection of recipes torn open and rent as if such a sparagmos might reveal the secret at the center, it is Vasco who has discovered his secret, his love for Martha and Martha's love for him. Referring to rumors of the Count's impotence and homosexuality, Vasco has detected the Count's vulnerability, his desire for Martha. The Count rather than Petri is the true old god/king of the drama, Vasco the new one.

> VASCO: All Right, right away. —you're not silent 'cause it ain't true, but cause it *is* true, and 'cause I hit where it hurts. Well, let people talk, I thought to myself. Let 'em say the Count hasn't got a heart. I knew that he has, and that I hit it. Did I, tell me now, did I?
> THE COUNT: Yes Vasco, you did. You're an explorer after all.
>
> (P. 267)

The Count's sacrifice is delayed as Vasco turns Martha over to him, sacrificing his own love in the process.

> STACH: But you're looking after them as though they were abandoning you. Why?
> VASCO: So they'll think of me. So I'll be like beef stuck in their teeth.
>
> (P. 270)

The real sacrificial victim of the birthday party is Vasco. His aunt's death suggests the death of his ties to traditional religion. Now giving up Martha to the love he recognizes she and the Count share allows him to realize the value of what he is giving up. While Stanley is destroyed by the initiation in Pinter's *The Birthday Party*, his women taken from him, Vasco willingly takes on the role of sacrificial victim and helps along the concluding stages of his own initiation and renewal. At the end of the play, when he watches the Count and Martha together, his realization of their love and their sacrifice of themselves in a world that values power over love is what completes his initiation and what makes the recipe his.

In *The Wicked Cooks*, however, the successful end of the search, the finding of Godot, does not lead to any state of transcendental peace. The Count and Martha's paradise is short-lived, and Vasco, hugging his secret to him, exits running. The new god/king, like the old, and like the actors in the ritual that Frazer describes so dramatically in *The Golden Bough*, are forever vulnerable, forever restless, and never free.

None of which is cause for despair in Grass's play. As Norris W. Yates notes in his study of Grass, man is primarily a seeker, and the quest is an archetypal theme in his work. "Man is a pilgrim neither entirely secular nor wholly religious, disordered within by the tensions between belief and unbelief, but seldom giving way to despair.... The country of Grass may be disordered, grotesque, and full of obscenity, blasphemy, pathos, and terror, but it is too exciting a world in which to despair."[34]

Although Günter Grass is less well known and appreciated for his drama than for his novels, *The Wicked Cooks* is not only his most interesting[35] or most significant play.[36] I believe it is also a play that may take its place with those of Beckett, Pinter, Ionesco, and Genet as it explores modern dilemmas. No less than *The Tin Drum*'s Oscar, questing with his drum and willing to grow only on his own terms,[37] Vasco, as a fingerbiting antihero, determined to explore the frightening world he inhabits, is busily mapping out a path through the labyrinth of the absurd; and like Vladimir and Estragon, who serve as they stand and wait, Vasco surely also serves as he runs. "Like his poems," writes Keith Miles of Grass, "his plays provide no categorical answers, no neat solutions. They glorify uncertainties, anxieties, unpalatable truths. They institute a search."[38] Godot may be an illusion, but if he is part of what the Count calls "an experience," that experience resides, in some measure, in the search itself.

NOTES

1. Martin Esslin in *The Theatre of the Absurd* refers to it as "probably his finest play" (p. 174).
2. Eugène Ionesco, *The Killer* in *The Killer and Other Plays by Eugène Ionesco*, trans. Donald Watson (New York: Grove Press, 1960), p. 11. All subsequent references to *The Killer* are from this edition.
3. Günter Grass, *The Wicked Cooks*, trans. Leslie Willson in *Four Plays* (New York: Harcourt, Brace and World, 1967), p. 201. All subsequent references to *The Wicker Cooks* are from this edition.
4. Richard N. Coe, *Eugène Ionesco*, p. 73.
5. Eugène Ionesco, "Why Do I Write? A Summing Up," in *The Two Faces of Ionesco*, ed. Rosette C. Lamont and Melvin J. Friedman, p. 9.
6. Leonard Pronko, *Eugène Ionesco*, p. 26.
7. See Esslin, *Theatre of the Absurd*, p. 152.
8. Coe, *Eugène Ionesco*, p. 14.
9. In Harold Pinter's *A Slight Ache*, Edward is similarly forced to look within himself as he confronts the silent matchseller.
10. Mircea Eliade, "Eugène Ionesco and 'La Nostalgie Du Paradise,'" in *The Two Faces of Ionesco*, ed. Rosette C. Lamont and Melvin J. Friedman, pp. 23–26.
11. Ibid., p. 26.
12. Rosette C. Lamont, "*L'Homme Aux Valises:* Ionesco's Absolute Stranger," in *The Two Faces of Ionesco*, ed. Rosette C. Lamont and Melvin J. Friedman, p. 252.
13. Alexandre Rainof, "Ionesco and the Film of the Twenties and Thirties: From Groucho to Harpo," in *The Two Faces of Ionesco*, ed. Rosette C. Lamont and Melvin J. Friedman, pp. 71–72.

14. Ibid., p. 72.
15. Ionesco, "Why Do I Write?" p. 7.
16. Eugène Ionesco, *Present Past Past Present: A Personal Memoir*, p. 39.
17. Germain Brée, "Ionesco's Later Plays: Experiments in Dramatic Form," in *The Two Faces of Ionesco*, ed. Rosette C. Lamont and Melvin J. Friedman, p. 102.
18. Thomas R. Whitaker, *Fields of Play in Modern Drama*, p. 37. Whitaker, for example, says of Hedda Gabler, "But it's clear that she tries to become both playwright and audience as she maneuvers others towards a 'beauty' that embodies her secret desire for death" (pp. 53–54).
19. Ahab Hassan, *The Dismemberment of Orpheus: Toward a Postmodern Literature*, p. 251.
20. Ibid., p. 23.
21. Eugène Ionesco, quoted by Rosette Lamont, "*L'Homme Aux Valises,*" p. 253.
22. Peter Brook, "Freud's Masterplot," *Yale French Studies* 55/56 (1977): 295.
23. Ibid., p. 297.
24. Ibid., p. 294.
25. Ionesco, "Why Do I Write?", p. 7.
26. Milan Kundera, Interview in *The Book of Laughter and Forgetting*, p. 233.
27. Ibid., p. 234.
28. Ibid., p. 233.
29. See Rosette C. Lamont, "Father of the Man," in *The Two Faces of Eugène Ionesco*, ed. Rosette C. Lamont and Melvin J. Friedman, pp. 31–52, and Katherine H. Burkman, "Opening Walls: Two Stories by Eugène Ionesco," *The Midwest Quarterly* 21, no. 4 (Summer 1980).
30. Ionesco, "Why Do I Write?" p. 19.
31. Esslin, *Theatre of the Absurd*, p. 298.
32. Kurt Lothas Tank, *Günter Grass*, p. 65.
33. Keith Miles suggests in his book *Günter Grass* that one reading of the play, which he rightly sees moving on a number of levels, may have to do with the "dilemma of the artist. The Count desperately tries to preserve his artistic integrity and his individuality in the face of a menacing conformism" (p. 45). In the Berlin premiere of the play (1962), the Count apparently wore a mask that made him look like Grass himself (p. 46). While Miles goes on to point out political and commercial parallels with cooks as political tyrants or business tycoons, he concludes, "Grass's effervescent fantasy finds in the clownish villainy of its cooks, a perturbing microcosm of Germany" (p. 46).
34. Norris W. Yates, *Günter Grass: A Critical Essay*, p. 5.
35. Esslin, *Theatre of the Absurd*, p. 298.
36. Yates, *Günter Grass*, p. 16.
37. Irene Leonard in her book *Günter Grass* says of Oscar that his drumming "however moral in its intention is merely a signpost to morality, not morality itself; it remains a quest" (p. 83).
38. Miles, *Günter Grass*, p. 47.

7

And Who's Godot When He's at Home?

The quest for Godot, which takes an active form in *The Killer* and *The Wicked Cooks,* is the dominant theme if not the dramatic shape of all the plays so far explored. Whether the characters wait for Godot, accept or reject him as a false messiah, exorcise him as an evil force, or go out looking for him, the desire for his presence, even though sometimes ambivalent, is the driving force of the plays.

But what of Godot himself? Or herself? Godot is not always an absent force. We have seen him ineffectually present as the mute orator of *The Chairs,* and as the hollow shell of the Young Man in *The American Dream;* and we have seen him, too, in Ibsen's Gregers Werle and O'Neill's Hickey playing the role of false messiah. Godot has appeared as well as an evil presence to be exorcised as Madame in *The Maids* and as Anna in *Old Times.*

In none of these plays, however, is Godot the protagonist. In each case he or she remains an intruding figure with whom the protagonist must deal. Only Beckett, who tends to keep Godot in the wings in most of his plays, allows a few of his protagonists to assume the savior role themselves. Mr. Rooney in *All That Fall,* Hamm in *Endgame,* and Krapp in *Krapp's Last Tape,* all would-be artists, have taken on something of the Godot role themselves (see chapter 3). But as the role of Godot shifts in these plays from an absent force to the protagonists themselves, they have evinced an inability to carry through on their creativity—to arrive. Struggling with the cycle of birth, death, and rebirth, only Hamm, to some degree, is able to accept a death that offers some promise of new life.

Godot, who fails to arrive in several of Beckett's plays, always puts in an appearance or takes indirect, decisive action in the plays of Harold Pinter. While Godot hovers in the wings in *Waiting for Godot,* teasing Estragon and Vladimir, through a frightened messenger boy, with the promise of salvation or the threat of damnation, Pinter's Monty/Godot acts decisively if maliciously in *The Birthday Party,* sending his messengers in for the kill. And while Godot continues to hover in the wings in such Beckett plays as *Act Without Words I*, *Act Without Words II*, and *Happy Days*, operating indirectly from backstage through a control of properties, Pinter sends his reluctant Godot on stage in *A Slight Ache* as an intruding Matchseller who brings renewal to Flora, death to her philosopher husband. Because Pinter's characters increasingly lack their Beckett counterparts' relationship to an exterior force or god, they have tended more and more to assume the role of Godot themselves, fighting out the battles of existence to decisive ends.

There is no arrival of Godot, however, in Pinter's *No Man's Land* (1975). Here, the playwright leaves his own territory with its numerous tragicomic renewals and its cyclical rhythms to enter Beckett's purgatorial arena in which, to borrow and elaborate on a notion of Estragon's, crucifixion is so slow that renewal is out of the question, or at best remains a question. Here the younger playwright moves from his own confessed interest in exploring people "at the extreme edge of their living where they are living pretty much alone"[1] to Beckett's interest in exploring people at the extreme edge of the void.

If, however, Godot fails to arrive in *No Man's Land,* Pinter does not banish him to Beckett's wings. He chooses, rather, to follow his mentor's example in *All That Fall, Endgame,* and *Krapp's Last Tape* by exploring Godot as protagonist. Godot does not arrive in *No Man's Land* because he is already there. Hirst is Godot, the god of his own world, and what he confronts in the intruding Spooner is his double, a mirror image of some of his own possibilities.

The self-awareness that Spooner brings about in Hirst, who has brought him home after a chance meeting in a public house, comes about as Spooner defines himself. On the realistic level of the play's action, Spooner engages in such self-definition in his effort to make Hirst's home a haven for his own old age. He would usurp the parasitic positions of Foster and Briggs, Hirst's other doubles, to become the old man's general servant or housekeeper. On a deeper level of the play's action, however, Spooner confronts himself in Hirst, even as Hirst confronts himself in Spooner, and it is that mutual confrontation that reveals the dynamics of Hirst/Godot's inaction.

Spooner presents himself to his host as a free man, whose freedom derives from the indifference of others to him, though he also gains his strength from being unloved, particularly by his mother. His freedom derives as well, he says, from his ability to distance himself from life's experience. He is, he notes, a voyeur, a "betwixt twig peeper"[2] who spies on others, always keeping his distance. ". . . And when you can no longer maintain an objective relation to matter, the game's not worth the candle," he assures Hirst, "so forget it and remember that what is obligatory to keep in your vision is a space, space in moonlight particularly, and lots of it" (p. 19). Such a stance apparently gives him the poet's unscrupulous freedom to "do any graph of experience you wish, to suit your taste or mine" (p. 20).

"It's a long time since we had a free man in the house" (p. 21), is Hirst's response to Spooner's indirect offer of freedom. Hirst himself is clearly not free. Much like Godot, who Vladimir and Estragon speculate cannot answer their vague supplications without consulting his friends, agents, correspondents, books, and bank account, Hirst is unable to make decisions without consulting his servants, Foster and Briggs. They plan his day, lock in his guest for the night, and help Hirst to change the subject to winter at the play's end, burying him forever in the no-man's-land they share with him, and from which Spooner offers to save him.

Spooner notices the "we" in Hirst's "It's a long time since we had a free man in the house," but it is not until later that a sense of the imprisonment of Hirst's prison guards emerges. Foster and Briggs are a retired Pozzo and Lucky, whose peregrinations have clearly led them nowhere. They have met, Briggs tells Spooner, on a street corner (the *Godot* road?) at which Foster asked Briggs for directions to Bolsiver street. The particular vision of the void that Briggs then describes with hilarious detail as a street "in the middle of an intricate one-way system" has apparently led the two younger men, as the system does, to "life At A Dead End" (p. 62). Unlike Pozzo and Lucky, however, who go "on" in the face of the boundaryless void that Pozzo has discovered life to be, Foster and Briggs have elected to give up the stasis of wandering in an exitless labyrinth for the stasis of living with and off of Hirst. Toward the play's end, when Spooner offers to relieve Foster of his secretarial duties, thus allowing the young poet to travel, join the navy, and explore life, Foster responds, "I've sailored. I've been there and back. I'm here where I'm needed" (p. 83).

Aware of his guards' lack of freedom as well as his own, Hirst also has reason to doubt Spooner's definition of himself as a free poet; hence he doubts his own potential for freedom. Spooner's definition of himself as a free poet by way of observation rather than participation in life is as spurious as is Teddy's position as a detached philosopher in *The Homecoming*, a position of impotence that lands Teddy out on the street. And how different can Spooner be from the self-seeking Foster and Briggs if he is willing to "graph experience" in any way Hirst wishes, either helping him to a final retreat from life or to a joyous embrace of it.

> I could advance, reserve my defenses, throw on a substitute, call up the cavalry, embody in essence Von Kleist's retreat from the Caucasus (the wittiest and most subtle systematic withdrawal known to man) or

throw everything forward out of the knowledge that when joy overfloweth there can be no holding of joy. The point I'm trying to make, in case you've missed it, is that I am a free man.

(P. 21)

Spooner may not be as free as he thinks he is, but he does offer Hirst a kind of choice here between retreating to death and throwing everything forward as he advances toward it. His credentials for offering the possibility of renewal include the vision he has had of a scene he encountered on a beautiful day when he sat by a canal in an Amsterdam café. Spooner shares this vision of potency with Foster and Briggs.

At another table, in shadow, was a man whistling under his breath, sitting very still, almost rigid. At the side of the canal was a fisherman. He caught a fish. He lifted it high. The waiter cheered and applauded, the two men, the waiter and the fisherman, laughed. A little girl, passing, laughed. Two lovers, passing, kissed. The fish was lofted, on the rod. The fish and the rod glinted in the sun, as they swayed. The fisherman's cheeks were flushed, with pleasure.

(P. 39)

Spooner admits that he has never painted the picture of the scene that he had planned to create, and the authenticity of his artist's credentials are questioned further by Foster, who manages to get Spooner to confess, indirectly, that he may not be an artist at all. Foster asks Spooner what he thinks of an incident he experienced in the East when "a kind of old stinking tramp" (much, one would gather, like Spooner) and his dog, who seem to have "about one eye" between them (p. 42), begged a coin from Foster, threw it back, and made it disappear before Foster could put his hands on it. Spooner labels the beggar, and by implication himself, as a con artist. Whether Spooner is operating now as artist or con artist becomes the question.

The subtextual battle between Spooner and Hirst that ensues and structures the play has to do with the potency of the fisher-king. T. S. Eliot's *Waste Land* imagery, with its dependence on Jessie Weston's treatment of the fisher-king in her *From Ritual To Romance* has already been evident in Spooner's vision of a potent fisher-king he wishes to paint and in Foster's one-eyed beggar (Eliot's one-eyed merchant). Now Spooner explains that Hirst suffers from the "great malt which wounds" (p. 82). Hirst is not only a drunk; he is a wounded fisher-king whose potency is the major issue. At the same time that he offers to save Hirst from the living death he inhabits with Foster and Briggs, Spooner continually challenges his potency. When Hirst responds to Spooner's questions about the past bucolic life they shared with memories of virginity and purity, suggesting that the garlands that were hung in his village church on the beams in honor of dead virgins were hung for young men as well as for young women and for "old men of the village who also died maiden" (p. 30) as well, Spooner responds with a strange fury. Hirst, he suggests, is far more the cuckold than the virgin he professes to be. "Do forgive me my candour," he says to Hirst. "It is not method but madness. So you won't, I hope, object if I take out my prayer beads and my prayer mat and salute what I take to be your impotence?" (p. 33).

Although such undercutting of his manhood brings Hirst to an exit on hands and knees, he counters in act 2 with memories of cuckolding Spooner, whom he now addresses as his long-lost friend, Charles Wetherby. When Spooner replies with further stories that undermine Hirst's masculinity, it does indeed seem to be madness not method that he employs if he would win favor with Hirst. His real aim would seem to be to replace Hirst, not to save him, and on a realistic level that probably is his aim. As his double, however, Spooner's effort to replace Hirst is an attempt to save him. The Matchseller who replaced Edward in *A Slight Ache* was just as much another part of Edward that continued in his place as he was the usurper who replaced him. The fact that the virility Flora detected in the Matchseller is not detected in Spooner by any character but himself does, however, reinforce the notion of Spooner as a spurious savior. The questioning of the potency of both challenged and challenger by each other in *No Man's Land* casts tremendous doubt on the possibility of this Godot's renewal.

Hirst's inability to accept his own mortality is at the heart of the problem. Spooner offers to help him with his paradoxically life-giving task several times, both directly and indirectly. Just after saluting his impotence, Spooner offers his friendship to Hirst as a Charon who will usher him to his death, and near the end of the play Spooner makes a similar offer: "I will accept death's challenge on your behalf. I shall meet it, for your sake, boldly, whether it be in the field or in the bedchamber" (p. 89).

The first offer is surrounded with digs at Hirst's virility and only leads Hirst to define the no-man's-land that he chooses over the death-renewal of which Spooner speaks. "No man's land . . . does not move . . . or change . . . or grow old . . . remains . . . forever . . . icy . . . silent" (p. 34), is his reply. The second offer, in which Spooner suggests that he will replace Hirst, dying for him rather than ushering him to death, is accompanied by an invitation to a creative comeback, a poetry reading in a public house, which Spooner assures Hirst will put him back in touch with the young and, by implication, with his youth. This, too, Hirst declines, settling into the subject of winter, a living death that precludes seasonal change, creativity, and life—but also death.

There are two other ways, less direct, in which Spooner offers Hirst a renewal of his feelings and creative power, both of which are also rejected by this Godot. Hirst has invited Spooner, as the Charles Wetherby that Hirst now calls him, to go through his photograph album. The dead faces, he says, "possess all that emotion . . . trapped. Bow to it. It will assuredly never release them, but who knows . . . what relief . . . it may give to them . . . who knows how they may quicken . . . in their chains, in their glass jars" (p. 79). Foster and Briggs are horrified at the offer. "They're blank, mate, blank. The blank dead" (p. 79), Briggs insists. And after Spooner offers to go through the album with Hirst and "put names to the faces. A proper exhumation could take place" (pp. 83–84), Foster insists, "Those faces are nameless, friend" (p. 84). Hirst, who is protected from his own invitation to new life by his henchmen, retreats. "There are places in my heart . . . where no living soul . . . has . . . or can ever . . . trespass" (p. 84), he says, giving up. What Hirst denies, then, is the very thing he asked Spooner to help him with, a release of trapped feelings, a renewal of the past, bringing it into the dynamics of time where it might be a source of new creativity. Now he will not be able to keep his appointment with those who wait for him.

Perhaps the most important and profoundly symbolic offer that Spooner makes to Hirst, which the old man also rejects, is that of himself as the drowning person in Hirst's dreams. Hirst struggles throughout the drama with a dream of drowning that he first suggests by his very denial might have been a drowning of the self. "There's a gap in me. I can't fill it. There's a flood running through me. I can't plug it . . . It's a muff. A muff, perfumed. Someone is doing me to death" (p. 46). After this suggestion of his own possible victimization, Hirst rejects the idea: "There's no water. No-one is drowning" (p. 46). When Spooner insists, "It was I drowning in your dream" (p. 47), Hirst collapses, doubtless recognizing his kinship with his other self and the reality of his own drowning self. But by rejecting the whole memory of the drowning, Hirst turns his back on the possible renewal involved in such a vision. Water dreams, according to Freud, often suggest birth, and dreams that involve rescue from water suggest giving birth.[3] "Throwing into, or drenching with, water is a well-known part of 'fertility' ritual; it is a case of sympathetic magic, acting as a rain charm."[4] By rejecting his dream, and by rejecting Spooner, spurious though he may be, Hirst rejects his own possible rebirth.

If Hirst were to appear on the Godot road, Estragon and Vladimir, who once mistook Pozzo for Godot, would be very apt to mistake Hirst for him as well. Resting in their mistaken identification, they would doubtless have all their expectations and anxieties about the nature of their potential savior confirmed. Like Godot, who the messenger boy has told Vladimir does nothing, Hirst does nothing. Like Godot, whom

Estragon and Vladimir see as imprisoned by those he must consult, Hirst is the prisoner of Foster and Briggs. And like the Godot whom Lucky defines in his "think" speech as a personal God "who from the heights of divine apathia divine athambia divine aphasia loves us dearly" (p. 28), Hirst also seems to lack the capacity to feel, to be amazed or terrified, and, in the sense that he can no longer write, the capacity for speech.

In *Waiting for Godot*, when Estragon asks where Vladimir and he "come in" in relationship to the all-powerful Godot, Vladimir suggests, "On our hands and knees" (p. 13). But if they saw this Godot, who like their Godot and like themselves does nothing, and who like their Godot and like themselves lacks freedom, they might find him, like their Godot, to be nothing but a kind of mirror image of themselves. Indeed, they might even meet, Hirst crawling out in act 1 of *No Man's Land,* the others, in Vladimir's metaphor, crawling in, all on their hands and knees, nose to nose.

There are, of course, differences. In *Waiting for Godot,* Estragon fondly remembers that Vladimir once saved him from a suicidal drowning. The implied rebirth was in the past; suicide is a speculation rather than a viable alternative in the present, but the memory is accepted, and despite all they are true friends. Not so, Spooner and Hirst. Foster and Briggs belittle Spooner's claim of friendship by calling him Mr. Friend, and Hirst turns down all of Spooner's offers of friendship. Hirst has failed to save whoever was drowning in his dream, possibly himself, and Spooner, who may or may not be the friend he professes to be, has failed to save Hirst.

In a sense, then, Pinter's *No Man's Land* is an even bleaker territory than Beckett's and might suggest a regression to the early Pinter world of Stanley's entrapment in nonlife in *The Birthday Party*. While Stanley was victimized by Monty as an outside force in the play, however, Spooner, ambiguous as his motives and attributes are, is clearly an inner potentiality; Hirst chooses his retreat from life. And despite Hirst's negative choice, Spooner has had some effect on him. Before his final submission to eternal stasis, Hirst hears birds singing, which he says he never heard in his youth. Spooner may never paint his picture, but he has had a vision of the fisher-king in all of his potency, and he has shared something of that vision with Hirst.

Beckett's land has long been familiar territory to Pinter. He discovered and appreciated it far before Beckett's dramatic realizations of Eliot's wasteland had permeated the modern consciousness. With *No Man's Land* he actually enters that territory, leaving behind, at least for this drama, the tragicomic dying gods of his other plays and their tragicomic rebirths in favor of an exploration of the dynamics of the stasis of Beckett's landscape.

The resemblance of Hirst to Beckett's Godot in *Waiting for Godot* is surely not a conscious choice on Pinter's part and may be pure accident; the two playwrights do inhabit and depict the same world. Godot, however, has become such a potent image for our times that it would be surprising if Pinter had not unconsciously been influenced to explore Godot's nature from his own perspective. In so doing his treatment remains characteristically more decisive than Beckett's. Beckett's Godots, when they are at home, remain indecisive; Godot won't come today, but he'll surely come tomorrow, the messenger boy tells Didi and Gogo. *No Man's Land* is an endgame with a more certain defeat than that in Beckett's *Endgame*,[5] in which Clov's presence undermines Hamm's determination and the young boy he has cited remains a potentiality. There is no doubt, however, that Beckett has charted the lands that Pinter explores here, just as there is no doubt that Pinter has shed some new light on the enigma of Beckett's Godot. Illuminating Beckett's landscape from his own particular angle, Pinter makes it clear that his Hirst/Godot will never more arrive and why. Turning his back on his creativity, his audience, and his life, Hirst's retreat does, however, in Pinter's hands, become a work of art itself, one that may even rival Von Kleist's "retreat from the Caucasus," which Spooner had labeled "the wittiest and most subtle systematic withdrawal known to man" (p. 20).

NOTES

1. Quoted by Roger Manvell, "The Decade of Harold Pinter," *Humanist* 132 (April 1967): 114.
2. Harold Pinter, *No Man's Land* (New York: Grove Press, 1975), p. 18. All subsequent references to *No Man's Land* are from this edition.
3. Sigmund Freud, *The Interpretation of Dreams*, trans. and ed. James Strachey (New York: Avon Books, 1965), pp. 435–37, 459.
4. Jessie L. Weston, *From Ritual to Romance*, p. 51.
5. Two articles that compare *No Man's Land* to *Endgame* are John Bush Jones's "Stasis as Structure in Pinter's *No Man's Land*," *Modern Drama* 19, no. 3 (September 1976): 291–304, and Ruby Cohn's "Words Working Overtime: *Endgame* and *No Man's Land*," *Yearbook of English Studies* 9 (1979): 188–203.

8

Godot Arrives: *The Homecoming*

The decisive action of Godot in several of Harold Pinter's dramas already explored has been largely negative. His merciless messengers defeat Stanley in *The Birthday Party*, and, although defeated, Godot appears with malign intentions in *Old Times*. Finally, the death-in-life that Hirst-Godot embraces in *No Man's Land* leaves those who look to him for new life homeless, exiles in their own no-man's-land.

But in some of his plays, Pinter, more than any other modern dramatist, has offered an authentic arrival of Godot. In these plays Godot is neither a malign force nor a false messiah but a true savior. *The Homecoming* (1965), possibly the playwright's masterpiece and certainly his most written-about play, is, as its title suggests, a drama of arrival, one in which modern man's and woman's exile comes to an end and one which celebrates an authentic arrival of Godot.

In previous chapters of this study, Godot has sometimes stood metaphorically for the king-priest-god of Nemi, defending his realm against any new gods who would take his power or dying as one god only to rise himself as the new deity. In Frazer's version of the Nemi ritual, the drama takes place in Diana's grove, and as fertility goddess, Diana unites with the new god. But in most of the plays explored, the women have failed to fill the role of fertility goddess: the ineffective, seductive mother-protector in *The Birthday Party*, the seductive, castrating mother in *The American Dream*, the creative-destructive parody of a Great Mother in *The Chairs*.

In *The Maids* and *Old Times*, the only dramas discussed in which women enjoy the role of protagonist, the salvation that Claire, Solange, and Kate achieve has involved the exorcism of female Godots, Madame and Anna. Here the metaphor shifts slightly as Godot is a part of the women who are struggling to attain their roles as fertility goddesses, rather than being the goddess's male consort. Although these plays go beyond the parody of rebirth that informs some of the other dramas, moving to a more authentic experience of renewal, the peripheral nature of the men in them prevents a full celebration, just as the parody of women/goddesses in the other plays has been a measure of the lack of an authentic arrival. Monsieur, in *The Maids,* is an off-stage figure. Although the maids can combat their servitude by playing out their drama of exorcism, their self-sacrifice leaving them with a sense of self-possession, they have really only given birth to their potential role as fertility goddess. And as Kate exorcises that part of herself which allowed her husband to enslave her, the discarding of that husband leaves her again self-possessed but alone.

For an authentic arrival of Godot with its saving rebirth, the union of male and female is necessary. The shifting metaphor of Godot as arriving god or budding goddess must give way to a new one that involves a mutual arrival. Although the savior figure in Pinter's *The Homecoming* is a woman, Ruth, salvation is worked out in terms of the male/female dynamic. The Count has reminded the cooks in *The Wicked Cooks* that salvation is not a formula but an experience. Vasco undergoes that initiatory experience only when he sees the Count and Martha together in a sacred union in which Martha plays the role of the biblical Ruth. When he hears the shots signifying their self-sacrifice, Vasco is reborn—it is as if they have given birth to him. And so to explore the nature of Godot's arrival in *The Homecoming,* one must look beyond Ruth's arrival as savior to the union of Ruth with her new consorts and the mutual arrival that they achieve.

Of course, if *The Homecoming* is read on a realistic level, its events are shocking to say the least. After six years' absence in America, Teddy, a university professor of philosophy, visits his English family, introducing them to his wife Ruth whom they proceed to keep, sending Teddy back to America. For a husband to stand calmly by as his family make love to and make plans for keeping his wife is outrageous. One does not know which is more unnerving, the flagrant lust that Teddy's father, Max, and his brothers, Lenny and Joey, exhibit regarding Teddy's wife, along with their calculated willingness to "put her on the game" of prostitution, which will allow her to support herself while living with the family, or Teddy's understated reaction to their plan. "She'd get old . . . very quickly,"[1] he observes from the sidelines as they formulate their "deal" with Ruth; but he then tells Ruth of their invitation to keep her and of their expectations. "Or you can come home with me" (p. 76), he adds, somewhat as if she were to choose between muffins or cake with her tea.

There is, perhaps, nothing more shocking about this family situation than the one that Peter Barnes creates in *The Ruling Class* (1968), another play in which Godot arrives. Here, when the mad son of the thirteenth Earl of Gurney is brought out of a lunatic asylum at his father's death to assume his role as the fourteenth Earl, his delusion that he is God is considered dangerous by his family on numerous levels, especially since he preaches the kind of Christian brotherly love and leveling of social rank that would undermine their way of life. Their rejection of this Godot, and their outrageous plotting against him is no less darkly comic than their subsequent acceptance of him when his doctor returns him to supposed sanity. As he now mouths the kind of philosophy they espouse, they are totally unaware that Jack now believes himself to be Jack the Ripper and is acting out his fantasy, killing first his aunt, for which deed he allows the butler to take the blame, and then the wife with whom his "loving" family has provided him.

Here Barnes is working in a satirical mode, however, commenting less, perhaps, on the family than on the barbarities of the privileged class and admonishing us, as we reject Godot, about the monsters we then create in our own image. "Oh God, that madest this beautiful earth, when will it be ready to receive Thy saints? How long, O Lord, how long?"[2] Shaw's Saint Joan cries out in an indictment of his time. "Never," comes back Barnes's Shavian-Pirandellian answer[3] in *The Ruling Class* as he indicts his time—our time: not as long as the upper classes fashion the kind of Godot that suits their vicious, coldblooded needs.[4]

Pinter's play, however, is both realistic and surrealistic,[5] and though it is filled with a kind of social satire, it is not of the Peter Barnes variety. His characters are not so much the Barnes stereotypes, who are more related to the caricatures of Albee's *The American Dream* than to Pinter's drama, for they are archetypal in nature. On a naturalistic level, the transfer of Ruth from her husband to his father and brothers, for whom she will play the role of wife, mother, and whore, is shockingly outrageous. On an archetypal level, her assumption of the role of fertility goddess who brings renewed life to a family of impotent men comes to seem logical, inevitable, and even cause for celebration.

Pinter's play is really an elaboration of an earlier drama, *A Slight Ache* (1962), in which the disposing of an old husband and the taking on of a new one is enacted in realistically absurd but archetypically logical terms. Why does Flora, the middle-class wife of her middle-class husband, who spends his leisure time writing philosophical essays, dispose of him, taking on instead an ugly, stinking, old Matchseller, who never speaks and who seems to spend the whole time of the play in a catatonic trance? Because Edward, despite his aristocratic pretensions, is out of touch with the garden over which Flora, as tragicomic fertility goddess, presides and is the embodiment of winter, whereas Barnabus, whose name means summer,[6] despite his unlikely appearance, heralds the advent of the new season and promises her new life.

The focus in this earlier play, despite its comic and absurd style, is on the death and rebirth of Edward as Godot, its emphasis on Edward's growing awareness of his tragic and comic predicament. In *The Homecoming*, however, Pinter shifts his focus to the figure of the fertility goddess. The basic plot of *The Homecoming* is a mutual conquest that, as painful as it is comic, results in the rebirth of Max's dead wife Jessie in Ruth.

When Jessie was alive, the household of male energies—her sons Teddy, Lenny, and Joey, as well as Max, Max's brother Sam, and Max's friend Mac—revolved around her. As the play opens we see the chaos of Max's impotent rule against the background of this lost, golden world: Max cannot put a sneering Lenny in his place and cannot function, as he tries to do, as both mother and father to the family. Sam and Joey are both put down as if they threatened him and then sent off without dinner. When Ruth enters with Teddy, she automatically fills the vacuum left by Jessie; Lenny, the pimp, grapples with her in an attempt to seize control of this potent new force, but instead is captured by it. Max, with stunned surprise, tries to eject Ruth, but having successfully (for the moment) asserted his authority over the family, welcomes her. Ruth extends her conquest to include Joey; her open acceptance of Joey's sexual interest, with the collaboration of Lenny, marks not only her conquest of Joey but her separation from Teddy; she finally agrees to accept Jessie's old role as mother, wife, and whore and sends Teddy back to America where, as his generation's version of Max, he will rule over a houseful of unfulfilled male impulses in himself and his three sons.

In the opening section of the play (there are five sections, marked off by blackouts), one comes to see Max's household, over which he exerts a shaky patriarchal rule, against the background of the lost world of Jessie. When Max's demands on Lenny are met with curses and sneers, he responds in a way that is to be repeated throughout the play, especially by Max and Lenny—the flight into fantasy by the spinning of yarns.[7] Here, as elsewhere, the story projects a situation in which the speaker's desired relationship with his listener is implied. Max "recalls" the day when he and his friend MacGregor were the toughest men in the West End of London: "We'd walk into a place, the whole room'd stand up, they'd make way to let us pass. You never heard such silence" (p. 8). We know from the shaking of his stick (p. 7) that Max would dearly love to assert his patriarchal authority over Lenny by physical assault.

Max then launchs into a description of his prowess with horses, and as the subject narrows from horses to fillies the latent association between horse and woman is firmly established. Max is asserting the former vigor of his sexuality and comparing it sneeringly with Lenny's; he is foreshadowing, too, his ability to pick a "stayer," to recognize the kind of woman who can perform in Jessie's old role.

But I was always able to tell a good filly by one particular trick. I'd look her in the eye. You see? I'd stand in front of her and look her straight in the eye, it was a kind of hypnotism, and by the look deep down in her eye, I could tell whether she was a stayer or not. It was a gift. I had a gift.

(P. 10)

Max's stick, the scepter he uses both as weapon and as crutch, symbolizes accurately the ambiguity of his rule, and Lenny scorns it as an empty remnant of Max's faded power: "Oh, Daddy, you're not going to use your stick on me, are you? Eh? (p. 11)

Max fares somewhat better with Sam, although as the best driver in his firm and a steady breadwinner Sam presents a dangerous claim—which he offers at some length (pp. 11–14)—to being Max's superior as a man. He brings home a box of first-class cigars to back up his extended boasting: He is not only the best driver, but he fought in the war alongside his illustrious Yankee passenger; and soldiering as well as cigars are symbols of vigorous manhood recognized in this circle. Max is at pains throughout the rest of the play to counter these claims, but at the moment he puts Sam down by taunting him for his lack of sexual experience.

> MAX: It's funny you never got married, isn't it? A man with all your gifts.
> *Pause.* Isn't it? A man like you?
>
> (P. 14)

Sam capitulates: his real love was Jessie, but he was only her admirer, her chauffeur, whom Max could trust.

If Lenny seems quite out of control (though not himself dominant over Max) and Sam put down only with some difficulty, Joey, the youngest son, is still a dutiful child. There is an implied threat in his avocation of boxing, but as Max tells him, "You don't know how to defend yourself, and you don't know how to attack. Once you've mastered those arts you can go straight to the top" (pp. 17–18). Like Sam, Joey has come home looking for his dinner, but Max has been so mercilessly taunted by Lenny for his feminine role that when either mentions food or hunger he sets off a storm of irritation, and neither ever gets his dinner. "Who do you think I am, your mother? Eh? . . . Go and find yourself a mother" (p. 16). Joey disappears upstairs, but Max's line will, by the end of the play, acquire a prophetic dimension.

The second "home" presented in this first section, the lost world of Jessie, included the three sons, Teddy, Lenny, and Joey, but there are more glimpses from that time of the other three satellites, Max, Mac, and Sam. The very names indicate their kinship. Mac is not a brother, but Sam comes close to identifying him as such: "You wouldn't have trusted any of your other brothers. You wouldn't have trusted Mac, would you?" (p. 18). Looking at the names, one is tempted to see Mac as a double of Max, and Sam as some kind of reversal. Sam is, at any rate, a neuter in Jessie's male harem, as against the more aggressive male role of the other two, and Max does continually use Mac as a way of putting down Sam, and therefore of raising his own stock: "We took you into the butcher's shop, you couldn't even sweep the dust off the floor. We took MacGregor into the shop, he could run the place by the end of the week" (p. 39). "Do you want to know who could drive? MacGregor! MacGregor was a driver" (p. 48).

Whatever their differences, however, Max and Sam share an ambivalence in their attitude toward Jessie. "Nothing like your bride . . . going about these days. Like Jessie" (p. 16), Sam admits, recalling the "delightful evenings" in which he drove her about in his cab. The memory, however, conjures up the painful scene, which he reveals only at the end of the play, when "MacGregor had Jessie in the back of my cab as I drove them along" (p. 78). Max's ambivalent memory of Jessie may be seen in his first mention of her as "not such a bad woman. Even though it made me sick just to look at her rotten stinking face, she wan't such a bad bitch" (p. 9).

Indeed, Max rejects his feminine role when it threatens his paternity, but sometimes when the sense of the past as an ideal time is shattered he takes on the fantasy of himself as always having been the mother. At the beginning of the second act, for example he tells Ruth a tale of the days when Jessie was the backbone of the family and when he himself was the breadwinner: in the story Jessie sits with her feet on the pouf, Max stands beside her, and the boys kneel at their feet. One of the essential features of the story is that Max was making opulently generous promises to Jessie (as a result of his "negotiations with a top-class group of butchers with continental connections"), and when Ruth punctures the whole fantasy by asking what became of the group of butchers, Max's mood veers immediately; he stubs out his cigar, attacks Sam on the question of his breadwinning skills, and then, in the same mood, claims the maternal functions for himself. "A crippled family, three bastard sons, a slutbitch of a wife—don't talk to me about the pain of childbirth—I suffered the pain, I've still got the pangs—when I give a little cough my back collapses" (p. 47).[8]

The same combination of maternal and paternal roles that, at least in his blacker moods, Max claims for himself is attributed to his own father in the final speech of the first section, where Max pictures himself as an infant:

> Our father? I remember him. Don't worry. You kid yourself. He used to come over to me and look down at me. My old man did. He'd bend right over me, then he'd pick me up. I was only that big. Then he'd dandle me. Give me the bottle. Wipe me clean. Give me a smile. Pat me on the bum. Pass me around, pass me from hand to hand. Toss me up in the air. Catch me coming down. I remember my father.
>
> (P. 19)

This speech comes out of Max's irritation with Sam who insists that he, too, has a place in his mother and father's house. "Look what I'm lumbered with. One cast-iron bunch of crap after another" (p. 19) is Max's response, followed by the tirade on his father. Max's remembrance of his father is bitter, the most negative, despairing statement of cycle in the play. It not only reflects Max's sense of helplessness as a child in the arms of a father-mother,[9] but also his sense of helplessness in his present situation as he attempts to repeat that double role in his family. The speech is suggestive not only of the absence of Jessie as a wife, but also of the absence of a mother in a yet earlier generation. As such, it is a fitting conclusion for the first section of the play and is logically followed by the entrance of Teddy with a new mother-wife and a new source of life—Ruth.

For Max, then, the present situation requires that he make contradictory claims to buttress his faltering authority: he is both father and mother, and his memory of the past oscillates as one or the other side of his present life is called forward. For Sam, too, the past is not only a paradise whose demise has made the present an empty, longing time, but also the source of an agonizing memory.

The setting of the play is also used to help evoke the past. Since Jessie's death, some changes in the geography of the house have taken place. Lenny has moved downstairs and now occupies the room adjacent to the "open living area" in which the action of the play takes place. An arch remains as a reminder of the old days when a wall and door separated the hall from the living room. "We knocked it down . . . years ago . . . to make an open living area. The structure wasn't affected, you see. My mother was dead" (p. 21). The arch hovers over the room and over the family (and over the audience) as an unconscious reminder of that structural principle that, though missing and so ambivalently remembered, is still essential.

A third "home," Teddy's America, is only sketched in the first section, in association with Sam's Yankee passenger, who is so rich—one might almost say rich in his easy manliness, or at least in its symbols—that he gives away a whole box of cigars; even his overflow is enough to raise Sam's family stock. America is the locus of men with impressive titles, "big business-men, men of affairs" (p. 13)—colonels, navigators, and aeronautical engineers, who are all eventually taken to London Airport. In the next section, when Lenny mentions that Teddy has not only been living in America but also bears one of those impressive titles, the situation seems all set up for him to take his remote and superior stance with them, and for them to take steps against it.

The second section opens with Teddy sneaking back into the house, just as, six years before, he had sneaked away to marry Ruth and emigrate to America. He still has the key. His first concern is to determine whether his place in the family structure is still open—that is, whether his room is still there. "It can't have moved" (p. 20), Ruth tells him, and Lenny confirms the point later in the play, although his tone makes that confirmation doubtful.

> We do make up a unit, Teddy, and you're an integral part of it. When we all sit round the backyard having a quiet gander at the night sky, there's always an empty chair standing in the circle, which is in fact yours.
>
> (P. 65)

Ruth senses more clearly than Teddy the fatalities operating in the situation and offers Teddy his last chance to escape before he gives up the key, but Teddy says they are "bound" to stay. Even to leave for a walk is unthinkable for him; "The last thing I want is a breath of air" (p. 24). Teddy hugs his limitations to him.

If Ruth can outflank Teddy, in a few moves, of his attempt to put her to bed, it takes even less time for Lenny to maneuver him up the stairs, leaving the stage free for his encounter with Ruth. Lenny's having taken over the room next to the "open living area," comes to seem more and more appropriate for him as the play progresses. As pimp, Lenny operates in the world as a kind of doorkeeper to the activities of others, watching and manipulating. Nothing happens without his cognizance from his "study, workroom cum bedroom next door" (p. 25).

Lenny, however, is more than doorkeeper and pimp. In an ironical usurpation of each other's roles, Teddy becomes the pimp who hands Ruth over to his family to fulfill their needs while Lenny becomes the philosopher, the seeker of that truth which the more narrow philosopher, Teddy, insists is outside his province. Questioning everyone in the self-mocking manner of Mick in Pinter's *The Caretaker*, Lenny covers his sensitivity by his crude banter, but nevertheless reveals his suffering spirit of inquiry.

Lenny greets his returning brother with his sleeplessness: "It's just that something keeps waking me up. Some kind of tick" (p. 25). In his first interchange with Ruth, Lenny refuses to identify the tick, as his brother has, as the clock.

> The trouble is I'm not all that convinced it was the clock. I mean there are lots of things which tick in the night, don't you find that? All sorts of objects, which, in the day, you wouldn't call anything else but commonplace. They give you no trouble. But in the night any given one of a number of them is liable to start letting out a bit of a tick. . . .
> (P. 28)

Lenny might be describing the play's action with his awareness of life's undercurrents, the impending doom that lurks beneath the commonplace.

Lenny prepares to receive Ruth by bringing in the clock, but even before he can open with this ploy the subject of time is upon him:

LENNY: Good evening.
RUTH: Morning, I think.
LENNY: You're right there.
(P. 27)

Change has come upon him; even their difference of costume points up the fact that Ruth is operating in a new time: "Isn't it funny? I've got my pyjamas on and you're fully dressed?" (p. 29). There is also a hint of imminent change in Lenny's intimation that if there were anything worth celebrating there would be alcoholic drinks rather than water in the sideboard. One can measure the progression of the understanding established between Lenny and Ruth from this point on by the fact that in the middle of the second act Ruth's demand for whiskey has been anticipated.

Lenny asks to hold Ruth's hand—"just a touch" (p. 30). When she asks why, he answers with a story of himself under an arch beating up a woman who has made him a proposal that he refuses because the lady "was falling apart with the pox" (p. 30); he knocks her down, and only decides not to kill her to avoid the bother of getting rid of the corpse. Ruth's question, "How did you know she was diseased?" (p. 31), has the effect of puncturing Lenny's picture of himself as dominant—if the woman is not pox-ridden, there is no reason for not accepting her proposal.

Lenny's second story, of himself shoveling snow, bigheartedly offering to help an old lady move an iron mangle and then beating her up when it turned out to be too heavy for him, is presented as an illustration of people desensitizing him by making "unreasonable demands"; Lenny seems to be anticipating here, as in the first story, Ruth's coming assault on him, feeling its approach, no doubt, in the quiet self-assurance of her series of curt answers and questions that continually undercut his nervous chatter. The second story is another threat: the woman who loads him down with an impossible task will be "clumped." It is worth mentioning that while in the story it is Lenny who is invigorated by fresh air, in the scene it is Ruth.

Lenny's threatening stories work on a more poignant level, however, which again suggests the lost child beneath the hardened pimp. He is asking for contact, and Ruth hears him. When he forces a direct confrontation by demanding Ruth's glass, a symbol, the erotic possibilities of which are increasingly capitalized on as the scene progresses, she both defeats his aggressions and makes her own invitation by the simple maneuver of stepping into the place of Jessie:

LENNY: You've consumed quite enough, in my opinion.
RUTH: No, I haven't.
LENNY: Quite sufficient, in my own opinion.
RUTH: Not in mine, Leonard.
   Pause
LENNY: Don't call me that, please.
RUTH: Why not?
LENNY: That's the name my mother gave me.

(P. 33)

Lenny's tactic throughout the scene has been to try to identify Ruth as a whore and to use this identification as a source of power over her. She counters by insinuations as to his lack of masculinity, then by claiming maternal power over him, and when that succeeds, by using her potency as a whore to complete her work of humiliation. With her exultant draining of the glass of water, Ruth asserts her own full-bodied sexuality in the face of his impotence, although Lenny's draining of his own glass of water after she exits suggests the possibility of his redemption through Ruth from that condition. Ruth's taking of Lenny is not only the decisive first step in her acquisition of the whole family, but is a monad of the play: the conflict of sexes produces victory for Ruth by the simple, inevitable expedient of assuming the robes of Jessie.

Ruth's initial victory over Lenny, however, is an ambituous one, which does not leave her fully exultant. If Max has been revealed as incomplete as a patriarch in the first section of the play, Ruth is revealed as incomplete as the matriarch in the second. Her draining of the glass of water followed by her comment, "Oh, I was thirsty" (p. 35), takes on greater significance in the fourth section of the play, in which the aridity of her life in America with Teddy is brought into focus. And the depths of her thirst are discovered in the remainder of the play as she moves to take on Teddy's family, choosing the jungle over the desert. Lenny can touch Ruth only by stroking her hair as she grapples with another man. He threatens her as a pimp and she can conquer him as a mother, but she cannot expect her thirst to be quenched by Lenny other than by permitting him to be her pimp. The victory has been established, but so have the limitations of the relationship.

The final scene of the second section, in which Lenny asks Max the "true facts" of the night of his conception, reaffirms Lenny's limitation. "I mean, for instance, is it a fact that you had me in mind all the time, or is it a fact that I was the last thing you had in mind?" (p. 36), Lenny inquires. The speech is yet another expression of Lenny as referee in the sex game; and the sneering tone in which he envisions men made in the image not of god but "of those two people at it" (p. 36) comes out of the rough handling he has just received from Ruth. Beneath the sneer, however, is the search for new beginnings. If, as Mircea Eliade suggests, "the return to origins gives the hope of rebirth,"[10] Lenny's curiosity about his own birth reveals his search for renewal in the wasteland he inhabits. Beneath the mask of the sadistic pimp is the frightened child seeking in the darkness of his life for what might be more ideal origins in some long-lost paradise.

The third section seems to return to the beginning of the play: Max is irritated because Joey will not go to the football game with him and because Sam's scraping out of his "leavings" seems to him to be loaded with antagonistic implications—as it no doubt is. The effect of this brief recapitulation is to inject Teddy and Ruth into the very midst of the household dynamics in full operation and to play into the continuing themes. Teddy, for example, jokingly demands his breakfast, a request not designed to delight Max, as already seen in the experience of Sam and Joey the evening before.

Max is faced with what seems an all-out assault; his oldest son invades the house in the night with a woman who cannot help upsetting the delicate balance of forces. His initial rejection of Ruth, like Lenny's rejection of her "proposal," plays directly off Lenny's first story: Teddy delivers Ruth to the arch (Pinter carefully specifies that they "stop just inside the room" [p. 40]), and Max uses Lenny's own word, "pox-ridden," in pushing her away. Max anticipates the move Ruth has made in conquering Lenny by himself pointing out that in simply entering she steps into Jessie's place: "I've never had a whore under this roof before. Ever since your mother died" (p. 42). But the challenge to his authority implicit in Ruth's very presence seems to be effective—his demand that Joey, the boxer, throw them out is met with a direct refusal: "You're an old man." It is Max's moment to win or lose all, and he comports himself with skill: by outboxing Joey he proves his earlier assertion that Joey is not yet ready to "go straight to the top" (p. 18), and with his scepter he puts down Sam, whose attempt to help Max keep on his feet is a softened version of Joey's accusation. Again the action stops, and the tableau reads like a prediction of the rest of the play. Ruth stands flanked by her two henchmen, Teddy and Lenny, both liveried in dressing gowns, Joey kneels at her feet, Max grovels nearby. Sam is out of commission. But Joey fails, in this round, either to break Max's paternal control of him or to take precedence with Ruth.

Toward Ruth Max now shows the same ambivalence as toward the memory of Jessie; having rejected her as a whore, he now steps forward to accept her as a mother of three sons—making a reversal that parallels that which Ruth has forced on Lenny and which already contains an implicit threat to Teddy:

MAX: Miss.
RUTH *walks toward him.*
RUTH: Yes?
  He looks at her
MAX: You a mother?
RUTH: Yes.
MAX: How many you got?
RUTH: Three
  He turns to TEDDY.
MAX: All yours, Ted?

(P. 43)

Max now offers Teddy a "cuddle and kiss." In an earlier quarrel with Lenny, Max has offered to "give you a proper tuck up one of these nights, son" (p. 17), and the present invitation seems strongly mingled with the same threat of rough treatment. Teddy and Max, as the curtain ends the first act, are approaching one another with the stance of wrestlers. The struggle with Ruth involves, as a necessary adjunct, the struggle with Teddy over Ruth.

The fourth section of the play is decisive. While the terms of Ruth's contract with her new family are worked out in the final section, the move from Teddy's to Max's world is accomplished here; as the family takes Ruth, Ruth takes the family, and Teddy follows the line that inevitably excludes him.

The complexity of Ruth's choice, which is not simply between impotence (Teddy) and fertility (his family), is indicated here by what happens to the cigars that Max, Teddy, Lenny, and Sam are lighting as Ruth and Joey serve coffee: Max puts his out, Lenny's and Teddy's go out. Significantly, Joey does not have one. As Rolf Fjelde remarks, Joey is "the only one who neither shares nor needs the ritual cigar . . . of them all, Joey is the one healthy animal, whose approach to Ruth, as she recognizes, is directly natural, if unprincipled."[11]

Max seems to have forgotten the danger he sensed when he first saw Ruth, and he begins the section expansively as he advances from praise of Ruth's coffee to his most effusive praise of the memory of Jessie. "That woman was the backbone to this family. . . . I left a woman at home with a will of iron, a heart of gold and a mind" (p. 46). In this mood, Max launches into the story discussed above in which his role is that of the generous master dispensing the overflow from his important activities to a grateful, ornamental subordinate: like Lenny, Max tries to project the kind of relationship with women that he would like to establish with Ruth, and implicit as well is the old paternal mastery over his sons: "I remember the boys came down, in their pyjamas, all their hair shining, their faces pink, it was before they started shaving, and they knelt down at our feet, Jessie's and mine. I tell you, it was like Christmas" (p. 46)—with the admiring shepherds worshiping, from a safe distance, the holy pair. Jessie, as the Virgin, occupies on her pouf the central position in the tableau, but Max, with his money, controls it. Like Lenny's, Max's story informs Ruth of the terms of her acceptance in the home—and, as before, she punctures the image at the crucial point where it fails to correspond with the present: "What happened to the group of butchers?" (p. 46). Did Jessie ever get her dress in pale corded blue silk? Is Max really a provider?

Max responds instantaneously. He stubs out his cigar (which is suddenly "lousy"), attacks Sam for *his* incapacity as a breadwinner, and drives him out. Women suddenly are useless in the world of his fantasy-memories: Max is his own woman and Jessie a "slutbitch" who couldn't even bear his own children. But the driving out of Sam (as a genuine scapegoat, loaded up with Max's sins) relieves him, and he returns to his former conviviality.

Ruth now begins a tactic that is both a forcing of attention on herself and, simultaneously, a shifting away from her liason with Teddy. She was "different," she says, when she met Teddy. Teddy replies with a tactic similar to Max's, building up and trying to impose his image of Ruth and her place in his life on Ruth and his family:

> She's a great help to me over there. She's a wonderful wife and mother. She's a very popular woman. She's got lots of friends. It's a great life, at the University . . . you know . . . it's a very good life. We've got a lovely house . . . we've got all . . . we've got everything we want. It's a very stimulating environment.
>
> (P. 50)

Lenny challenges Teddy at this point, noting that his cigar has gone out, but so, Teddy points out, has Lenny's. Lenny's sexual impotence, already explored in section two, is seen now in counterpoint with the more intellectual sterility of Teddy. As an intellectual, Teddy puts himself at odds with the crudeness of his family, but in so doing he places himself outside the realm of the living. Teddy is a dead man, and Ruth has experienced a near-death in her relationship with him. Teddy operates, he explains, "on things and not in things." His critical works, beyond the comprehension of his family, are based on this power of his to remain uninvolved.

Life with Teddy, then, has held no reality for Ruth, who rejects his noninvolvement for the movement of life. When Lenny tries to engage Teddy in philosophical discussion about the nature of being, Teddy hedges as to what is in his province; but Ruth enters the discussion, just as she chooses to enter the family.

> Don't be too sure though. You've forgotten something. Look at me. I ... move my leg. That's all it is. But I wear ... underwear ... which moves with me ... it ... captures your attention. Perhaps you misinterpret. The action is simple. It's a leg ... moving. My lips move. Why don't you restrict ... your observations to that? Perhaps the fact that they move is more significant ... than the words which come through them. You must bear that ... possibility ... in mind.
>
> (Pp. 52–53)

Ruth follows this declaration for sheer instinctual being with a description of America as a wasteland, a desert. "It's all rock," she says "and sand. It stretches ... so far ... everywhere you look. And there's lots of insects there" (p. 53).

Ruth's speech on the movement of her leg and her lips is crucial to the action and the meaning of the play. Through it she is not only calling attention to herself but offering herself to the family as something of special and mysterious value, even as she has offered herself in the glass of water to Lenny. Ruth is sexually starved, and she may, as so many critics have observed, be using her sexuality as a means of entering and manipulating the family,[12] but her desires are more complex; they include the need for power and sex, but they also include the need to be part of a family, to be loved, and to be whole, needs that she recognizes in those to whom she now offers herself.

Lenny now says:

> I've got a couple of friends of mine, we often sit round the Ritz Bar having a few liqueurs, and they're always saying things like that, you know, things like: Take a table, take it. All right, I say, *take* it, *take* a

table, but once you've taken it, what are you going to do with it? Once you've got hold of it, where you going to take it?

(P. 52)

"Taking a table" is grappling with things, engaging one's whole being—and since, as far as the play is concerned, the only significant relationships are domestic and sexual, taking a table is, for Lenny, taking a woman—so the speech expresses again his inability, thus far, to make that engagement. Max tags him as a pimp: "You'd probably sell it." Lenny answers that "You wouldn't get much for it," and Joey, the demolition man, throws in his appropriate comment, "Chop it up for firewood" (p. 52).

Ruth interrupts all this discourse on "taking" by doing just that: her opening line, "Don't be too sure though," refers back to Lenny's "You wouldn't get much for it" and is, therefore, an oblique reference forward to Lenny's idea of "putting her on Greek Street," where he maintains his "stable" of prostitutes. Ruth proceeds to draw attention to where it belongs: to the movement of her body and her lips. "Perhaps the fact that they move is more significant . . . than the words which come through them. You must bear that . . . possibility . . . in mind" (pp. 52–53). Ruth's proposal here—she has advanced a step toward explicitness from the proffered glass of water—is two-edged: "Take me, I am worth something," as well as "Why don't I just take you."

Silence, as the men are, in fact, taken. Teddy, who finally senses the overall movement of the action in which he is involved, stands; this is the beginning of his long, slow exit from his home. Ruth goes on to a decisive rejection of America: she was born "quite near here"; it is her home. America is all rock and sand and insects. Another silence. *"She is still."*

It is this stillness of Ruth that wins her all battles. In his excellent book, *Harold Pinter: The Poetics of Silence,* James R. Hollis notes that Pinter "assembles words to remind us that we live in the space between words."[13] Hence, it is by exploiting the pause and silence that Pinter makes silence a dramatic "presence."[14] "The unspoken gestures of the play do not imply ignorance so much as recognition of that which lies beyond language."[15] Ruth leaves behind the words that Pinter has called "stratagems to cover nakedness" and presents the men with the mysteriousness of being.

In this instance the silence is too much for the men. Negotiations have been carried on too far under the surface for them to make as yet the direct confrontation demanded by Ruth, and they simply leave—Lenny to make a strategic circle back to his observation post.

In a scene that reverses his first scene with Ruth, Teddy is now eager to leave and tries again to paint the bright picture of America: "Think of it. Morning over there. Sun. We'll go anyway, mmnn? It's so clean there" (p. 54). Ruth rejects that cleanliness, and when Teddy asks whether she didn't have "a good week" in Venice, she rejects that too in favor of the Venice that Lenny had imagined for her when she first met him. Lenny had told her, "I've always had a feeling that if I'd been a soldier in the last war—say in the Italian campaign—I'd probably have found myself in Venice" (P. 30). Ruth now says to Teddy, "But if I'd been a nurse in the Italian campaign I would have been there before" (p. 55). The image of Venice is never "explained," but from its contexts it is made to stand in polar opposition to the cleanliness and sterility of America. Teddy closes the scene with his unfailing—and unavailing—plea to Ruth: "You just rest" (p. 55).

The Argus-eyed Lenny slides in from his lair; conversation between him and Ruth again opens with the time, recalling the beginning of their first scene together; but now both agree on the imminence of change: "Winter'll soon be upon us. Time to renew one's wardrobe" (p. 56), Lenny remarks, and Ruth agrees that "that's a good thing to do." The fertility goddess must look to the new year, forsaking the old as the seasons change: and Teddy is brushed off by the family like a fallen leaf.

Subtextual negotiations begin: Ruth likes clothes, a change of clothes. The tone of Lenny's storytelling shifts radically; rather than his earlier threats, he picks up the gist of Max's story of Jessie with a tale of a hat given to a girl. Ruth for once does not ask the question that shatters the likelihood or relevance of the story but instead launches into a tale of her own, a description of her work as a model before she met Teddy and went to America. Here, if anywhere, one hears Ruth's description of her sense of the word "home": the England of her fantasy is not Teddy's "filthy urinal" but a large white water tower, trees, a path to a lake, and a cold buffet. Her story seems to be an indirect attempt to tell Lenny that home is here where, as she has said, she was born.

In any case, Lenny and Ruth have reached an understanding. When Teddy demands that Ruth come with him, they answer with a kiss, certainly not the expression of impending sexual entanglement, but rather more like the demonstration—to Teddy and to one another—of their mutual accord, the "touch" Lenny had asked for at the beginning. As his immediate turning over of Ruth to Joey demonstrates, Lenny stands to Ruth as servant to mistress, pimp to whore, and priest to goddess. "LENNY *sits on the arm of the sofa. He caresses* RUTH's *hair as Joey embraces her*" (p. 59). He becomes a master of ceremonies, and he and Ruth even have private signals between them:

JOEY *clasps her.* LENNY *moves to stand above them. He looks down on them. He touches* RUTH *gently with his foot.* RUTH *suddenly pushes* JOEY *away. She stands up.*

(P. 60)

But the signal does not mean that Lenny is giving orders. If Ruth becomes a sacrificial victim, she becomes a figure of divinity as well. Rising from the couch on which she has submitted to Joey's advances as victim, Ruth becomes the imperious victor demanding food and drink. What Ruth orders is the Saturnalia Lenny had tacitly promised in their first meeting: "We haven't got a drink in the house. Mind you, I'd soon get some in, if we had a party or something like that. Some kind of celebration . . . you know" (p. 28). Just as Max and his kitchen had in the first act produced nothing and in the second, under Ruth's influence, a "very good lunch" (p. 45), now the sideboard has turned its water into whiskey.

Teddy ends the fourth section standing aside (one can almost say cast aside), feverishly explaining why it is good not to "take a table":

It's a way of being able to look at the world. It's a question of how far you can operate on things and not in things. I mean it's a question of your capacity to ally the two, to relate the two, to balance the two. To see, to be able to *see!* I'm the one who can see . . . You're just objects. You just . . . move about. I can observe it. I can see what you do. It's the same as I do. But you're lost in it. You won't get me being . . . I won't be lost in it.

(Pp. 61–62)

Standing in direct opposition to Ruth's "philosophy," Teddy will neither take nor be taken.

But the beginning of the final section of the play indicates with bitter humor that Teddy's philosophy is not adequate to the situation—that he is not outside it; he rather must operate "in things" to the extent of retaliating against Lenny by stealing his cheese roll. Lenny's long reproach is to this effect: the expansive opportunities of America have not released Teddy but made him "a bit inner" (p. 65).

When Joey comes downstairs ("with a newspaper") from an inconclusive, two-hour bout with Ruth, asserting that "now and again . . . you can be happy . . . without going any hog" (p. 68), Lenny finds it necessary, with the story of the two birds had by himself and Joey in the rubble, to attempt for Teddy's benefit the kind of projection of himself and Joey as tough, virile males that he had tried in his opening ploy with Ruth. The story is clearly a lie:

LENNY: Tell him about the last bird you had, Joey.
Pause.
JOEY: What bird?

(P. 66)

But the story does foreshadow what is about to happen to Teddy: "We got out . . . and we told the . . . two escorts . . . to go away . . . which they did" (p. 68).

The story, too, is an image of the situation in the play. Lenny prompts Joey on the setting until they agree on a bombed site "in the rubble," and the point of Lenny's story is that Joey insisted on "having" the girl without her desired contraceptive protection. The image is Beckett's, one of birth astride of a grave, although here it is the attempt on the level of a pimp's joke to evoke a sense of renewal in a wasteland. Lenny's image remains true to his profession, that of a rape, but it reflects, as well, his search for new life.

While Joey needs prompting from Lenny about his fantasized conquest, he is quite positive in his insistence that he is satisfied with his unconsummated time with Ruth. Her conquest of Joey has advanced from that of the "tart" he called her earlier to a more particular and individual affection—now he is upset at the thought of sharing her or of anyone else "getting the gravy."

Max's suggestion that Ruth be invited to stay comes out of the discussion of Joey's frustration, and out of his own. He has evidently failed to take sufficient warning from Ruth's destruction of his story of Jessie-on-the-pouf, and he imagines the continuation of his rule with this old structural member replaced: "Perhaps it's not a bad idea to have a woman in the house. Perhaps it's a good thing" (p. 69). Ruth fuses with Jessie in his mind. On first seeing Ruth, Max had said, "I've never had a whore under this roof before. Ever since your mother died" (p. 42). Now the full implication of that line is clear: Max first rejects Ruth as a whore, but now he accepts her as a whore-wife-mother; it is what the family table of organization calls for.

MAS: . . . Listen, I'll tell you something. Since poor Jessie died, eh, Sam? We haven't had a woman in the house. Not one. Inside this house. And I'll tell you why. Because their mother's image was so dear any other woman would have . . . tarnished it. But you . . . Ruth . . . you're not only lovely and beautiful, but you're kin. You're kith. You belong here.
Pause.
RUTH: I'm very touched.
MAX: Of course you're touched. I'm touched.

(P. 75)

Godot Arrives: *The Homecoming*

Ruth calls the tune in the negotiation of the contract, bringing up specific earlier points of discussion such as her wardrobe and the promises implicit in Max's story of Jessie and Lenny's story of the hat he bought for a girl: "You would have to regard your original outlay simply as a capital investment" (p. 77). On the other hand, Ruth's earning her own money satisfies her qualms that Max (and by extension the family) is not a trustworthy provider.

As negotiations begin to finalize themsleves, Sam suddenly spills the information he has been with difficulty harboring throughout the play—and evidently for years before—that "MacGregor had Jessie in the back of my cab as I drove them along" (p. 78). His announcement comes as the final expression of resistance to the acquisition of Ruth. Sam sides with Teddy; the opening of the final section shows him whispering his affection to Teddy, and suggesting that he stay so that they "could have a few laughs" (P. 63). Sam never once speaks to Ruth; the only indication in the play of any communication is his shaking hands with her (p. 48) when Max drives him out. His reaction to the question whether Teddy "gets the gravy" is an indignant "He's her lawful husband. She's his lawful wife" (p. 69), and he brands as "silly" the idea of keeping Ruth (p. 70).

Sam's near-fatal outburst is equivalent to Max's lament over the cyclical nature of his troubles, "One cast-iron bunch of crap after another. One flow of stinking pus after another" (p. 19). He sees the stealing of Ruth as the return of the wheel of generations to the most painful point in his life. Sam is the eternal chauffeur. He likes to keep his car clean, to carry Yankees like Teddy who respect him for his ability to do his job without "taking liberties" (p. 13),[16] or to carry Jessie when he can do so within the established bounds of propriety. To live in an atmosphere of unleashed sexual vitality is, to use Teddy's terminology, outside Sam's province.

Such vitality is also, of course, foreign to Teddy; and if one asks why Teddy came home at all, the answer must be, despite his resentments and the counterattack on the cheese roll, that he came to deliver Ruth. His life as a thinker, as one disengaged, is almost by definition outside the orbit of the all-engaging wife-whore-mother whose demand is quite simple: "Look at me" (p. 52). The image of Ruth that he builds up—helping him write his lectures—is not borne out by anything else seen of her. To be sure, Teddy seems panic-stricken when he realizes that Ruth's involvement with his family is becoming too deep for him, but when it reaches a certain irretrievable depth, he grows more and more amenable. Although he fails to take up Lenny's offer to make him the American branch pimp (p. 74), it is he who opens negotiations for them with the comment, "If you like the idea I don't mind. We can manage very easily at home . . . until you come back" (p. 75), and he has the last word in outlining her family duties: "Keep everyone company" (p. 78). Ruth's final words to him, "Don't become a stranger" (p. 80), are both amusing and poignant; the warning comes a bit late.

Teddy's exit leaves us with a final tableau—almost the same, in fact, as that which resulted at the end of the first act from Max's hitting Joey and Sam: Lenny stands aside and watches as Max and Joey grovel at the feet of Ruth (one might say in both tableaux that Sam is simply out of it). The difference is that while the first tableau resulted from Max's violent assertion of authority, this one is the adequate expression of the motivation of each character, and Joey is now receiving the attentions of Ruth.

Lenny, the pimp, is as chauffeurlike as Sam, and his profession as midwife to the passions of others is carried out both within and outside the family. On one subtextual level he has been in conflict with Teddy over the possession of Ruth and with Ruth over the terms of his service to her; but at a deeper level he, like Teddy, has carried out the functions assigned to him by the fatalities of his nature.

All the males in the play are sterile; as Lenny says, "We've got rocks. But they're frozen stiff in the fridge" (p. 61). But Joey's case seems curable—immimently so. Joey is the spiritual descendant of Mac, and his present problem is not impotence but virginity. He has been held under the paternal/maternal hand of Max throughout the whole play; even during the time when Lenny and Max are considering the idea of keeping Ruth, and Joey is very excited, Max can control him with a parental tone: "Well, you *are* going to have to share her! Otherwise she goes straight back to America. You understand?" (p. 73). But Joey has also been subjected to some peremptory orders from Ruth (p. 60), and the indications at the end of the play are that Max's reign over him has come to an end.

Sam is right that the cycle of generations has returned the home to what it was in the lost golden age; the pattern is, in fact, schematically perfect:

$$\text{RUTH} \Longleftarrow \begin{matrix} \text{TEDDY} \\ \text{LENNY} \\ \text{JOEY} \end{matrix} \quad \begin{matrix} \text{(husband, father, cuckold)} \\ \text{(chauffeur-pimp)} \\ \text{(stud)} \end{matrix} \quad \begin{matrix} \text{MAX} \\ \text{SAM} \\ \text{MAC} \end{matrix} \Longrightarrow \text{JESSIE}$$

Although absent, Teddy is indeed still "an integral part of it" (p. 65), as Max had been when he was "going all over the country to find meat" (p. 46); and one can project Teddy homeward where he will rule his three restive sons until, presumably, one of them brings home a woman to dethrone him.

"I'm too old, I suppose" (p. 81). Max's complaint, which opens and closes the play and against which he makes a successful last stand as he first greets Ruth, finally convicts him—the table of organization has no place for him. He has lost Joey, and if Lenny is not monarch he is at least prime minister. The final line of the play, "Kiss me," is a fulfillment of the first line, "What have you done with the scissors?" Max has found them, but he does not have them. They have him.

The repetition of the cycle, the return to the relationships in the golden age of Jessie, does more, however, than enthrone Ruth as the dominant force in a power struggle. It is a cycle that suggests an inevitable series of relationships that are essential for survival. In ritual terms the woman as fertility goddess moves from the aging, dying god-king (winter) to the young or new god-king (spring), from the husband to the son. Inevitably, the wife and mother is also the whore. Through the aid of Sam, Jessie moved from Max to Mac. Through the aid of Lenny, Ruth moves from Teddy (and Max) to Joey.

SAM: She's got three children.
MAX: She can have more! Here. If she's so keen.
TEDDY: She doesn't want any more.
MAX: What do you know about what she wants, eh, Ted?

(P. 90)

As a fertility goddess, Ruth's choice must be for creation.

The image of Venice is never explained—we know its import only functionally in its opposition to America and in its appeal to Lenny and Ruth. Similarly, the whole world of Max's England is never defined as an alternative to America but is built up in a long series of associations. Ruth's action in crossing worlds "means" this whole complex of choices, but essentially it is less a choice between good and evil than a choice between life and death. Teddy operates on things, Ruth chooses to operate in things. England is the place where one's archetypal reality finds direct and powerful expression. England is, in fact, on-stage, while America is off-stage. America does not exist, nor does Teddy when he departs. Max's England, on the other hand, is palpable, with a role that Ruth begins to play simply by entering the stage.

Ruth's struggle is for more than power, then; it is a struggle for life. And the action that enthrones her is treated with both satire and sympathy. As Ruth contracts to stay on with the family, she beats them at their own game, and the civilized aspect of the contract is but a satirical exposue of the barbarities in civilization itself. Ruth is presented as both victorious and agonized, however, torn between the various roles she is compelled as woman to play. "It's about love and levels of love," Pinter has said of the play. "The people are harsh and cruel to be sure. Still they aren't acting arbitrarily but for very deep-seated reasons." The characters, he says, act "out of the texture of their lives and for reasons which are not evil but slightly desperate."[17] Pinter's satire is mixed with sympathy for his own version of that alien biblical Ruth who comes home in despair and makes her desperate choice for life.

Like the biblical Ruth, Pinter's Ruth is an outsider who chooses to leave her own people to follow in the footsteps of her mother-in-law. Although Ruth's husband in *The Homecoming* is not literally dead, Teddy is as dead as the biblical Ruth's husband for all intents and purposes. Whatever legal claim he may have, he relinquishes even as the nearest kinsman, Mr. So and So, relinquishes his claim in the biblical story. What seems, then, to be a lack of loyalty on Ruth's part is actually a deep loyalty akin to the biblical Ruth's that leads her to perpetuate the family of which she has become a part. Hugh Nelson points out as well the similarity of Ruth's late-night encounter with Lenny, in which he is aware that she is making "some kind of proposal," to the biblical Ruth's foray to the threshing floor where she proposes that her kinsman, Boaz, become her husband.[18]

The forwardness and the sexual aggression of both Ruths signify not only their strong motivation to survive but also their desire to contribute to the survival of the family. Seen in this light, the behavior of Pinter's Ruth is not so shocking, for as Steven Gale suggests, she operates in the play as a life force. "Max, Lenny, and Joey represent elements (food, sex, battle) necessary to forge a society with enough leisure and ease to permit philosophers and chauffeurs (inessential thought, luxury) to exist; and Ruth is the element out of which life is created and is, therefore, the most important and strongest of all forces, for she is closest to the basic drives of life (without which the others are meaningless)."[19]

Indeed, the potential is there at the play's end, it seems to me, for more than survival. Beneath the crudeness of Lenny is the inquiring philosopher, and beneath the stupidity of Joey as stud is a growing awareness of love. We do not know about Jessie's capacity for love, but we do know about Ruth's meaning to Joey; the theme of touching in the play gives the particular turn of the cyclic wheel a particular meaning for the individuality of the characters. When Max accepts Ruth as "kin" and "kith," they are both "touched," and beneath the mocking tone is the possibility of celebration. Lenny may not be able to receive or give the touch he originally demands, and Max may not be able to receive the kiss that is his final demand, but they find a place in her family; and Ruth's final action as *"she continues to touch Joey's head, lightly"* (p. 82) is in the form of a blessing.[20]

Vera Jiji, who notes "that the play is based upon the emotions and feelings of man at a very primitive stage of development," helps to clarify the universality of *The Homecoming*'s action and the nature of its celebration. In Freudian terms, she notes, what we have is "a living through again" of the basic "rebellion against the father, even as his ways are reaffirmed by repetition," as well as "the reconquest of the woman." What makes this "living through again" of primal actions positive is its ritual nature, the ritual having the kind of positive attributes assigned it by Eric Erikson, the interplay of its pattern allowing for "mutual recognition" and the certification of a sense of self allowing "for the expression of aggression and the reaffirmation of love."[21]

The individual fates of the men in their relationship with Ruth are less important in the play's final effect than their participation in the ritual in which they are more than individuals.

> The final tableau is a dramatization of silence. Teddy's protests have been stilled; Sam lies prostrate on the floor; Lenny, Joey, and Max are almost literally bowing before the seated Ruth. Their silence is a sign of recognition, a token of homage not so much to Ruth as to the train of collective associations which she carries behind her. The silence of the conclusion is the silence of kenosis wherein each of the characters has emptied himself in order to become fuller. Each of the characters, together the composite man, participates in something larger than the self. Each participates in the archetype of original unity, the return to the source, the homecoming.[22]

With the mutual homecoming so enacted, Godot arrives.

NOTES

1. Harold Pinter, *The Homecoming* (New York: Grove Press, 1965), p. 75. All subsequent quotations are from this edition.
2. George Bernard Shaw, *Saint Joan* in *Seven Plays by Bernard Shaw* (New York: Dodd, Mead & Co., 1951), p. 911.
3. *The Ruling Class* has many echoes of Pirandello's treatment of madness in his *Henry IV*.
4. Bernard Dukore in *The Theatre of Peter Barnes* writes, "In this elegantly wrought 'baroque comedy,' as Barnes subtitles *The Ruling Class*, the first act climaxes with the arrival of a newly born boy, the second with another type of birth, the arrival in society [as Jack the Ripper] of that child's father who is welcomed as a true member of the ruling class" (p. 25).
5. Pinter says of his own writing, "If you press me for a definition, I'd say that what goes on in my plays is realistic, but what I'm doing is not realism" ("Writing for Myself," *Twentieth Century* 169 [February 1961]: 174).
6. The day of Saint Barnabas, June 11 in the old-style calendar, was the day of the summer solstice, and Barnaby-bright is the name for the longest day and the shortest night of the year.
7. See Kristan Morrison's *Canters and Chronicles: The Use of Narrative in the Plays of Samuel Beckett and Harold Pinter* for a discussion of the use of such "yarns" or narratives in both Beckett's and Pinter's plays.
8. Earlier in the play Max comments, "I gave birth to three grown men. All on my own bat" (p. 40).

9. Paul Rogers, who initially played the part of Max, was guided by Pinter in his delivery of this speech. "If you read it the way it comes out," Rogers told John Lahr in an interview, "you get a picture which we often forget. How terrifying grown-ups are in sheer size to a little child. Poor little bugger didn't know if he'd come down in one piece . . ." (*A Casebook on Harold Pinter's The Homecoming*, ed. John Lahr [New York: Grove Press, 1971], p. 152).

10. Mircea Eliade, *Myth and Reality*, p. 30.

11. Rolf Fjelde, "Plotting Pinter's Progress," in *A Casebook on Harold Pinter's The Homecoming*, ed. John Lahr (New York: Grove Press, 1971), pp. 102–3.

12. Rolf Fjelde writes, "She has but one and the same nature, as Teddy has to learn: amoral, wide open, overtly the victim, covertly the aggressor—she will in time undoubtedly 'do the dirty' on them" ("Plotting Pinter's Progress," p. 105). Ruth, according to Steven M. L. Aronson, uses sex as "a way station toward complete dominance" ("Pinter's 'Family' and Blood Knowledge," in *A Casebook on Harold Pinter's The Homecoming*, ed. John Lahr [New York: Grove Press, 1971], p. 82. Hugh Nelson also finds "a total absence of values" in the characters' "animal struggle to survive and perpetuate itself" ("*The Homecoming:* Kith and Kin," in *Modern British Dramatists*, ed. John Russell Brown [Englewood Cliffs, N.J.: Prentice-Hall, 1968], p. 163).

13. James R. Hollis, *Harold Pinter: The Poetics of Silence*, p. 13.

14. Ibid., p. 17.

15. Ibid., p. 109.

16. Teddy, in fact, steps neatly into an identification with the Yankee who gave Sam the cigars by commenting over Sam's prostrate body that "I was going to ask him to drive me to London Airport" (p. 79).

17. Henry Hewes, "Probing Pinter's Play," *Saturday Review*, 8 April 1967, p. 56.

18. Nelson, *"The Homecoming"*, p. 156. The sexual ambiguity or inconclusiveness of Ruth's encounter upstairs with Joey is also akin to the inconclusiveness of the biblical Ruth's meeting with Boaz on the threshing floor; in each case certain legal proceedings must precede consummation.

19. Steven H. Gale, *Butter's Going Up: A Critical Analysis of Harold Pinter's Work*, p. 148.

20. An idea suggested by Professor Dorothy Laming.

21. Vera Jiji, "Pinter's Four Dimensional House: *The Homecoming*," *Modern Drama* 17, no. 4 (December 1974): 441.

22. Hollis, *Harold Pinter*, pp. 109–10.

9

Awakenings

At the climactic moment of Samuel Beckett's *Waiting for Godot,* after Pozzo and Lucky have made their second exit, Vladimir replaces high tragedy's traditional, Aristotelian moment of recognition with a tragicomic recognition that he will probably never have recognition. He wonders about the nature of his reality, of all reality.

> Was I sleeping, while the others suffered? Am I sleeping now? Tomorrow, when I wake, or think I do, what shall I say of to-day? That with Estragon my friend, at this place until the fall of night, I waited for Godot? That Pozzo passed with his carrier, and that he spoke to us? Probably. But in all that what truth will there be?
>
> (P. 58)

The Keatsian question lingers romantically on in modern drama—"Fled is that music:—Do I wake or sleep?"—but the twilight zone between day and night, waking and sleeping, life and death has become a frightening no-man's-land in which exiled characters listen in vain for the beautiful song of the nightingale. An antiromantic attitude disrupts the lyrical strain, and a new poetry emerges in which death, for example, is resisted only because it's impractical; one will not be admitted to the Eiffel Tower so ill-dressed or the rope is not strong enough to do the job. Shelley's moon rises at a rapid speed, and yet, "nothing happens, nobody comes, nobody goes, it's awful."

The moment of recognition for which Vladimir longs is that Sophoclean one in which Oedipus's discovery of himself affirms a mysterious order in the universe. In Beckett's plays as well as the others explored, Godot's arrival would confer that sense of existence, order, and wholeness for which, fragmented as we all are, we long. Ionesco writes, he insists, mainly to cry out that somehow he has existed, and Vladimir's final message to Godot is that he exists. "Tell him . . . *(he hesitates)* . . . tell him you saw me and that . . . *(he hesitates)* . . . that you saw me . . ." (p. 59). He has told Estragon that he felt seen by the blind Pozzo, but

Estragon assures him that he was dreaming. Perhaps, though, Pozzo was Godot and they did not recognize him. The agony of the play is that the uncertainty about the nature of Godot is an uncertainty about the self that continues to preclude a final awakening and the sense of arrival it would confer. Ionesco ends his parody of a recognition scene in *The Bald Soprano* with a brilliant stroke. After Mr. and Mrs. Smith deduce, through a long line of coincidences including the sharing of the same bed, that they are man and wife, they promptly fall asleep!

There are, of course, moments of arrival in *Waiting for Godot* and the other plays we have explored. Pozzo has located and accepted his position as an aimless wanderer, an eternal exile; the void has taken on a sacred quality for him that allows him to claim the "gleam" of light between birth and death as his. In O'Neill's *The Iceman Cometh* and in Ibsen's *The Wild Duck,* Larry and Old Ekdal experience similar arrivals, moments of acceptance in which they waken from their dreams, give up their illusions, and accept the dark, mysterious justice that in each play calls for a bloody sacrifice—in the one case of the guilty (Parritt-Hickey), in the other of the innocent (Hedvig).

But Pozzo, Old Ekdal, and Larry are significantly not the protagonists of their dramas, and so the arrivals at the dark knowledge of self and reality that they attain do not make salvation, even on their bleak terms, central to the experience of the plays. Emphasis is, instead, on the nonarrival of Godot or the arrival of false messiahs, such as Gregers and Hickey, who bring death or a death in life to most of the others in the plays.

Such peripheral awakenings, do, however, remain important elements in the plays. Even characters such as the Old Man and Old Woman of Ionesco's *The Chairs,* who like Harry Hope and his crew and the Ekdal family live on illusion, have their moments. Unrecognized by the invisible Emperor, separated even in suicide, Ionesco's elderly couple do unite briefly as they recall their arrival in Paris. Whether Paris existed or not and whether they arrived or not is immaterial. What counts is the feeling they have as they laugh together that they did arrive. The laughter they share as part of their nightly ritual of remembrance allows them to transcend their defeated lives and their mute orator; their return to the source of their joy is their momentary participation in the sacred. The tragicomic affirmation of the absurd unites illusion with reality as the couple travel on that borderline between the waking and sleeping state until they arrive, and with their "words" create Paris and Godot. Maddy and Dan Rooney share a similar moment in *All That Fall,* laughing at their own plight, at the very idea that God will uphold those who fall, and Nag laughs in *Endgame* at his own joke about the inferiority of God's creation to that of a tailor. The arrivals are minimal, fleeting, and absurd, but they are arrivals nevertheless.

And even when the plays lack authentic arrivals, like *The American Dream, The Birthday Party,* or *The Killer,* plays in which nightmare abounds, the playwrights confront the audience with an experience that challenges them to recognize that nightmare and hence to waken from it. Grandma leads us through the nightmare of *The American Dream,* sacrificing herself, departing rather than living in the nightmare, presenting us with her death as a means to help us awaken from the nightmare. There is no such guide in Pinter's *The Birthday Party,* but in both plays the parody of rebirth, which retains its ritual sacrifice, and the biting satire that attends the parody fling the challenge of awakening at us. As we experience the failure of Bérenger's search in Ionesco's *The Killer,* we are forced to confront Ionesco's vision of the nightmare of modern life, to move through it. Just as Vladimir refuses to hear Estragon's nightmares, we may refuse to hear Ionesco's, but there is no awakening from a nightmare that one denies. When Hirst refuses to accept his dream of drowning in *No Man's Land,* he elects that state between dreaming and waking, life and death, which gives the play its name.

Similarly lost in time and space, Krapp returns again and again in *Krapp's Last Tape* to his "Farewell to love" tape, yearning in vain for that womblike state in which he was moved gently by water while lying on the breast of his beloved. The inability truly to return to such ideal somnolence makes him a far more pathetic figure than the more heroic Hamm who, refusing to be discarded, chooses to discard his increasingly meager means to survival, awakening to a new sense of life even as he prepares for the great sleep of death. Krapp gives up his new birthday tape; Hamm finishes his chronicle. As in *The Chairs,* words, it seems, art, can save.[1]

In the plays we have explored in which Godot has been perceived as at the heart of the nightmare, a force to be exorcised, an experience of awakening has come with the completion of the rite of exorcism. Breaking through the layers of illusion that have imprisoned them in their fantasy world in *The Maids,* Claire's suicidal/murderous act liberates the sisters, giving them a new sense of identity in their defeat. Speaking of Claire, Oreste F. Pucciani writes, "She has by a triumph of imagination which requires her death become Madame. But at the same moment, though very briefly, she has become Claire. She has acquired a self. The scapegoat is a strange being, a sort of God; a myth. Claire is about to escape before our eyes into eternity. She will take Solange with her, for she is Claire, Solange, Madame, and myth."[2] By remembering her former roommate as "dead," a roommate who clearly, on some level, is a part of herself, Kate in *Old Times* emerges from the sleep of her past, speaks of a long purifying bath, and takes possession of herself.

Another kind of arrival is the one in Grass's *The Wicked Cooks* in which Vasco gains the Godot recipe only when he realizes that it is not a recipe and that the love that the Count and Martha share is not one of possession at all. The mutual conquest of Pinter's *The Homecoming* may involve power conflicts over possession, but here, too, the nightmare is mitigated by love, and the acceptance of the nightmare fabric of life allows that rebirth of Ruth as Jessie which promises new life to the family and to Ruth as a part of the family.

The peripheral and fleeting arrivals that are part of the fabric of so many of the plays give way to a full exploration of arrival in *The Homecoming*. The play does not end, as the biblical Book of Ruth does, with a genealogy, but just as the Book of Ruth suggests that her union with Boaz led eventually to the salvation of her adopted people through her great grandson, David, so *The Homecoming* suggests a possible redemption for the modern family as it regroups around its Ruth. "The ultimate adventure," Joseph Campbell says, speaking of his hero with a thousand faces, "when all barriers and ogres have been overcome, is commonly represented as a mystical marriage . . . of the triumphant hero-soul with the Queen Goddess of the World. This is the crisis at the nadir, the zenith, or at the uttermost edge of the earth, at the central point of the cosmos, in the tabernacle of the temple, or within the darkness of the deepest chambers of the heart."[3]

In *The Homecoming* this "ultimate adventure" takes place at the center, the home, and it involves bringing to light the darkest of feelings. In Campbell's terms, Ruth comes to represent all that can be known by the hero who must accept her in her duality and in her multiplicity of roles if together they are to be "released from every limitation. The hero who can take her [the goddess] as she is, without undue commotion but with the kindness and assurance she requires, is potentially the king, the incarnate god, of her created world."[4] With Ruth and her new family's mutual acceptance of each other, we celebrate the potential freedom of an authentic arrival of Godot.

In Pinter's most recent short dramas, collected in a volume he calls *Other Places*, the arrival of Godot is again in question. The young man of *Family Voices* is subject to the fatalities of an Oedipal dilemma that makes movement to other places and a homecoming impossible.[5] But if the Young Man is trapped in a no-man's-land, the characters in *A Kind of Alaska* and *Victoria Station* are again on the move, and the arrival of Godot is again connected with an awakening.

In *A Kind of Alaska,* Deborah is just returning from other places that her doctor designates as "a kind of Alaska." On a literal or realistic level, Deborah is the disoriented victim of a sleeping sickness who has fallen into a trancelike state in her adolescence, at the age of sixteen, emerging twenty-nine years later as a forty-five-year-old woman. On a less literal, archetypal level, Deborah's disorientation is akin to that of the characters in *Waiting for Godot*. Her inability to grasp her age, the place, or time and to recognize those about her suggests the fragmentation of the modern predicament. As in *Godot*, her disorientation seems to express both her lost condition and a progress toward a fundamental reorientation and rebirth, a true awakening.

Deborah, in fact, clings to the idea that she is soon to have a birthday, and her doctor promises her a party much as Lenny promised Ruth liquor in *The Homecoming* should there be cause for celebration. As with the other absent or present birthday parties in the plays explored, this birthday party hovers in the play, suggesting the struggle with rebirth, sometimes successful, sometimes not, that is a vital part of its action.

As Deborah awakens from her long sleep in *A Kind of Alaska*, she does not, like the Sleeping Beauty of the fairy tale, accept the hand of the prince—"And you are my Prince Charming. Aren't you?"[6]—who has awakened her. Deborah is clearly not the fairy tale Sleeping Beauty to whom feminist writers have so often objected as a figure of feminine passivity, one who depends upon the arrival of Prince Charming for her awakening and her happiness.[7] Nor is Pinter's Deborah the victim of a patriarchal society such as Anne Sexton depicts in her poem "Briar Rose (Sleeping Beauty)," one who awakens to total nightmare. "Each night I am nailed into place/and I forget who I am," grieves Sexton's heroine, who goes on to identify her Prince Charming as an incestuous father "thick upon me/like some sleeping jellyfish,"[8] and to agonize over her awakening.

Pinter's Deborah is as antiromantic and as aware of herself as a sacrificial figure as Sexton's heroine is, but she is not as despairing. In *The Uses of Enchantment*, Bruno Bettelheim considers male and female fairy-tale heroes to be "projections onto two different figures of two (artificially) separated aspects of one and the same process which *everybody* has to undergo in growing up. While some literal-minded parents do not realize it," he claims, "children know that, whatever the sex of the hero, the story pertains to their own problems."[9] While Deborah is clearly dealing with the sexual awakening that Bettelheim interprets the Sleeping Beauty fairy tale to be about,[10] she becomes more than an ill-used women; in her combination of physical age and mental youth and in her Beckettian struggle to become truely awake, Deborah comes to represent the effort of all of us, male and female, to move to some meaningful kind of rebirth.

In *A Kind of Alaska,* the role of Prince Charming devolves upon Dr. Hornby, who has left his wife, Deborah's sister, in order to watch over Deborah. Dr. Hornby is questioned and examined by Deborah even as he seeks to question her about her experience. While it seems to the doctor that Deborah has "ventured into quite remote . . . utterly foreign . . . territories" (p. 35), his effort being to chart her "itinerary," it seems to Deborah at her awakening that she is in a very strange, foreign territory now and that she must learn to chart her present itinerary. Her first words, "Something is happening" (p. 5), which she repeats after Hornby explains that she is waking from a sleep of many years and that her mind has been suspended "in a kind of Alaska," seem like an echo of *Endgame*'s "Something is taking its course" (p. 13). The suggestion in both plays is that the action is moving on a deep, unconscious level, just as life moves on that deeper level, and that we sense or are at times in touch with that level.

When Hornby asks to be recognized—"Do you know me? . . . Can you hear me? . . . Who am I?" (pp. 5–6)—Deborah responds, "No-one hears what I say. No-one is listening to me." When the doctor persists in asking for recognition, she informs him that he is "no-one" (p. 6). Hornby, it seems, has failed as a Prince Charming to penetrate to her world, to hear her, and his present explanations seem to her remote and strange—nothing. When Deborah complains that the dog who has awakened her with his "turning about" is dreaming and "not himself up" (p. 7), the suggestion is that the doctor who has awakened her is himself dreaming and not himself awake.

In one sense Hornby is nothing or dead since he proclaims his wife a widow. "Your sister Pauline was twelve when you were left for dead. When she was twenty I married her. She is a widow. I have lived with you" (p. 35). In *Victoria Station,* also a short piece in *Other Places,* a cab driver conversing with his controller suggests at one point that he has a wife and daughter at home. His wife, he says, is "probably asleep,"[11] and when questioned about his daughter he says he thinks "that's what she is" (p. 55). But at the present he has a passenger in the car asleep on the back seat with whom he is deeply in love and with whom he plans to spend his life. In each case, why this bizarre fascination with a sleeping woman? Symbolically, these men desire to share in the forthcoming awakening, possibly the awakening of some more feminine part of themselves, but certainly an awakening that will bring them out of their own kind of Alaska, the one in which, to some degree, we all dwell.

Deborah's awakening is replete with the conflicts of any adolescent coming into womanhood, aggravated in this case by womanhood's sudden arrival. She is fascinated with Hornby, whom she imagines has violated her and whom she suspects she has encouraged in some way that would bring on the disapproval of her mother.

> You shouldn't have touched me like that. I shan't tell my mother. I shouldn't have touched you like that.
>
> (P. 10)

When informed that her mother and father brought her to the place where she has been awakened by Dr. Hornby, Deborah imagines herself as a sacrifice. "Did they sacrifice me to you?" (p. 12). She insists that he has "ruined" her, and she vacillates between her feeling of guilt—"I've obviously committed a criminal offense and am now in prison" (p. 17)—and her sense of her own desires—"I think I love you" (p. 20). To protect herself from her mixed feelings, she uses the clichés that have surrounded her youth.

> I've had enough of this. Find Jack. I'll say yes. We'll have kids. I'll bake apples. I'm ready for it. No point in hanging about. Best foot forward. Mummy's motto. . . .
>
> (P. 20)

On a psychological level, then, Deborah seems to be suffering from adolescent, Oedipal conflict. Her sister Pauline is a "bitch" for suggesting that her father has a mistress, and Pauline also suspects Deborah of the worst sexual abandonment. "Pauline always says I'll end up as part of the White Slave Traffic" (p. 14). The "something" that is happening has in some way to do with her growing up and becoming a woman. It is while moving a vase the better to see her father that Deborah is overtaken with her illness. "Daddy is kind and so is Mummy. We all have breakfast together every morning in the kitchen. What's happening?" (p. 21).

The depth of Deborah's conflict may, it seems, even have caused her to escape into sleep. She identifies herself with her two sisters—"We're very close. We love each other. We're known as the three bluebells" (p. 13)—but is critical of Pauline for being too talkative and witty—"You'll bite your own tongue off one of these days and I'll keep your tongue in a closed jar and you'll never ever ever ever be witty again" (p. 13). Pauline, though, she assures us, is all right, while Estelle, her other sister, is "deep" and "sen-su-al." Apparently both characteristics are dangerous. The depth of Deborah's fear of her own self-expression and sensuality may then be assessed as she claims she does not want to see Pauline. "People don't want to see their sisters," she explains. "Sisters are diabolical. Brothers are worse. One day I prayed I would see no-one ever again, none of them ever again . . ." (p. 18). Deborah's prayer has very nearly come to pass.

Her description of her long sleep, which she relives at moments during the play, suggests a tremendous repression of Deborah's emerging sensuality and her ambivalent feelings. "Nothing has happened to me. I've been nowhere" (p. 17), she insists when questioned. While dancing in slow motion, she explains that she has "been dancing in narrow spaces . . . Like Alice" (p. 24). The dancing, like Alice's experiences in Wonderland, has been arduous, "like dancing with someone dancing on your foot all the time" (p. 25), although apparently there were breaks in the space which "opened and became light," allowing her to become light and to dance "till dawn night after night after night, night after night . . ." (p. 26). Later she senses that the walls are closing in on her, and she feels as if she is in a vice. "I'll tell you what it is. It's a vast series of halls. With enormous interior windows masquerading as walls. The windows are mirrors, you see. And so glass reflects glass. For ever and ever" (p. 39).

Water is dripping, and Deborah explains that she had been unable to communicate with them in her "vast hall of glass with a tap dripping" (p. 39). Since the walls that have closed her in are really mirror/windows, it would appear that she is closed in by her own image, the dripping water suggesting an even more regressive return to the womb. The various other references in the play to water suggest the rebirth process through which she is going. "Why is everything so quiet? So still? I'm in a sandbox. The sea? Is that what I hear?" (p. 13), she asks early in the play, later deciding to plunge into life. "I'm going to run into the sea and fall into the waves. I'm going to rummage about in all the water" (p. 33). Here is both regression, a return to the womb, and progression, a new reaching out and exploration of the waters of life.

One may be tempted to view Deborah as merely an adolescent unable to deal with her emerging womanhood who has regressed into a state of latency from which she is seen to reemerge. But like the characters in almost all of Pinter's dramas, Deborah is more than a psychological case. She is the sacrificial victim she has sensed herself to be, the scapegoat who is to redeem those who circle around her. She is a part of Estelle, who, like Antigone, takes care of a blind father, and she is part of Pauline, bereft of a husband. As a scapegoat, Deborah's tale is less one of a ludicrous disease, a special case history, and more one of an archetypal struggle for a true awakening.

The question of sleep as such is universalized in the play in several telling ways. I have already mentioned the sleeping dog that Deborah says is waking her up but is himself still asleep, a clear reference to Dr. Hornby. Pauline, however, makes another reference to a long sleep. When she lies to Deborah about her parents' and her other sister's absence, Pauline locates them on a cruise, traveling, like Deborah has, on water. "Estelle also . . . needed a total break" (p. 28), she explains, not seeming to notice that the "also" must refer to Deborah and her total break with the everyday reality they endure. Yet another reference to sleep is made by Deborah in connection with Pauline. When Pauline's presence is announced by Hornby, Deborah protests that she should not be there at this time of night. "I'm always telling her. She needs her beauty sleep. Like I do, by the way" (p. 16). The doubling among the sisters is clear here, as Deborah's long sleep becomes both a "total break" and a "beauty sleep," which we may all need at times.

Indeed, Bruno Bettelheim reminds us of the virtues of "The Sleeping Beauty" in which the passivity of sleep may be interpreted in a positive way. We tend today, Bettelheim notes, to fear periods of "quiet growth" as if accomplishments were only measurable in what can be seen. But "the Sleeping Beauty tells that a long period of quiescence, of contemplation, of concentration on the self, can and often does lead to highest achievement."[13]

Such achievement is difficult to measure as Deborah wakes up, but she does transcend her disoriented sense of secular time. When Dr. Hornby tries to calm her down as she recalls her hate for her sisters and imaginary brothers, he suggests that "Tomorrow . . . is another day." She resists; "No it isn't. No it isn't. It is not!" (p. 18). Like Pozzo, Deborah senses that "they give birth astride of a grave." Although she yearns for a birthday with presents she can keep that, unlike her, will not become lost, she knows, like Pozzo, that tomorrow and today are "the same day," and that the past and future are both a living part of the mysterious present that she so struggles to claim. At the end of the play, Deborah tries to assess her situation.

> You say I have been asleep. You say I am now awake. You say I have not awoken from the dead. You say I was not dreaming then and am not dreaming now. You say I have always been alive and am alive now. You say I am a woman.
>
> (P. 40)

Once again we recall Vladimir in *Waiting for Godot* watching the sleeping Estragon and wondering about the degree to which he himself is awake or alive or real. Dr. Hornby has explained to Deborah that she has been "nowhere" and "it is we who have suffered" (p. 34). Vladimir has wondered if he, like Estragon, was sleeping while the others suffered. Having been to other places, Deborah is no longer sure of this place. All of the things that she has been told and that she repeats become questions rather than certainties. They tell her that she is a woman, but what is it to be a woman? Surely the play explores the complexities and uncertainties of being a woman or rather of becoming a woman and of becoming a person. And what we experience as we watch Pinter's Sleeping Beauty wake up and assess her situation is an assessment of our own.

Selecting some of the lies and some of the "truths" they have told her, Deborah looks first at Pauline and then at Hornby, completing her rebirth with an acceptance of the world she is offered.

> She is a widow. She doesn't go to her ballet classes any more. Mummy and Daddy and Estelle are on a world cruise. They've stopped off in Bangkok. It'll be my birthday soon. I think I have the matter in proportion.
> *Pause*
> Thank you.
>
> (P. 40)

If the speech were not so poignant, it would be simply ludicrous, since her arrangement of the facts she has been offered falls so short of accounting for Deborah's experience or for life. On another level, however, the words are adequate to the experience and to life. Widowhood, loss—there will be no Prince Charming; the end of ballet classes and the loss of youth; the absence of family, who, like Deborah, are traveling the world—more loss. And yet there will be a birthday. Deborah accepts herself in what seems to be the strange proportions of this world, and she is even thankful. If Deborah is able to find herself amid so much loss, then her trip to a kind of Alaska has not been in vain and her return may offer us a new awakening.

At the inception of modern drama, Ibsen's Hedda Gabler, trapped in a repressed society, makes a point of not showing her leg; Hedda can rebel only through surreptitiously cruel acts and suicide. Pinter's Ruth, however, calls attention to her leg; Ruth finds value in herself and the desperate needs of the family, which Ibsen has satirized, but with which Pinter has identified and to which Ruth responds. In its evolution modern drama has not been without its suicides—Hedvig, Parritt, the Old Couple in *The Chairs,* Claire, the Count and Martha in *The Wicked Cooks,* to name but a few we have encountered, have all, for a variety of reasons, taken their place as ritual scapegoats, embracing their own deaths. But the possibilities of rebirth have actually grown stronger as Godot has taken many forms to which the protagonists of modern drama respond.

When the controller in *Victoria Station* cannot seem to remain in control—the driver, number 274, has never heard of Victoria Station and is not interested in picking up the passenger with a limp, fishing equipment, and a feather in his hat, the wounded fisher-king of old, who waits for him there—the controller finally sets forth to find the driver. The driver is parked by a "dark park" next to what he envisions as the Crystal Palace, which the controller informs him "burnt down years ago, old son" (p. 57). He is guarding his own sleeping beauty in the back seat of his cab. Infuriated by the driver's recalcitrance, and increasingly obsessed with him, the controller, who is "alone in this miserable freezing fucking office" (p. 58), unloved, and on the verge, he says, of death, valiantly sets forth to find him.

> CONTROLLER: Don't move. Stay exactly where you are . . . I'll be right with you.
> DRIVER: No, I won't move.
> *Silence.*
> I'll be here.
> *Light out in office.*
> *The DRIVER sits still.*
> *Light out in Car.*
>
> (P. 62)

The old god/king has become as irrelevant as Victoria Station where he must be stranded. The new god/king sits still in his cab, his sleeping passenger a part of his own potential awakening. Ruth has left her American family, the driver has left his wife and child at home, and the controller leaves all logic, all his dying values behind as with a leap of faith, he sets forth in search of Godot.

NOTES

1. The struggle of Beckett's plays, in a Lacanian sense, is between the regressive behavior of Krapp, who yearns to be reunited with the m(other), and the effort to accept the words or language that come with the Oedipal phase and the Law of the Father. See Ellie Ragland-Sullivan, "Jacques Lacan: Feminism and the Problem of Gender identity," *Sub-Stance* 11, no. 36 (1982): 6–20 for an unusually clear discussion of this conflict.

2. Oreste F. Pucciani, "Tragedy, Genet, and *The Maids*," *Tulane Drama Review* 7, no. 3 (Spring 1963): 58.

3. Joseph Campbell, *The Hero with a Thousand Faces*, p. 109.

4. Ibid., p. 116. Ann Rowlett led me to Campbell's account of the meeting with the goddess as it applies to *The Homecoming* in her seminar paper, "The Function of the Female in Yeats' *On Baile's Strand* and *Purgatory* and in Pinter's *The Homecoming*," 30 Nov. 1984.

5. See my chapter, "*Family Voices* and the Voice of the Family," in *Harold Pinter: Critical Approaches*, ed. Steven H. Gale, for a full discussion of the play.

6. Harold Pinter, *A Kind of Alaska* in *Other Places: Three Plays by Harold Pinter* (New York: Grove Press, 1981, 1982), p. 19. All subsequent references to *A Kind of Alaska* are from this edition.

7. In *Kiss Sleeping Beauty Good-bye*, Madonna Kulbenschlag, for example, not only sees the Sleeping Beauty as "a symbol of passivity"; she sees her as well as "a metaphor for the spiritual condition of woman—cut off from autonomy and transcendence, from self-actualization and ethical capacity in a male-dominated milieu" (p. 5).

8. Anne Sexton, "Briar Rose (Sleeping Beauty)," in *Transformations*, p. 112.

9. Bruno Bettelheim, *The Uses of Enchantment: The Meaning and Importance of Fairy Tales*, p. 226.

10. Ibid., p. 233.

11. Harold Pinter, *Victoria Station* in *Other Places: Three Plays by Harold Pinter* (New York: Grove Press, 1981, 1982), p. 55. All subsequent references to *Victoria Station* are from this edition.

12. In Martin Esslin's chapter on Jean Genet in *The Theatre of the Absurd,* "A Hall of Mirrors" (pp. 200–233), he suggests that Genet's account of a friend caught in a hall of mirrors at a fairground is a key to the playright's theatre. "The image expresses the essence of Genet's theatre, the image of man caught in a maze of mirrors, trapped by his own distorted reflection, trying to find the way to make contact with the others he can see around him but being rudely stopped by barriers of glass" (p. 200).

13. Bettelheim, *The Uses of Enchantment,* p. 226.

Works Cited

Albee, Edward. *The American Dream*. In *The American Dream and The Zoo Story: Two Plays by Edward Albee*. New York: The New American Library, Signet Books, 1961.

Anders, Gunther. "Being Without Time: On Beckett's Play *Waiting for Godot*." In *Samuel Beckett: A Collection of Critical Essays*. Edited by Martin Esslin. Englewood Cliffs, N.J.: Prentice-Hall, 1965.

Aristotle. *Aristotle's Poetics*. Translated by S. H. Butcher. Edited by Francis Fergusson. New York: Hill & Wang, 1961.

Aronson, Steven M. L. "Pinter's 'Family' and Blood Knowledge." In *A Casebook on Harold Pinter's The Homecoming*, edited by John Lahr. New York: Grove Press, 1971.

Artaud, Antonin. *The Theatre and Its Double*. Translated by Mary Caroline Richards. New York: Grove Press, 1958.

Aslan, Odette. *Jean Genet*. Théâtre de tous les temps 24. Paris: Éditions Seghers, 1973.

Balliett, Whitney. "Off Broadway: Three Cheers for Albee." *The New Yorker*, 4 February 1961, pp. 63–66.

Beckett, Samuel. *Endgame*. New York: Grove Press, 1958.

———. *Krapp's Last Tape and Other Dramatic Pieces*. New York: Grove Press, 1957.

———. *Proust*. New York: Grove Press, 1970.

———. *Waiting for Godot*. New York: Grove Press, 1954.

Bettleheim, Bruno. *The Uses of Enchantment: The Meaning and Importance of Fairy Tales*. New York: Alfred A. Knopf, 1976.

Brée, Germain. "Ionesco's Later Plays: Experiments in Dramatic Form." In *The Two Faces of Ionesco*, edited by Rosette C. Lamont and Melvin J. Friedman. Troy, N.Y.: The Whitson Publishing Co., 1978.

Brook, Peter. "Freud's Masterplot." *Yale French Studies* 55/56 (1977): 280–300.

Brooks, Curtis M. "The Mythic Pattern in *Waiting for Godot*." *Modern Drama* 9, no. 3 (December 1966): 292–99.

Brustein, Robert. *The Theatre of Revolt: An Approach to the Modern Drama*. Boston and Toronto: Little Brown & Co., an Atlantic Monthly Press Book, 1964.

Burkman, Katherine. "*Family Voices* and the Voice of the Family in

Pinter's Plays." In *Harold Pinter: Critical Approaches*, edited by Steven H. Gale. Rutherford, N.J.: Fairleigh Dickinson University Press, 1986.

———. "Opening Walls: Two Stories by Eugène Ionesco." *The Midwest Quarterly* 21, no. 4 (Summer 1980): 412–22.

Busi, Frederick. *The Transformations of Godot*. Lexington: The University Press of Kentucky, 1980.

Calarco, N. Joseph. *Tragic Being: Apollo and Dionysus in Western Drama*. Minneapolis: The University of Minnesota Press, 1969.

Campbell, Joseph. *The Hero with a Thousand Faces*. Princeton: Princeton University Press, 1972.

Camus, Albert. *The Myth of Sisyphus and Other Essays*. Translated by Justin O'Brien. New York: Vintage Books, 1955.

Carmier, Ramono, and Pallister, Janis L. *Waiting for Death: The Philosophical Significance of Beckett's En Attendant Godot*. University, Ala.: The University of Alabama Press, 1979.

Cetta, Lewis. *Profane Play, Ritual and Jean Genet: A Study of His Drama*. University, Ala. The University of Alabama Press, 1974.

Chabrowe, Leonard. "Dionysus in *The Iceman Cometh*." *Modern Drama* 4, no. 4 (February 1962): 377–88.

Coe, Richard N. *Eugène Ionesco*. 1st Evergreen ed. New York: Grove Press, Evergreen Pilot Books, 1961.

Cohn, Ruby. *Edward Albee*. Minneapolis: University of Minnesota Press, 1969.

———. "Words Working Overtime: *Endgame* and *No Man's Land*." *Yearbook of English Studies* 9 (1979): 188–203.

Driver, Tom F. *Romantic Quest and Modern Query: A History of the Modern Theatre*. New York: Delacorte Press, 1970.

Dubois, Jacques. "Beckett and Ionesco: The Tragic Awareness of Pascal and the Ironic Awareness of Flaubert." *Modern Drama* 9, no. 3 (December 1966): 283–91.

DuKore, Bernard F. *The Theatre of Peter Barnes*. London and Exeter: W. H. Heinemann, 1981.

Eliade, Mircea. "Eugène Ionesco and 'La Nostalgie du Paradis'." In *The Two Faces of Ionesco*, edited by Rosette C. Lamont and Melvin J. Friedman. Troy, N.Y.: The Whitson Publishing Co., 1978.

———. *Myth and Reality*. Translated by Willard R. Trask. New York: Harper Colophon Books, Harper & Row, Publishers, 1975.

———. *Rites and Symbols of Initiation: The Mysteries of Birth and Rebirth*. Translated by Willard R. Trask. The Library of Religion and Culture, edited by Benjamin Nelson. New York: Harper Colophone Books, Harper & Row, Publishers, 1975.

———. *The Sacred and the Profane: The Nature of Religion*. Translated by Willard R. Trask. New York: A Harvest Book, Harcourt, Brace & World, 1957.

Esslin, Martin. "Godot and His Children: The Theatre of Samuel Beckett and Harold Pinter." In *Modern British Dramatists: A Collection of Critical Essays*, edited by John Russell Brown. Twentieth Century Views. Englewood Cliffs, N.J.: Prentice-Hall, 1968.

———. ed. *Samuel Beckett: A Collection of Critical Essays*. Englewood Cliffs, N.J.: Prentice-Hall, 1965.

———. *The Theatre of the Absurd*. 3d ed., rev. and enl. New York: Penguin Books, 1983.

Fergusson, Francis. *The Idea of a Theater: A Study of Ten Plays*. Princeton: Princeton University Press, 1968.

Fjelde, Rolf. "Plotting Pinter's Progress." In *A Casebook on Harold Pinter's The Homecoming*, edited by John Lahr. New York: Grove Press, 1971.

Frazer, Sir James George. *The Golden Bough*. Abridged ed. in 1 vol. New York: The Macmillan Co., 1951.

Freud, Sigmund. *The Interpretation of Dreams*. Translated and edited by James Strachey. New York: Avon, Discus Books, 1965.

———. "The Theme of the Three Casketts." *The Standard Edition of the Complete Psychological Works of Sigmund Freud*, vol. 12. Translated and edited by James Strachey. London: The Hogarth Press, 1938.

———. "The 'Uncanny.'" *The Standard Edition of the Complete Psychological Works of Sigmund Freud*, vol. 17. Translated and edited by James Strachey. London: The Hogarth Press, 1938.

Frye, Northrop. *Anatomy of Criticism: Four Essays*. Princeton: Princeton University Press, 1971.

Gabbard, Lucina P. *The Dream Structure of Pinter's Plays: A Psychoanalytic Approach*. Rutherford, N.J.: Fairleigh Dickinson University Press; London: Associated University Presses, 1976.

Gale, Steven H. *Butter's Going Up: A Critical Analysis of Harold Pinter's Work*. Durham, N.C.: Duke University Press, 1977.

Ganz, Arthur. *Realms of the Self: Variations on a Theme in Modern Drama*. New York: New York University Press, 1955.

Gelb, Arthur, and Gelb, Barbara. *O'Neill*. Abridged ed. New York: Dell Publishing Co., Laurel ed., 1965.

Genet, Jean. *Les Bonnes*. In *Les Bonnes & Comment Jouer Les Bonnes*. Paris: L'Arbalète, Marc Barbezat, 1963.

———. *The Maids*. In *The Maids and Deathwatch: Two Plays by Jean Genet*. Translated by Bernard Frechtman. New York: Grove Press, 1962.

Gitenet, Jean. "Profane and Sacred Reality in Jean Genet's Theatre." Translated by Janie Vanpée. In *Genet: A Collection of Critical Essays*, edited by Peter Brooks and Joseph Halpern. Twentieth Century Views Series, edited by Maynard Mack. Englewood Cliffs, N.J.: Prentice-Hall, a Spectrum Book, 1979.

Gontarski, Stanley E. "Birth Astride of a Grave: Samuel Beckett's 'Act Without Words 1.'" *Journal of Beckett Studies* (Winter 1976): 37–40.

Gorden, Lois C. *Stratagems to Uncover Nakedness: The Dramas of Harold Pinter*. Columbia: University of Missouri Press, 1968.

Grass, Günter. *The Wicked Cooks.* Translated by Leslie Willson. In *Four Plays.* New York: Harcourt, Brace & World, 1967.

Hassan, Ahab. *The Dismemberment of Orpheus: Toward a Postmodern Literature.* 2d ed. Madison: University of Wisconsin Press, 1982.

Hesla, David H. *The Shape of Chaos: An Interpretation of the Art of Samuel Beckett.* Minneapolis: The University of Minnesota Press, 1971.

Hewes, Henry. "Probing Pinter's Play." *Saturday Review,* 8 April 1967, p. 56.

Hinchcliffe, Arnold P. *Harold Pinter.* Twayne's English Author Series. New York: Twayne, 1967.

Hollis, James R. *Harold Pinter: The Poetics of Silence.* Crosscurrents/Modern Critiques, edited by Harry T. Moore. Carbondale and Edwardsville: Southern Illinois University Press, 1970.

Holtan, Orley I. *Mythic Patterns in Ibsen's Last Plays.* Minneapolis: University of Minnesota Press, 1970.

Hubbs, Clayton A. "Chekhov and the Contemporary Theatre." *Modern Drama* 24, no. 3 (September 1981): 357–66.

Hughes, Alan. "'They Can't Take That Away From Me': Myth and Memory in Pinter's *Old Times*." *Modern Drama* 17, no. 4 (December 1974): 467–76.

Hurt, James. *Cataline's Dream: An Essay on Ibsen's Plays.* Urbana: University of Illinois Press, 1972.

Ibsen, Henrik. *The Wild Duck.* In *Henrik Ibsen, Plays: One.* Translated and introduced by Michael Meyer. The Master Playwrights series. London: Eyre Metheun, 1980.

Innes, Christopher. *Holy Theatre: Ritual and the Avant Garde.* Cambridge: Cambridge University Press, 1981.

Ionesco, Eugène. *The Chairs.* In *Four Plays by Eugène Ionesco.* Translated by Donald M. Allen. New York: Grove Press, 1958.

———. *Les Chaises.* In *Eugène Ionesco Theatre I.* Paris: Gallimard, 1962.

———. *The Killer.* In *The Killer and Other Plays by Eugène Ionesco.* Translated by Donald Watson. New York: Grove Press, 1960.

———. *Tueur Sans Gages.* In *Theatre D'Eugène Ionesco II.* Paris: Gallimard, 1962.

———. "Why Do I Write" A Summing Up." Translated by Rosette C. Lamont. In *The Two Faces of Ionesco,* edited by Rosette C. Lamont and Melvin J. Friedman. Troy, N.Y.: The Whitson Publishing Co., 1978.

Jiji, Vera. "Pinter's Four Dimensional House: *The Homecoming*." *Modern Drama* 17, no. 4 (December 1974): 433–42.

Jones, John Bush. "Stasis as Structure in Pinter's *No Man's Land*." *Modern Drama* 19, no. 3 (September 1976): 291–304.

Kluckhohn, Clyde. "Myth and Ritual: A General Theory." In *Myth and Literature: Contemporary Theory and Practice,* edited by John B. Vickery. Lincoln: University of Nebraska Press, 1966.

Kulbenschlag, Madonna. *Kiss Sleeping Beauty Good-Bye.* New York: Doubleday and Co., 1979.

Kundera, Milan. *The Book of Laughter and Forgetting.* Writers From the Other Europe series, edited by Philip Roth. Penguin Books, 1981.

Lahr, John. "An Actor's Approach: An Interview With Paul Rogers." In *A Casebook on Harold Pinter's The Homecoming,* edited by John Lahr. New York: Grove Press, 1971.

Lamont, Rosette C. "Father of the Man." In *The Two Faces of Ionesco,* edited by Rosette C. Lamont and Melvin J. Friedman. Troy, N.Y.: The Whitson Publishing Co., 1978.

———. "*L'Homme aux Valises:* Ionesco's Absolute Stranger." In *The Two Faces of Ionesco,* edited by Rosette C. Lamont and Melvin J. Friedman. Troy, N.Y.: The Whitson Publishing Co., 1978.

Leonard, Irene. *Günter Grass.* New York: Barnes & Noble, 1974.

McMahon, Joseph H. *The Imagination of Jean Genet.* Yale Romantic Studies, Second Series, 10. New Haven and London: Yale University Press, 1963.

Malpas, Edward. "A Critical Analysis of the Stage Plays of Harold Pinter." Ph.D. dissertation, University of Wisconsin, 1965.

Manvell, Roger. "The Decade of Harold Pinter." *Humanist* 132 (April 1967): 112–15.

Maughlin, Susan. "The Play Within the Play in *Endgame.*" A student paper written for my course in modern drama, 1983.

Mercier, Vivian. *Beckett/Beckett.* New York: Oxford University Press, 1977.

Metman, Eva. "Reflections on Samuel Beckett's Plays." In *Samuel Beckett: A Collection of Critical Essays,* edited by Martin Esslin. Englewood Cliffs, N.J.: Prentice-Hall, 1965.

Mihalyi, Gabor. "Beckett's 'Godot' and the Myth of Alienation." *Modern Drama* 9, no. 3 (December 1966): 277–82.

Miles, Keith. *Günter Grass.* Vision Critical Series, edited by Anne Smith. London: Vision Press Ltd., 1975.

Morrison, Kristan. *Canters and Chronicles: The Use of Narrative in the Plays of Samuel Beckett and Harold Pinter.* Chicago: The University of Chicago Press, 1983.

Nelson, Hugh. "*The Homecoming:* Kith and Kin." In *Modern British Dramatists: A Collection of Critical Essays,* edited by John Russell Brown. Twentieth Century Views. Englewood Cliffs, N.J.: Prentice-Hall, 1968.

Nichols, Dudley. "Dudley Nichols on *The Iceman Cometh.*" In *Twentieth Century Interpretations of The Iceman Cometh,* edited by John Henry Raleigh. Englewood Cliffs, N.J.: Prentice-Hall, 1968.

Nietzsche, Friedrich. *The Birth of Tragedy and the Case of Wagner.* Translated by Walter Kaufmann. New York: Vintage Books, 1967.

Nigro, Don. "In Search of Lost Krapp." Paper read at the First Annual Symposium in the Humanities, Samuel Beckett: Humanistic Perspectives, 8 May 1981, at The Ohio State University.

Northam, John. *Ibsen: A Critical Study*. Cambridge: Cambridge University Press, 1973.

Oates, Joyce Carol. "Chekhov and the Theatre of the Absurd." In *Drama and Discussion*, 2d ed., edited by Stanley A. Clayes. Englewood Cliffs, N.J.: Prentice-Hall, 1978.

O'Neill, Eugene. *The Iceman Cometh*. New York: Vintage Books, 1946.

Paolucci, Anne. *From Tension to Tonic: The Plays of Edward Albee*. Crosscurrents/Modern Critiques, edited by Harry T. Moore. Carbondale and Edwardsville: Southern Illinois University Press, 1972.

Pinter, Harold. *A Kind of Alaska*. In *Other Places: Three Plays by Harold Pinter*. New York: Grove Press, 1981, 1982.

―――. *The Birthday Party*. In *The Birthday Party and The Room: Two Plays by Harold Pinter*. New York: Grove Press, 1960.

―――. *The Homecoming*. New York: Grove Press, 1965.

―――. *Old Times*. New York: Grove Press, 1971.

―――. *Victoria Station*. In *Other Places: Three Plays by Harold Pinter*. New York: Grove Press, 1981, 1982.

―――. "Writing for Myself." In *Twentieth Century* 169 (February 1961): 172–75.

Pronko, Leonard. *Eugène Ionesco*. New York: Columbia University Press, 1965.

Pucciani, Oreste F. "Tragedy, Genet and *The Maids*." *Tulane Drama Review* 7, no. 3 (Spring 1963): 42–59.

Ragland-Sullivan, Ellie. "Jacques Lacan: Feminism and the Problem of Gender Identity." *Substance* 11, no. 36 (1982): 6–20.

Rainof, Alexandre. "Ionesco and the Film of the Twenties and Thirties: From Groucho to Hayes." In *The Two Faces of Ionesco*, edited by Rosette C. Lamont and Melvin J. Friedman. Troy, N.Y.: The Whitson Publishing Co., 1978.

Reid, Alec. *All I Can Manage, More Than I Could: An Approach to the Plays of Samuel Beckett*. Rev. ed. New York: Grove Press, 1971.

Robinson, Michael. *The Long Sonata of the Dead: A Study of Samuel Beckett*. New York: Grove Press, 1969.

Rosen, Steven J. *Samuel Beckett and the Pessimistic Tradition*. New Brunswick, N.J.: Rutgers University Press, 1976.

Rowlett, Ann. "The Function of the Female in Yeats' *On Baile's Strand* and *Purgatory*, and in Pinter's *The Homecoming*." A student paper written for a seminar in modern drama, 30 November 1984.

Saint-Leon, Claire. "*Les Bonnes* de Jean Genet: Quelle Version Faut-il Jouer?" In *Studies in Language and Literature: The Proceedings of the 23rd Mountain Interstate Foreign Language Conference*, edited by Charles L. Nelson, pp. 513–16. Richmond: Eastern Kentucky University Press, 1976.

Sartre, Jean-Paul. "Introduction." *The Maids and Deathwatch: Two Plays by Jean Genet*. Translated by Bernard Frechtman. New York: Grove Press, 1954.

Schechner, Richard. "Godotology: There's Lots of Time in Godot." *Modern Drama* 9, no. 3 (December 1966): 268–76.

———. "Puzzling Pinter." *Tuland Drama Review* 11, no. 2 (Winter 1966): 176–84.

Sexton, Anne, "Briar Rose (Sleeping Beauty)." *Transformations*. Boston: Houghton Mifflin Co., 1971.

Shaw, George Bernard. *Saint Joan*. In *Seven Plays by Bernard Shaw*. New York: Dodd, Mead & Co., 1951.

Skloot, Robert. "Putting Out the Light: Staging the Themes of Pinter's *Old Times*." *Quarterly Journal of Speech* 61, no. 3 (October 1975): 265–70.

States, Bert O. *The Shape of Paradox: An Essay on Waiting for Godot*. Los Angeles and Berkeley: University of California Press, 1978.

Tank, Kurt Lothas. *Günter Grass*. Translated by John Conway. Modern Literature Monographs. New York: F. Ungar Publishing Co., 1969.

Thody, Philip. *Jean Genet: A Study of His Novels and Plays*. New York: Stein and Day, 1969.

Tolpin, Marian, M.D. "Eugène Ionesco's *The Chairs* and the Theatre of the Absurd." *American Imago* 25, no. 2 (Summer 1968): 119–39.

Turner, Victor. *The Ritual Process: Structure and Anti-Structure*. Chicago: Aldine Publishing Co., 1969.

Vickery, John B. "*The Golden Bough:* Impact and Archetype." In *Myth and Symbol: Critical Approaches and Applications*, edited by Bernice Slote. Lincoln: University of Nebraska Press, 1963.

Weston, Jessie L. *From Ritual to Romance*. New York: Doubleday Anchor Books, 1957.

Whitaker, Thomas R. *Fields of Play in Modern Drama*. Princeton: Princeton University Press, 1977.

Wilson, J. S. "Interview with O'Neill by J. S. Wilson." In *Twentieth Century Interpretations of The Iceman Cometh*, edited by John Henry Raleigh. Englewood Cliffs, N.J.: Prentice-Hall, 1968.

Yates, Norris W. *Günter Grass: A Critical Essay*. Contemporary Writers in Christian Perspective. Grand Rapids: Eerdmans, 1967.

Index

Absurd, the, 127, 150; definition of, 30 n.3; playwrights of, 15
Absurd(ist): classic, 14; drama, 16, 62; hero, 16, 18, 38; play, 17; protagonist, 16; world, 61
Absurdists, 13, 15, 16
Act Without Words I (Beckett), 77, 117
Act Without Words II (Beckett), 117
Albee, Edward, 13, 18, 29, 62, 64, 70; *The American Dream*, 54–58, 59, 62, 66, 70, 87, 113, 117, 125, 127, 150; *The Sandbox*, 57–58, 62
All That Fall (Beckett), 72–79, 150
American Dream, The (Albee), 54–58, 59, 62, 66, 70, 87, 113, 117, 125, 127, 150
Aristotle, 16, 17, 31 n.20
Arrabal, Fernando, 15
Artaud, Antonin, 17, 18, 64, 87

Bald Soprano, The (Ionesco), 108, 150
Barnes, Peter: *The Ruling Class*, 126–27
Beckett, Samuel, 13, 14, 15, 17, 18, 25, 26, 29, 30, 33, 34, 39, 42, 44, 47, 48, 50, 54, 72, 73, 80 n.14, 88, 93, 98; *Act Without Words I*, 77, 117; *Act Without Words II*, 117; *All That Fall*, 72–79, 150; *Endgame*, 15, 17, 18, 38, 72–80, 124, 150, 151, 154; *Happy Days*, 62, 93, 117; *Krapp's Last Tape*, 72–79, 151; *Waiting for Godot*, 14, 17, 26, 29, 30, 33, 34–51, 54, 57–58, 62, 75, 83–84, 87, 88, 93, 96, 99, 103, 106, 109, 117, 119, 122, 123, 124, 149, 150, 151, 153, 157
Bettelheim, Bruno, 153, 157
Birthday Party, The (Pinter), 13, 66–72, 88, 92, 114, 117, 123, 125, 151
Birthday(s), 3, 15, 18, 21, 25, 27–29, 30, 66, 68, 72, 113, 153, 158. See also *All That Fall; Birthday Party, The; Endgame; Iceman Cometh, The; Kind of Alaska, A; Krapp's Last Tape; Wild Duck, The*

Blacks, The (Genet), 83–84
Brecht, Bertolt, 14
Bree, Germain, 106
Brook, Peter, 107
Brooks, Curtis M., 48
Brustein, Robert, 14, 18, 33, 87

Campbell, Joseph, 152
Camus, Albert, 33, 39, 42, 44; on absurd hero, 30 n.3, 38
Caretaker, The (Pinter), 132
Chabrowe, Leonard, 29
Chairs, The (Ionesco), 55–65, 70, 77, 78, 109, 111, 125, 150, 151, 158
Chekhov, Anton, 13, 14, 15, 16, 93; *The Cherry Orchard*, 13, 16, 47–48; *The Three Sisters*, 66
Coe, Richard, 98, 101

Dismemberment, 65 n.4
Driver, Tom, 16
Dubois, Jacques, 39
Dumb Waiter, The (Pinter), 114
Dying-and-reviving gods, 18, 19, 48, 54–58, 59–65, 113, 123, 145. See also Frazer

Earth Mother, 91, 93
Eliade, Mircea, 34–35, 36, 37, 40, 74–75, 105, 135; *Myth and Reality*, 74; *The Sacred and Profane*, 46
Eliot, T. S., 74; "The Waste Land," 120, 123
Endgame (Beckett), 15, 17, 18, 38, 72–80, 124, 150, 151, 154
Esslin, Martin, 15, 59, 109
Exorcism(s), 30, 117, 125, 126. See also *Maids, The; Old Times*

Family Voices, The (Pinter), 52, 152
Fergusson, Francis, 16, 17, 30; *Idea of a Theater, The*, 16

Index

Fertility goddess: in *The Homecoming,* 125, 128, 140, 145; in *A Slight Ache,* 127. *See also* Earth Mother; Great Mother
Frazer, Sir James George, 18, 19, 84–85, 125; *The Golden Bough,* 18, 54–55, 114; and the Cambridge School of Anthropology, 33. *See also* Dying-and-reviving gods
Freud, Sigmund, 122
Frye, Northrop, 17, 18

Gale, Steven, 146
Genet, Jean, 13, 14, 17, 18, 29, 87–88, 93, 115; *The Blacks,* 83–84; *The Maids,* 81–88, 89, 91–94, 94 n.1, 95 n.3, 125, 126, 151
Ghost Sonata, The (Strindberg), 107
Gitenet, Jean, 87
Godot as metaphor, 14–15, 30, 66, 78, 79, 96; in *Act Without Words I and II,* 117; in *All That Fall,* 117–18; in *The American Dream,* 57; in Beckett plays, 73; in *The Birthday Party,* 67, 69, 72, 92, 125; in *The Chairs,* 58–65, 117; in *Family Voices,* 152; in *Happy Days,* 117; in *The Homecoming,* 125–47, 152; in Ibsen and O'Neill, 18–19, 117; in *The Iceman Cometh,* 25, 26, 28, 150; in *The Killer,* 104, 106, 107, 108; in *Krapp's Last Tape,* 117–18; in *Old Times,* 92, 94, 117, 125; in O'Neill, 117, 150; in Pinter's plays, 88; in *The Ruling Class,* 126–27; in *The Sandbox,* 58; in *Six Characters in Search of an Author,* 87; in *A Slight Ache,* 117; in *Waiting for Godot,* 93, 117; in *The Wicked Cooks,* 96–97, 109, 112, 114, 117; in *Victoria Station,* 151, 158, 159. *See also* Savior figure(s)
Godot myth, 34, 43, 47, 50, 51, 51 n.3. *See also* Godot as metaphor
Golden Bough, The (Frazer), 18, 54–55, 114
Gontarski, Stanley, 77
Gordon, Lois, 71
Grass, Günter, 13, 29; *The Tin Drum,* 115; *The Wicked Cooks,* 13, 96–97, 109–15, 117, 152, 158
Great Mother, 62

Hamlet (Shakespeare), 104
Happy Days (Beckett), 62, 93, 117
Hassan, Ihab, 106–7
Hollis, James R., 139
Holtan, Orley I., 24; *Mythic Patterns in Ibsen's Last Plays,* 24

Homecoming(s), 13, 14, 30, 108. *See also* Homecoming, The
Homecoming, The (Pinter), 89, 119, 125–48, 152, 153, 158
Hubbs, Clayton A.: "Chekhov and the Contemporary Theatre," 48
Hurt, James, 22

Ibsen, Henrik, 14, 31 n.37, 69, 70, 106; *Hedda Gabler,* 158; *The Wild Duck,* 18–29, 66, 67, 71, 72, 73, 117, 150
Iceman Cometh, The (O'Neill), 18, 25–29, 31 n.38, 31 n.39, 66, 78, 106, 117, 150
Initiation(s), 29, 30, 34–35, 91, 99, 102, 107, 113, 114, 126. See also *Waiting for Godot*
Innes, Christopher: *Holy Theatre: Ritual and the Avant Garde,* 17
Ionesco, Eugene, 13, 18, 29, 58, 59, 70, 115, 149; *The Bald Soprano,* 108, 150; *The Chairs,* 55–56, 66, 70, 78, 109, 111, 125, 150–51, 158; *The Killer,* 13, 87, 96–109, 110, 112, 117, 151; *The Lesson,* 108; *The Rhinoceros,* 104, 108; *Story Number I* and *Story Number II for children under three years old,* 109; *The Stroll in the Air,* 108

Jiji, Vera, 146

Kafka, Franz, 56; *The Trial,* 45, 56, 68, 99
Kafkaesque, 15, 51
Killer, The (Ionesco), 13, 87, 96–109, 110, 112, 117, 151
Kind of Alaska, A (Pinter), 152–58
Kluckhohn, Clyde, 33–34
Krapp's Last Tape (Beckett), 72–79, 151
Kundera, Milan, 108

Lamont, Rosette C., 105
Lesson, The (Ionesco), 108

Maids, The (Genet), 81–88, 89, 91–94, 94 n.1, 95 n.3, 125, 126, 151
Maimed rite, 22, 23, 29. *See also* Ritual
Maughlin, Susan, 77–78
Metman, Eva, 47, 76
Miles, Keith, 115
Miss Julie (Strindberg), 86
Myth: defined, 33–34; in *The Chairs,* 63; in Chekhov, 48; in *The Maids,* 151; of the messiah, 106; relationship to ritual, 33
Myth critic(s), 33

Nemi ritual, 19, 125
Nietzsche, Friedrich, 13, 14, 18, 88
No Man's Land (Pinter), 118–24, 151
Northam, John, 23

Oates, Joyce Carol, 15
Oedipus the King (Sophocles), 21, 77, 99
Old Times (Pinter), 81–82, 88–94, 125–26, 152
O'Neill, Eugene, 14, 15, 19, 20, 31n.37, 67, 69, 70, 71, 72, 73; *The Iceman Cometh*, 18, 25–29, 31n.38, 31n.39, 66, 78, 106, 117, 150
Other Places (Pinter), 152, 154

Pierce, Roger, 72
Pinter, Harold, 13, 17, 18, 25, 29, 62, 93; *The Birthday Party*, 13, 66–72, 88, 92, 114, 117, 123, 125, 151; *The Caretaker*, 132; *The Dumb Waiter*, 114; *The Family Voices*, 52, 152; *The Homecoming*, 89, 119, 125–48, 152, 153, 158; *A Kind of Alaska*, 152–58; *No Man's Land*, 118–24, 151; *Old Times*, 81–82, 88–94, 125–26, 152; *Other Places*, 152, 154; *The Room*, 88; *A Slight Ache*, 118, 121, 127; *Victoria Station*, 152, 154, 158–59
Pirandello, Luigi, 14; *Six Characters in Search of an Author*, 78, 96
Pronko, Leonard, 100
Pucciani, Oreste F., 151

Rainof, Alexandre, 105
Rhinoceros, The (Ionesco), 104, 108
Rite. *See* Ritual
Ritual(s), 19, 63; defined, 33–34, 48, 49, 50, 51, 54, 63, 69, 71, 73, 75, 105, 113. *See also* Birthday(s); Exorcism(s); Homecoming(s); Initiation(s)
Ritual patterns, 18, 25, 29, 64. *See also* Ritual(s)
Robinson, Michael, 44, 47
Room, The (Pinter), 88
Ruling Class, The (Barnes), 126–27

Sacrifice, 20–25, 30, 60, 68, 70, 85, 114, 151, 155. *See also* Dying-and-reviving gods; Sparagmos
Sacrificial: rite(s), 17, 29, 84, 86, 94; ritual(s), 18. *See also* Sacrifice; Dying-and-reviving gods
Saint Joan (Shaw), 127
Salvation, 15, 16, 19, 20, 26, 27, 30; in *The American Dream*, 55, 59; in Beckett's plays, 76; in Book of Ruth, 152; in *The Chairs*, 59; Ionesco on, 106; in Kafka, 45; in *The Killer*, 96, 107; in *The Maids*, 86; in *Waiting for Godot*, 46, 47, 50, 52n.14; in *The Wicked Cooks*, 126
Sandbox, The (Albee), 57–58, 62
Sartre, Jean Paul, 83, 84
Savior figure(s), 14, 15, 18. *See also* Salvation
Scapegoat(s), 158; in *The Iceman Cometh*, 14, 16, 19, 28; in *A Kind of Alaska*, 156; in *The Maids*, 84–85, 151; in *Waiting for Godot*, 46. *See also* Dying-and-reviving gods
Schechner, Richard, 36
Sexton, Anne, 153
Shakespeare, William, 14; Hamlet, the character, 13, 14, 16, 103; *Hamlet*, 104
Shaw, George Bernard, 14; *Saint Joan*, 127
Shepard, Sam, 64
Six Characters in Search of an Author (Pirandello), 78, 96
Slight Ache, A (Pinter), 118, 121, 127
Sophocles, 16, 21, 25; *Oedipus the King*, 21, 77, 99; Sophoclean, 65n.4, 72, 149
Sparagmos, 56. *See also* Dismemberment; Dying-and-reviving gods
Stoppard, Tom, 14
Story Number I and *Story Number II for children under three years old* (Ionesco), 109
Strindberg, August, 14; *Miss Julie*, 86; *The Ghost Sonata*, 107
Stroll in the Air, The (Ionesco), 108

Thody, Philip, 86
Three Sisters, The (Chekhov), 66
Tin Drum, The (Grass), 115
Trial, The (Kafka), 45, 56, 68, 99
Turner, Victor W., 47

Vickery, John B., 18
Victoria Station (Pinter), 152, 154, 158–59

Waiting for Godot (Beckett), 14, 17, 26, 29, 30, 33, 34–51, 54, 57–58, 62, 75, 83–84, 87, 88, 93, 99, 103, 106, 109, 117, 119, 122, 123, 124, 149, 150, 151, 153, 157
"Waste Land, The" (Eliot), 120, 123
Weston, Jessie: *From Ritual to Romance*, 120
Whitaker, Thomas R., 106
Wicked Cooks, The (Grass), 13, 96–97, 109–15, 117, 152, 158
Wild Duck, The (Ibsen), 18–29, 66, 67, 71, 72, 73, 117, 150

Yates, Norris W., 114